An Officer in the First Afghan War

ROUTES OF THE AUTHOR in BELOOCHISTAN.

Scale of English Miles

C. & J. Walker Sculp. 9 Castle St. Holborn.

DESERT

SHIKARPORE

Khinpore

Jughun

Bigham

Khanpore

Jamschedum

Noushera

Lukhee

Pulloa

Sukkur

Rore

Indus River

Kyra Gurra

Nerun

Chandiah

New Dherra

Tali

Vree

Turskena

Wuslah Seah

Jaj Injharee

Sonmanee

Shamsebarr

Kumur

Lukhra

Sundeka

Abad

Rathore

Bharran

Kaffir Kalloon

Doct Musa

Cumbur

Pollitepun

Pinar

a hill

Teves

Sorabhe

F

Mushef

Wabee

Abu Sustan

Kekur

Bugnvan

Hulleylae

Hulleylae

Wad Mehmood

Darra

Bugnam Gur

Keziah

Zehree

Gaga

Bigwar

Beggeren

Mogrub

An Officer in the First Afghan War

Narrative of Services in Beloochistan &
Afghanistan, With the Army of the Indus,
and Beyond

Lewis Robert Stacy

LEONAUR

An Officer in the First Afghan War
Narrative of Services in Beloochistan & Afghanistan,
With the Army of the Indus, and Beyond
by Lewis Robert Stacy

First published under the title
Narrative of Services in Beloochistan and Affghanistan
In the Years 1840, 1841, & 1842

Leonaur is an imprint
of Oakpast Ltd

ISBN: 978-0-85706-377-9 (hardcover)
ISBN: 978-0-85706-378-6 (softcover)

http://www.leonaur.com

Publisher's Notes

Contents

To the Right Honourable
Hugh Baron Gough,
Baronet and Knight Grand Cross
of the Most Honourable Military Order of the Bath,
General and Commander in Chief of the British Army
in India, &c. &c. &c.
This Narrative is with His Lordship's Kind Permission,
Respectfully Inscribed,
by His Grateful Servant,
the Author.

Prefatory Note
by the Original Editor

The absence of Colonel Stacy from England rendered it indispensable that he should devolve the office of superintending the publication of his Narrative to an agent upon the spot, for whose guidance, or rather information, very particular directions were furnished by Colonel Stacy, accompanied by large discretionary power with respect to any passages or expressions in the work which might appear liable to objection, or even capable of misapprehension. The most distinct and peremptory of these directions was, that every passage which could be supposed to cast an injurious reflection upon others, and especially the late Sir William Nott, should be expunged.

The Editor has endeavoured to fulfil the intentions of the Author, upon this as well as other points, as far as practicable, consistently with the nature and object of the work, and the conscientious exercise of the discretion with which he was clothed: if, however, from a desire not to compromise the character of Colonel Stacy, or weaken his just claims, he has deviated from the letter or the spirit of his directions, it is but fair and right that the blame, if any, should fall, not upon the Author, but upon his Editor.

The object of the work is twofold, partly of a public, and partly of a private nature. Of the transactions in Kelat, during the years 1840, 1841, and 1842, and of the operations of General Nott's force in the bold movement from Candahar upon Ghuznee and Cabool,— both intimately connected with a very critical period of our Indian affairs,—no full, exact, and authentic records have yet been given to the public, and in such cases, misrepresentations and distortions of facts, the offspring of ignorance or malice, often usurp their place, disseminating and perpetuating error.[1] In this *Narrative*, the Author lays before the public, in the first place, an ample and truthful report of occurrences which are not devoid of intrinsic interest, and which possess much historical value; in the second place, an exposition of his own individual services, and those of his brave companions in arms, which this gallant officer believes (and the readers of his *Narrative* will probably concur with him) have not been adequately acknowledged and requited.

It is not improbable that the following passage in a letter to Colonel Stacy from an officer politically connected with the affairs of Kelat in 1841, which shews the impression made upon the minds of competent judges, may have furnished the hint which originated this work:

There has been a great deal of misrepresentation and false colouring by parties who were profoundly ignorant of the subject, with respect to Kelat affairs; individuals, like yourself, occupying prominent situations, have at the same time suffered; and I cannot help thinking, considering the important part you have had to play, that you should publish a plain narrative of events as they occurred; it cannot fail to be highly interesting.

The *Narrative* corresponds with this suggestion; it is written in a plain, frank, unadorned style, and whilst no facts are withheld which are essential to truth and to the character and conduct of the Author, a studious endeavour is apparent on his part not to disparage the services, or wound the feelings, of others.

Although the services of Colonel Stacy at Kelat and in Affghanistan are the staple subject of this *Narrative*, an imperfect idea would be formed of the merits of this veteran (whose military career verges upon half a century) if his subsequent services, which are slightly ad-

---

1. The public journals of British India teemed at the time with misstatements regarding the negotiations of Colonel Stacy with the Khan of Kelat and the Brahooe chiefs; and there appeared in the Calcutta *Englishman*, of the 1st December, 1842, an article relative to the passage of the retiring army through the Kyber, which, for its bold contempt of truth, is worth quoting: "A letter from the camp says, of the passage through the Kyber, that Colonel Wymer, who commanded the rear, had to fight through every inch of the defile, and the fellows had even the daring to follow him for some distance after he had cleared the pass; but he did not lose one camel-load of property. Of all the officers employed in important commands during the war, there is not one who has performed services superior to those rendered by Colonel Wymer, &c." Colonel Wymer must have smiled at this statement, if he ever saw it, for he well knew that he did not "command the rear," and it is believed that he did not see a shot fired in the Kyber!

verted to at the close of the *Narrative*, were not more conspicuously noticed.

In the latter part of the year in which the British forces returned from Affghanistan, he was engaged in the action with the Mahratta troops at Maharajpore, near Gwalior, on the 29th December, 1843. Brigadier Stacy, upon that occasion, commanded a brigade of infantry, with which it was the intention of the commander-in-chief (Sir Hugh Gough) to attack the centre of the enemy's very strong position; a change in their arrangements during the night made it necessary for Sir Hugh to alter his dispositions; but his Excellency, in his despatch, bears testimony to the "gallantry and exertions" of Brigadier Stacy in that severe conflict.

At the fiercely contested Battle of Sobraon, on the 10th February, 1846, in which the British army stormed the very strong intrenchments of the Sikhs, defended by 30,000 of their best Khalsa troops and a formidable artillery, the part taken by Brigadier Stacy was still more distinguished. His brigade formed part of Major-General Dick's division, and was appointed to commence and head the attack, and the commander-in-chief (Sir Hugh Gough) speaks in the highest terms of commendation of the manner in which Brigadier Stacy's brigade, which, he says, was "the brigade most hotly and successfully engaged," performed their duty: "the whole army," he writes in his despatch, "had the satisfaction to see the gallant Brigadier Stacy's soldiers driving the Sikhs in confusion before them within the area of their encampment."

Brigadier Stacy led his brave men, upon this occasion, *on foot*, and received a contusion. On the fall of Major-General Dick, early in the action, the command of the division devolved upon him, and he retained it until the termination of the campaign and the breaking up of the army. Sir Hugh Gough has further dedicated the following paragraph of his despatch to a very particular and prominent mention of the brigadier and his brave men:—

> Brigadier Stacy, C.B., I must commend to your special protection and favour. On him devolved the arduous duty of leading the first column to the attack, turning the enemy's right, encountering his fire before his numbers had been thinned or his spirit broken, and, to use a phrase which a soldier like your Excellency will comprehend, taking off the rough edge of the Sikhs in the fight. How ably, how gallantly, how successfully this

was done, I have before endeavoured to relate. I feel certain that Brigadier Stacy and his noble troops will hold their due place in your Excellency's estimation, and that his merits will meet with fit reward.

Having selected a brave and skilful man for an arduous duty, to lead the advance at both the pitched battles of Maharajpore and Sobraon, Lord Gough magnanimously awarded him his full share of praise; and such a tribute does honour to the giver as well as to the object of it. The terms employed by the governor-general (Lord Hardinge) are not less encomiastic.

It does appear strange, after such services, some of them so characterized by the highest authorities,—services special and civil, as well as military,—that the moderate expectations of Colonel Stacy should be disappointed. Some time (not immediately) after the battle of Sobraon, he was made a full colonel, *aide-de-camp* to Her Majesty, a distinction which he must have highly prized; but Colonel Stacy naturally expected that this distinction would have been ante-dated, and, as it always has done, have conferred rank; that he would have been created K.C.B. (having commanded the 3rd division of the Army of the Sutlej, after the fall of Major-General Dick), and have had brevet rank from the time of his bringing in the young *khan* of *kelat*; or, if that service should be considered purely civil, from the battle of Candahar, or the passage of the passes from Cabool, with civil honours for civil work.

Had brevet rank been given to Colonel Stacy for his services in Beloochistan in 1841 and 1842, or for his exertions in the Jugdulluk and Lundee Khana passes, in October and November, 1842, he would have been competent to take advantage of the next brevet; or, had brevet rank been given him for the general actions of Maharajpore and Sobraon, it would probably have secured him the full advantages of the recommendations of Lord Gough and Lord Hardinge, in their despatches from Sobraon.

The reason for refusing him the honour of K.C.B. was, probably, that his military rank precluded him from that grade of the Order; but he held the regimental rank of lieutenant-colonel at Sobraon, on the 10th February, 1846; and he was a colonel of the 1st March, 1846. Several officers in England, in Her Majesty's service, created K.C.B., were only lieutenant-colonels, though they were "Fane" major-generals in India. Besides, if that were the objection, there seems to be the more reason why Colonel Stacy should have brevet rank for his services in 1841 and 1842, advancing him four years nearer to the step or grade which would enable the Government, without any contravention of rule, to bestow upon him the honour for which, it is understood, he was recommended both by Lord Hardinge and Lord Gough.

Lest it should be surmised that pecuniary advantages or indulgences may have supplied a poor equivalent for those unpurchasable rewards which are the solace of a soldier's retirement, it may be right to state that, upon this head, if Colonel Stacy has experienced justice, it is of a most rigid and niggardly quality. The Indian Government, under Lord Ellenborough, retrenched the additional allowance of 270 *rupees* per month, whilst he was at Kelat, made to him by that of Lord Auckland (whose treatment of the gallant officer was throughout generous and kind), during the two months (from 7th March to 10th May, 1842) subsequent to bringing in the *khan*, until his arrival at Candahar, although he was still on special duty; and more recently the government construction of the rules of the service was applied to his case with still more severity.

On the 22nd February, 1846, Government general orders were promulgated, giving twelve months' *batta* to the Army of the Sutlej, as "a testimony of the approbation of the Government of India of the bravery, discipline, and soldier-like bearing" of that army. Upon this, Colonel Stacy drew for the commuted *batta* of a brigadier commanding a division of infantry, according to the Pay and Audit Regulations of 1840, which direct that the rate of donation *batta* shall be of the rank in which the parties were serving on the date of the Government order announcing the grant of the gratuity, which, in his case, was that of a *de facto* divisional commander, he having become so, by the chances of war, on the field of battle, and having continued so after the date of the order, by general orders of the commander-in-chief, dated 11th February and 8th March, 1846, until the breaking up of the army. Nevertheless, his donation *batta*, instead of being that of a divisional commander, or at least of a brigadier commanding a division of infantry, was restricted to that of a lieutenant-colonel.

Possibly Colonel Stacy may not approve of a reference to these details respecting subordinate parts of his case; but it seemed to the Editor that their entire omission might leave it imperfect.

London, May 31st, 1848.

Introduction

When the General Orders were issued by the Government of British India, in 1838, directing the formation of a force, denominated the Army of the Indus, I was lieutenant-colonel of the 32nd regiment of Bengal Native Infantry, in command of the station of Dacca. I volunteered immediately, in a letter to the military secretary of the commander-in-chief (Sir Henry Fane), and received a reply in very kind terms, expressing his Excellency's regret that he could not give me a regiment in the Army of the Indus, as every regiment included in that force had its commander. But, in about a fortnight after, I received another letter from headquarters, stating that, the command of the 5th regiment having become vacant, I should find myself in Orders as its lieutenant-colonel. Accordingly, in General Orders, dated "Simla, 20th October, 1838," my removal from the 32nd to the 6th regiment of native infantry was notified, and I was directed to proceed forthwith and join.

Without the delay of a halt between Calcutta and Loodiana, I reached the latter station the very day the General Orders appeared reducing the number of regiments in the Army of the Indus, the 5th being excluded. A few days after, the commander of the 43rd regiment having left the army on sick certificate. Sir Henry Fane,—who declared "he knew what officers he required,"—again removed me[1] from the 5th to the 43rd regiment. I overtook this corps the day it crossed the Indus, and served with it during the whole campaign under Major-General Sir William Nott, the 43rd being always in my brigade. General Nott was left at Quetta, in Shawl, to keep open the communication with the Indus, and to check Meer Mehrab Khan, of Kelat. On the 12th July, 1839, I was sent in command of a detachment, consisting of a troop of the *Shah's* horse artillery, 300 of the

---

1. G. O. Ferozepore, 15th December, 1838.

Shah's cavalry, the 43rd, and 100 men Shah's infantry, from Quetta to Candahar, to escort ten *lacs* of *rupees* and some stores for the army at Candahar. Notwithstanding the smallness of the force, and the crippled condition of the camels, this service was performed with the loss of only three men.

At the Kojuck Pass, the enemy had assembled in great force, having possession of the hill commanding the road, from which they were dislodged. In the night (which was dark) they commenced an attack upon our picquet, which they continued until near daybreak, when we crossed the Kojuck, and reached Chummun after midnight, with no other loss than a few men slightly wounded, and several camels, laden chiefly with grain, which dropped during the day exhausted. We arrived at Candahar on the 1st August. The 43rd regiment remained here, as part of the garrison, the command of which, as senior officer, devolved upon me, and I continued in command of Candahar until the arrival there of General Nott, on the 15th November, 1839.

On the 6th June, 1840, I accompanied the general into the Ghilzie country, returning to Candahar on the 21st, and on the 17th August I was sent down to Quetta, with a detachment, consisting of four guns Shah's horse artillery, 300 Christie's irregular cavalry, and the 43rd regiment of Native Infantry, to relieve that place, then threatened by Meer Mahomed Nasseer Khan, and afford protection to the town and province, in conjunction with the troops already there. Agreeably to instructions received from Cabool, I was required to refrain from all operations against the fortress of Kelat, without positive orders from the authorities of Cabool. I reached Quetta on the 29th, and assumed, under orders of General Nott, the command of all the troops there, until the arrival of the general, on the 22nd September. I had been in the meantime strongly urged by Captain Bean, the political agent at Quetta, to move upon Moostung, and "coerce" or "disperse" the rebellious tribes in the vicinity; but with this proposal I could not comply without acting in direct opposition to imperative orders from General Nott.

The fortress of Kelat,[2] it may be necessary to premise, had been taken by assault by a detachment of the Army of the Indus, under Major-General Willshire, on the 13th November, 1839. The reason assigned by the Government of India[3] for hostilities against the Khan

---

2. Called "Kelat-e-Kohistan," or "Kelat-e-Nasseer," to distinguish it from other places named Kelat.

3. General Order, by the Governor-General of India, dated "Camp, Deothanee, 4th December, 1839."

of Kelat was, "the many outrages and murders committed, in attacks on the followers of the Army of the Indus, by the plundering tribes in the neighbourhood of the Bolan Pass, at the instigation of their chief, Meer Mehrab Khan, at a time when he was professing friendship for the British Government, and negotiating a treaty with its representatives;" and the object of the hostilities was declared to be "the exaction of retribution from that chieftain, and the execution of such arrangements as would establish future security in that quarter;" or, as avowed in Major-General Willshire's despatch to be the scope of his instructions from our envoy and minister at Cabool, "the deposing of Mehrab Khan."

The Khan of Kelat being killed in the assault, the fortress was made over to Shah Newaz Khan, descended, collaterally with Mehrab Khan, from Abdoolla Khan, the founder of the family.[4] Lieutenant Loveday, of the 37th regiment of Bengal Native Infantry, who had been recently attached to the political agency of Shawl, as an assistant to Captain Bean, accompanied Major-General Willshire's force, and on the fall of Kelat he was left there (at the request of Shah Newaz Khan), with a small guard of 30 *sepoys*, as assistant Political Agent.

Meer Mahomed Nasseer Khan, the only legitimate son of the late Mehrab Khan, in July, 1840, succeeded in obtaining possession of the fortress; the Brahooe garrison having deserted the cause of Shah Newaz Khan, who abdicated in favour of Mahomed Nasseer Khan. On the 20th October, General Nott marched against Kelat, and I accompanied him. The fortress was found to be deserted, and it was reoccupied by the British troops on the 3rd November. On the retreat of the Brahooes from Kelat, and their discomfiture at Dadur, Lieutenant Loveday, who was taken with them as a prisoner, was murdered under circumstances which will be hereafter detailed. Upon the reoccupation of Kelat, I proceeded with the return force to Candahar.

Before leaving Kelat, I had written to Mr. Ross Bell, then Political Agent in Upper Scinde, offering to take political charge of the fortress, and to endeavour to induce the young *khan*, Meer Mahomed Nasseer, to disband his forces, come in, and acknowledge the supremacy of the East-India Company.

Leaving the 2nd regiment of the *Shah's* infantry at Moostung, and a troop of the *Shah's* horse artillery, and most of the cavalry, at Quetta, we reached, with the remainder of the troops, Killa Abdoolla on the 25th November, and next morning marched to the foot of the Kojuck

4. See the genealogy, Appendix, No. 1.

Pass. General Nott proceeded direct to Chummun, and I conveyed the two 18-pounders over the pass. The weather was miserably cold, with drifts of snow; the tackle was rotten; but the company of European artillery, and six companies of the 43rd, by dint of hard and constant labour, accomplished, without a halt, an undertaking which had occupied double and treble their numbers two and three days in performing, and everything was got into camp at Chummun on the 27th.

Upon going to make my report, I received orders from Major-General Nott to return and assume political charge of Kelat. An official letter from Mr. Ross Bell, addressed to the general, dated "Sukkur, 14th November, 1840," contained the following paragraph:—

The melancholy fate of Lieutenant Loveday, and the fact of a garrison having been left in Kelat, render it necessary that a prudent and intelligent officer should be placed in political charge of that place, pending a final settlement of affairs in Beloochistan. Your despatch under acknowledgment gave cover to a letter from Colonel Stacy, in which he offers to undertake the service in question; and should you be enabled to spare him, I need only say that I shall be able to place entire reliance on his judgment and discretion, and that I hope you will permit him to assume charge.

Kelat – From 27th November, 1840, to 13th October, 1841

The return force moved from Chummun towards Candahar on the morning of the 28th of November, 1840, and I retraced my steps, crossing the Kojuck for the fourth time. The natives were busily engaged in cutting up and carrying off the flesh and hides of the camels which had dropped the day before. They did not molest me; but their numbers made it prudent for me to wait for my baggage at the top of the pass. I reached Quetta on the 2nd December.

Here I remained for five days, expecting instructions from Mr. Ross Bell, as the political agent of Shawl (Captain Bean) considered my nomination to have been made under a misapprehension. I found here Mr. Charles Masson,[1] from whom I acquired much information, the characters of most of the *sirdars* and servants of the *khanat* of Kelat being well known to him. To his communications upon this head, and to his recommendation of Moolla Nasseer Oolla, Babee, whom I employed in my negotiations, I owe much of the success which attended them.

Leaving Quetta on the 7th December, I arrived at Moostung on the 9th, and sent for a man named Shadee Khan, Kumbararee, who had been recommended to me by Mr. Masson as well acquainted with the country and friendly to the young *khan*. After an hour's conversation with him, I despatched a note to Moolla Nasseer Oolla, who reached my tent next day. We conversed for some hours, and the moolla agreed to join me at Kelat and assist my negotiations with the young *khan*, of

---

1. Mr. Masson was at this time detained at Quetta by order of the late Sir Wm. Macnaghten, pending an inquiry respecting his supposed connection with the Brahooes, and the recapture by them of Kelat; the result of which inquiry was that he was "entirely freed from suspicion."

whom be was a personal friend, and he told me his relative, Moolla Faiz Ahmed, Babee (another person strongly recommended to me by Mr. Masson), was still more intimate with him, both having been disciples of a *syud* who had preached and propagated some new and popular doctrine. It was agreed that I should send an invitation to Faiz Ahmed, at Shorawuk, Captain Macan, who commanded at Moostung, being unable to afford me a guard, I accepted the services of Shadee Khan's brother, Moolla Dad Khan; we departed on the 11th December, and reached Kelat on the 13th.

The four days preceding the arrival of my *vakeel*, Moolla Nasseer Oolla, Babee, were occupied in necessary arrangements, and in inquiries respecting the *khan*, his *sirdars*, and the views and wishes of the different parties.

Nasseer Oolla joined me on the 17th, and on the 26th I received Mr. Ross Bell's instructions as to the object of my negotiations, namely, to induce the young *khan* to disband his forces, and to wait upon Mr. Bell at Baugh, under a guarantee of safe-conduct.

Having completed the necessary inquiries into the state of affairs, on the 4th January, 1841, I despatched Moolla Nasseer Oolla with a letter to the young *khan*, at Zeedee. He returned on the 21st with a very polite reply from the *khan*, stating that he had sent Sirdar Meer Esah Khan, Mhengal, and Darogah Gool Mahomed to confer with me at Kelat. The *moolla* assured me that the young *khan* was desirous to come in person, but the *sirdars* would not hear of it; and that there was very great distrust of the honour and sincerity of the British in the *khan's* camp. Gool Mahomed was with much difficulty prevailed upon to be one of the envoys.

I did not think it advisable to hold the conference within the walls of Kelat; the village of Toke, about fourteen miles distant, was proposed by Gool Mahomed, and fixed upon as the place of meeting. Accordingly, on the 23rd January, I proceeded towards the village, at an early hour, accompanied by Moolla Nasseer Oolla, and my *moonshee*, Moolla Mahomed; but, when about half-way, we were met by a horseman bearing a message from Gool Mahomed, that no supplies were to be had at Toke, the houses of which were unroofed, and that he had consequently moved to Rodenjoh, where he begged me to join him. It has since transpired, as I then suspected, that this plea was a mere artifice, the *darogah* suspecting that I intended to seize him, and would send *sepoys* in that direction.

On receiving the message, however, I struck off to Rodenjoh

(horsemen being observed on the tops of the hills, who disappeared as we neared them), and on my arrival, Sirdar Meer Esah Khan and Darogah Gool Mahomed came out to meet me. We embraced, and, after mutual salutations, entered the village, a miserable place, exhibiting every token of abject poverty.

It was evident that my appearance without a guard, or even a single *sepoy*, astonished the deputies; and that precautions had been taken on their part against a surprise. I accompanied them into a hovel, which had been carpeted for the occasion, and, after the customary courtesies, as soon as it could be done with propriety, I proposed that the object of the interview should be entered upon. The room was accordingly cleared, the *sirdar*, the *darogah*, the *moolla*, the *moonshee*, and myself being the only persons left. Gool Mahomed began the discussion; but his demands were so ridiculously extravagant, that I interrupted him, observing that the question was, whether the young *khan* desired to try his fortune once more in the field, or to accept terms; if the latter, he must first disband his army, and then wait upon Mr. Bell; and that I would guarantee his safety, and accompany him back to Zeedee or elsewhere, if he and Mr. Bell should not agree.

The *darogah* replied, they wished for terms, and were ready to disband their army and consent to Mr. Bell's proposals. They had a long list of grievances, commencing from the time our army crossed the Indus up to their own defeat at Kotroo,[2] which appeared to be the master grief. These, I said, were matters for after-consideration, and I pledged myself, on the part of Mr. Bell, that the young *khan* should be allowed to come unmolested to his paternal uncle, Meer Mahomed Azim Khan, at Zheree, where I would meet him.

I thought it expedient (and I still think it was so) to advert upon this occasion to the murder of Lieutenant Loveday, and the *darogah* made the following statement respecting that occurrence. He said that Meer Nasseer Khan and himself were riding from the field of battle after their defeat at Dadur,[3] and when they were some distance from the scene of action, and had slackened their pace, their friends joining them every minute, a body of Sheerwannees came up; that the young *khan* inquired about Lieutenant Loveday, and being told that he had been slain, exclaimed, "Then you have dishonoured me and my country!" that he loaded the Sheerwannees with invectives, forbade

2. Appendix, No. 2.
3. By Major Boscawen, on the 3rd November, 1840, after the Brahooes had made an unsuccessful attempt against Dadur, defended by Captain Watkins.

the tribe his presence, and although they subsequently came to the *durbar* with ropes round their necks imploring pardon, it was refused; and that, when my letter was received, Mahomed Khan, Sheerwannee, was excluded from the council.

The *darogah* denied that Lieutenant Loveday had been beaten or otherwise maltreated. This statement I afterwards related to Mahomed Khan, Sheerwannee, without mentioning from whom I received it, and inquired if it was true. He declared that there was not a word of truth in the story; that the oppressive conduct of Lieutenant Loveday's *moonshee* (Gholam Hussein), as farmer of the revenues at Moostung, had provoked the hatred of all classes, and, when the *moonshee* headed the *sepoys* and fired upon the people, they returned the fire and ultimately killed nearly all the *sepoys*. The subsequent trial of Kaissoo, who put Mr. Loveday to death, has established the accuracy of the Sheerwannee *sirdar*, Mahomed Khan.

I was detained so late at Rodenjoh that I did not reach Kelat until long after dark. On the 27th January, I started for Zheree, which I reached on the 30th, being accompanied by Moolla Nasseer Oolla and Moolla Mahomed Moonshee, without a single *sepoy*. The march from Capotah to Nechara is almost impracticable for any force. The Kund-e-Capotah is a very steep and difficult ascent over a narrow path on the side of a hill, leading up to a table-land. After passing the valley of Soorkun, we had to clamber over the Kund-e-Soorkun, and some miles beyond this, we came to the Chunneeree Pass, which for a very considerable distance is passable only with the greatest caution by camels lightly laden.

At the end of the Chunneeree is the well of Bader, the water in which remains at one particular height throughout the year, and further on is the famous Pass of Toongee, which for eighty yards is but a cleft in a rock, rent asunder apparently by some convulsion of nature, the road or path being not more than five to seven feet wide.

It is proper to notice, that Meer Mahomed Azim Khan, brother of the late Khan of Kelat, Meer Mehrab, whom I was about to visit at Zheree, had always been very inimical to the British; and as he would be jealous of Darogah Gool Mahomed's obtaining the credit of bringing the young *khan* to terms with us, it had been arranged at the conference at Rodenjoh that Sirdar Meer Esah Khan should escort the *khan* to Zheree, the *darogah* being the guarantee of my safety. But on the arrival of the *sirdar* and the *darogah* at Zheree, they discovered that Meer Azim Khan had written to the young *khan*, advising him not to trust the British, whereupon it was resolved that the *darogah* should return and disabuse the *khan's* mind, and escort him to Zheree, whilst my safety was to be entrusted to the *sirdar*. Meer Azim Khan openly declared that he would oppose any negotiation with the English, and, in the hope of thwarting it, resorted to a dastardly attempt upon my life, of which I was ignorant until some months afterwards, when it was divulged during some high words in camp.

It appears that, when Meer Azim Khan heard I was coming to Zheree without a single *sepoy*, he hired a man named Mallooke, a *shikaree* (hunter), to shoot me in the Soindah Pass, which opens direct upon Zheree. Meer Esah Khan, who had taken up his residence in the village of Nograma, the farthest from the pass, was informed of the intended assassination, and immediately encamped at the very mouth of the pass, with his Mhengals, whom he apprised of the fact, and that he was my guarantee. The tribe, accordingly, kept on the alert night and day, but Mallooke, to whom, as a *shikaree*, every sheep-track in the hills was known, gained the pass by a mountain-path, a mile to the eastward, unknown to the Mhengals.

On the 30th of January I started from Pundaran (the chief of which was an orphan boy, about nine years of age, his father having fallen with Mehrab Khan in the defence of Kelat), and our party halted for prayers about a mile from the mouth of the pass, whence I sent two horsemen on to give notice to Sirdar Meer Esah Khan of my approach. Whilst the party were engaged in their devotions, I walked back to examine the side of the pass, which had appeared to me to indicate some rich mineral production. My absence caused much alarm to the party, who remonstrated with me, and advised me not to leave the camp, as the hills thronged with straggling Brahooes; but, ignorant of the real motive of this advice, my restless curiosity was so highly excited by the attractions of a most romantic country, that I refused to pledge myself to adopt it.

Soon after, I was surprised to perceive Meer Esah Khan, with thirty or forty horsemen, coming towards us at a smart pace; they testified joy at finding me safe; and, as we emerged from the pass into the plain, I observed the *sirdar's* people close round me, which caused some alarm to my Brahooe *moonshee*. In this way we passed on to Nograma, where houses had been prepared for us. It seems that my party had halted a few hundred yards only from the spot where Mallooke had taken post; that my horsemen had stopped and questioned him; and, on delivering my message to Meer Esah Khan, related their meeting with the *shikaree*. The *sirdar* ordered every horse to be ready, and, instead of his *sowaree* camel, mounted a smart nag himself, though he had not been on horseback for years.

Led by the horsemen, they reached the spot where they had seen Mallooke, who had concealed himself amongst some underwood. He was discovered, confessed his object, and pleaded poverty as the inducement to undertake the deed. His matchlock was broken by Esah Khan's order, and he was dismissed with a few cuffs and kicks. When he first became acquainted with Meer Azim Khan's design upon me, the *sirdar* expostulated with him, but Azim angrily replied that, if the *shikaree* failed, he and his followers (whom he had summoned) would cut up both me and my party as we entered Zheree. Esah Khan retorted that I was under his protection, and if the slightest violence was offered to me, he and his Mhengals would destroy every man concerned in it. This threat had been the occasion of our being surrounded by the Mhengals as we came out of the pass, and thus to Meer Esah Khan was I indebted for my life.[4] On leaving Kelat, a bet of one hundred to one had been offered that I should be killed, like Lieutenant Loveday, and refused!

I had subsequently occasion to remonstrate with Meer Azim Khan on his conduct towards the young *khan* of Kelat, when I remarked (in the presence of the *meer's* father-in-law) that, if I were to disclose to the *khan* his attempts upon my life,—detailing the circumstances,—his honour would be forfeited. The *meer* did not deny the charge, but, as well as his father-in-law, nodded assent.

Foiled in these attempts, Meer Azim Khan did all he could to embarrass me, and forbade the villagers to supply me with grain, which subjected me to much inconvenience.

Darogah Gool Mahomed returned on the 4th of February, without the young *khan*. The distrust of the people at Zheree was incredible. Although I was unattended by a single *sepoy*, they feared a *chupao* (surprise, or sudden attack), and were continually sending out horsemen in every direction to reconnoitre, and even suspected me of treachery, defenceless as I was, believing I had *sepoys* concealed in the hills. The defeat of the Brahooes at Dadur, and our attack upon them at Kotroo, whilst negotiations were going on, had exasperated them, and the murder of their prisoner. Lieutenant Loveday, had inspired them with apprehensions of our vengeance; so that, at this moment, alone, in the

---

4. This *sirdar*, who was the real chief of the Mhengals (his eldest brother having left his country), died in 1845.

midst of the Brahooe camp, my life seemed scarcely worth an hour's purchase.

But from the day the commissioners of the young *khan* met me at Rodenjoh, not a hostile movement was made by the Brahooes, nor was a shot fired (except in the Quetta district) from the moment I boldly trusted myself amongst them until we quitted the country. After much discussion with the *darogah*, it was settled that the young *khan* should visit me the next morning, and that I should conduct him direct to my quarters. I went out to meet him accordingly on the 5th of February, and, after the usual exchange of compliments, he rode back with me. He had 500 or 600 men with him, on horses and camels; they forced themselves into my small apartment till it was crammed, refusing to quit it, though ordered to do so by the *khan* and the chiefs.

The young prince was uneasy at first, but his fears soon wore off, and he conversed freely on hunting, shooting, &c. Meer Mahomed Azim Khan attended him, and conducted himself in a very rude and indecorous manner. I caught part of an observation he made, "Friends with the English! Don't trust them, especially this one;" and, turning abruptly round, I asked the *khan* what the *meer* said. The young prince expressed strong displeasure by his countenance, but adroitly replied that the *meer* was only in jest. The *meer* was known to be an unprincipled man, a spirit-drinker, and without any title to notice, save his being the uncle of the *khan*.

The young *khan* having taken his departure to pray at the shrine of some saint, the *darogah* was left to talk with me on business. He commenced in the old strain,—descanted upon the eternal theme of the Kotroo *chupao*, the treacherous seizure of Beejar Khan,[5] &c. So inveterate appeared the impression amongst the chiefs of our treachery in the Kotroo affair (our own *vakeel* being in their camp at the moment of our attack), that, finding it impossible to get over this obstacle, I proposed that the young *khan* should go over to Mr. Ross Bell, at Baugh, and negotiate with him in person, whilst I remained as a hostage in the Brahooe camp. After some deliberation, this proposal was rejected, and I resolved, in compliance with the request of the *khan* and his chiefs, to go myself and procure from Mr. Ross Bell a formal guarantee that they might visit him with safety.

The following day, I paid a visit to the young *khan*, in his camp. His tent was a miserable, worn-out pal, lined with green baize. It was

5 Appendix, No. 3.

the only tent he possessed, he observed, and "he was ashamed to ask so great a man to enter it!" I had arranged, through my *vakeels*, that I should have a private interview with him before we met in *durbar*, and accordingly .we had a long conversation, the *darogah* and my two *vakeels*, Moolla Nasseer Oolla and Moolla Faiz Ahmed, being the only other persons present. The *khan* insisted on the necessity of attending to the advice of his chiefs in *durbar*, which was the law of the country. I represented to him that some of them had predetermined that he should not go to Mr. Ross Bell; that the advice of some was dictated by their own fears, not a regard for his interests; and, alluding to the fall of his father through the perfidious conduct of his servants, I urged the *khan* to think and act for himself. He still persisted in believing he was obliged to follow the advice of his *durbar*, more especially as he was so young.

At length, he took off his ring, and said, "Give this to Ross Bell Sahib; tell him to put it to any terms he may think proper, and I will agree to them; say I trust to his generosity; remind him that I am an orphan, having lost my father, my country, my all, though whatever I did was ill self-defence."

I gently put back his hand with the ring, observing it was impossible; and as the chief had resolved that he should not go with me to Mr. Ross Bell, I would go by myself and learn the particulars of the Kotroo affair. The *khan* said, "You say you will go to Ross Bell: may I ask you to do me two favours? Tell him, first, that I am not afraid of him, but of other people, and of another *chupao*; and secondly, that if he will release Meer Boheer, who is the friend of my heart, and send him to me, I shall be most grateful." Meer Boheer (taken prisoner at Kotroo) was not only a great favourite of the *khan*, but was the uncle of the girl betrothed to him. I promised I would mention both points favourably to Mr. Ross Bell, and thus ended our conference.

At the *durbar* which ensued, when the *khan*, the *sirdars*, and myself were left to business (Meer Azim Khan not being present), the former opened the discussion, speaking with considerable fluency. His attitude was good, his body reclining gently forward, his left arm resting upon his shield, which was on his lap. The whole scene was striking and dramatic. He began by describing the misery in which I had found him, and to which he had been reduced by the English; he alluded to the loss of his father and of the *khanat*; his wanderings; the persecutions he had endured from Lieutenant Loveday and Captain Bean; and his utter destitution after the *chupao* at Kotroo; he declared that his life was one of misery, and that he would cheerfully lay it down if his death could restore peace to his country.

Turning to me, he said he had heard from his own subjects at Kelat, and from the Candahar merchants, that they had experienced kind treatment at my hands, and this report, together with the confidence I had manifested in coming amongst them unattended, induced him to regard me as a true friend. He added, that his father and himself had experienced great harshness from the English, who had cherished their enemies, and that, since the *chupao* of Kotroo, and the seizure of Beejar Khan, who had come in on a promise of security, he could not rely upon our word. I spoke next, observing that the object of my visit was to bring about an interview between the *khan* and Mr. Ross Bell, who had given me authority to guarantee his and his *sirdars'* safety; and that I had brought with me, as my *vakeels*, two of the *khan's* best friends, who would pledge their lives for my sincerity.

Akoon Mahomed Sudeeq followed, objecting decidedly to the *khan's* visit to Mr. Ross Bell, at least without a perfect assurance of safety, and inveighing in bitter terms against our want of faith. After this, little order was observed, several chiefs speaking at once, and almost all being opposed to the interview, on the plea that the *khan* would be seized, like Beejar Khan. I repeated my offer to remain in the Brahooe camp as a hostage for the safety of the *khan* and his chiefs, but it was at once refused. All the speakers strove to avoid giving me personal offence, save Akoon Mahomed Sudeeq, who spoke of the treachery of the English in such offensive terms that he was rebuked by the *khan*. After the *durbar*, the *akoon* endeavoured to make himself agreeable to me, and subsequently sought the intervention of Moolla Nasseer Oolla, to make up a quarrel he had with Gool Mahomed.

The *khan* was highly gratified the next day by the receipt of a letter from Meer Boheer, announcing that Mr. Ross Bell had given him his *rooksut* (discharge), with handsome presents, and speaking in warm terms of that gentleman's treatment of him. The liberation of this chief (though 132 of his tribe, taken at Kotroo, still remained in prison) facilitated my negotiations with these people, by convincing them that they might place confidence in my promises and assertions. My difficulties, however, began to multiply. The Brahooes from the *khan's* camp (which was in a state of extreme misery), during the night, carried off the contents of a pit of *boosah*.

My anxiety to avoid anything that could bear the appearance of plunder induced me, when I sent Moolla Nasseer Oolla to Zheree with my first letter to the *khan*, to feed the deputies and their followers, rather than countenance extortion: this rule I observed throughout, and many blessings were invoked upon the justice of the Company.

It was arranged that the young *khan* should, on the 9th February, spend the day in my quarters, in order that measures might be devised to get rid of some of his hungry rabble, for whom it was impossible to find subsistence, and who, from morning till night, beset the *khan's* tent, clamouring for rations; one of the propositions tendered to the *khan* being the disbanding of his army. On this occasion the young prince told me his life was a burthen; that his people tormented him with cries that they were starving. Although only fourteen, his countenance exhibited traces of the misery he had undergone for the preceding two years. He related to me that, when Shah Newaz Khan (then ruler of Kelat) and Lieutenant Loveday were in pursuit of him, he and his party were driven to such straits, that but for one of his people shooting a dove, which was immediately cooked and given to him, he should have been unable to proceed.

The disbanding of his army had been readily agreed to by the *khan* and his chiefs; but the difficulty was to decide how this was to be effected. The number of the troops was full 6,000. Some of the minor chiefs agreed to retire if their expenses and those of their followers were paid; and some could be got rid of for five *rupees* and a little grain each. The *khan* was utterly destitute, and I candidly acknowledged that my means were small. It was resolved that, on the following day, further inquiries should be made, and in the meantime the visit to Mr. Bell was reconsidered. But I could obtain no concession. I could not detach the *khan* from the *sirdars*; I could find no opportunity of conversing with him alone; and the minds of the chiefs were so indelibly impressed with a notion of our treachery, by the seizure of Beejar Khan, and the affair at Kotroo, .that nothing but a distinct pledge of safe-conduct from Mr. Ross Bell himself would change their determination not to suffer the young *khan* to depart.

There were other allegations against our good faith, which, as I was ignorant of the circumstances, I could not disprove or explain; and, ultimately, I found it advisable to agree that I should proceed direct to Mr. Ross Bell at Baugh, accompanied by *sirdars* Meer Khamal Khan, Ittazee; Meer Esah Khan, Mhengal; and Meer Boheer Khan, Zheree; who were empowered by the *khan* to reply to all questions, and to make arrangements with Mr. Bell, in the *khan's* name, by which he would abide.

The difficulty of disposing of the *khan's* rabble was an impediment to our departure; some minor chiefs and many men had been got rid of, but there remained more than could be supported on our route.

On the 12th of February, I received a letter from Mr. Ross Bell, dated the 7th, enclosing one for the young *khan*, which I sent off, hoping to strengthen the efforts, in *durbar,* of Meer Khamal Khan and Meer Boheer Khan, who, I heard, wished the *khan* to proceed to Mr. Bell in person. The three *sirdars*, however, brought me word the same day, that an anonymous letter had been received in the *khan's* camp, from Kelat, stating that a *chupao* was setting out from thence to seize the *khan* and his *sirdars*, which threw their whole camp into consternation. This and other mischievous communications, whencesoever they originated, caused me much embarrassment. I convinced the *sirdars* that the anonymous report was entitled to no credit.

Nothing, however, could induce them to permit the *khan* to proceed to Mr. Bell until I had been at Baugh, although I appealed to them whether anything could be more friendly than the terms of Mr. Bell's letter to the *khan*, which the latter had sent to me. Further dissatisfaction was created by intelligence that Gundava, with 1,000 *rupees* a month, had been settled on Beebee Ganjan, the senior wife of the late Mehrab Khan. I urged that the difference between Meer Nasseer Khan and the Company was no reason why the Beebee should be left destitute; the answer was, "Gundava belonged to the *khan*, not to the Company; if Beebee Ganjan was to be assisted, it should have been with money."

I found that Meer Boheer's presence in the camp was not attended with the advantages I expected. He proved covetous and venal, and although to one party he lauded Mr. Ross Bell and the Company, it was evident that he had been tampered with successfully by the other, with whom he talked of his injuries at Kotroo, and the imprisonment of his followers.

The letter of Mr. Bell, I learned from my *vakeel,* Moolla Nasseer Oolla, had produced a great effect upon the *khan*, who, when it was read in *durbar*, declared his resolution to go to Baugh, in spite of the opposition of the *sirdars*, especially Meer Azim Khan and Meer Mahomed Khan, Ittazee. These two *sirdars*, however, succeeded in modifying his determination, and it was at length settled that the *khan's* camp and mine should move together the next morning, the 15th of February, to Nurh, where I was to leave the young *khan*, with a written security for himself and his camp, and proceed with Meer Khamal Khan, Meer

Esah Khan, and Meer Boheer, charged with a letter from the *khan*, who agreed to abide by any arrangements they might make with Mr. Bell. The *sirdars* of both parties insisted that it should be made one of the stipulations that I should remain with them.

Our march was delayed until the 16th, owing to the crippled state of my *godowns* (though the *khan's* rabble army had been reduced to a handful); and to a serious quarrel which had occurred in the *khan's* camp, in consequence of his having consented, at the instigation of Meer Boheer and his sister, to cancel the nomination of Meer Khamal Khan, as one of the deputies to Mr. Ross Bell. Khamal Khan was provoked at this slight, and expostulated with the young *khan*, telling him no Ittazee should saddle a horse by his orders; that he had pledged his word with me, and by that agreement he would stand; that he would "saddle " by my orders, not by the *khan's*. I succeeded in pacifying the *sirdar*, and sent Moolla Nasseer Oolla to remonstrate with the young *khan*, who readily reverted to the first arrangement, and I had the pleasure of seeing him, in the afternoon, riding into the camp on the same camel with Meer Khamal Khan.

In our journey it was evident that the famine had extended all over the country; the people were miserable objects, famishing with hunger, dwelling in scanty huts or sheds, open on all sides; yet, impoverished as they were, they seemed in perpetual dread of a *chupao*. The *sirdars* were likewise full of apprehensions of some treachery; horsemen would ascend the hills on our line of march, and the moment a halt was resolved upon, a chief and his tribe took possession of each road.

We reached Nurh on the 20th, where the *khan's* camp was to halt; and at the request of the *khan*, who was depressed in spirits at being left without "a white beard," Meer Esah Khan, with my consent, remained behind with him, the *meer's* eldest son. Khan Mahomed, proceeding with me in his stead. I had never seen the young *khan* in such a low condition as when we parted: "My fate," he said, "is in your hands."

We arrived at Kotroo about noon on the 25th of February. On reaching the tent of Lieutenant Wallace (the assistant political agent), he received us outside, in the sun. I introduced the chiefs, but he never asked us to enter his tent. They were more astonished than I was at such an apparent want of courtesy. We took leave, and were no sooner seated in Meer Khamal Khan's garden-house than they questioned me respecting the custom of the *sahib-loge* on such occasions. I could not deny that Lieutenant Wallace's behaviour (which is still a mystery to me) was extraordinary. The subject was dropped; but I suspect the incident will be long remembered.

The next day, having halted at this place, Moolla Rheimdad, the ex-*Naib* of Shawl, presented himself and asked my permission to join the *khan's* camp. I was sorry to see this man at large; I knew his character too well not to dread the result. In my private correspondence with Mr. Ross Bell, I told him that he would embroil everything, and wished he should be kept from my camp. I proposed to Rheimdad that he should remain at Kotroo until my return, and when he retired, I represented to the deputies the risk of allowing him to proceed to the *khan's* camp. Darogah Gool Mahomed, alone, backed his application; the others leaving the matter to my decision. In vain I warned the *darogah* of the consequences of allowing Rheimdad to go to Nurh; "Remember my words," I said; "he will jump on your neck and throw you down in the mire."

Gool Mahomed replied, "He is my son, and a faithful servant of the *khan*." In the sequel, he recalled to mind my slighted advice with pain and anguish.

On the 28th I started from Shoran, rain falling and the country under water, with the chiefs (leaving our baggage), for Baugh, which we reached by a most circuitous route, the roads being almost impracticable, and after a series of adventures (unnecessary to detail), on the 2nd of March. Mr. Ross Bell courteously received the chiefs, who, after an hour's conversation, were dismissed to a tent prepared for them near the town of Mungul-ke-Shuhr.

During the interval between the 2nd and the 9th, the deputies often visited the political agent, and on the 10th a *durbar* was held, previous to their taking leave, at which Bebee Ganjan was also present. As Mr. Bell was obliged to proceed up the Bolan Pass, it was arranged between him and the *sirdars* that Meer Nasseer Khan should meet him at Quetta. At parting, Mr. Bell, who had treated the deputies in a most friendly manner, desired them to convey to the young *khan* his assurances of friendship, and, after the Brahooe custom, he gave his hand to Sirdar Meer Khamal Khan, as the representative of Meer Nasseer Khan, and desired him to give it to the *khan*, as a token of the sincerity of the British agent. Mr. Bell, at the same time, delivered into my charge, before the assembled *sirdars*, a reply to the *khan's* letter, embodying the substance of what he had communicated to the chiefs. The latter, as will subsequently appear, were much gratified by their reception at Baugh.

We took our departure on the 11th of March, and reached Kotroo again on the 13th, where I found letters from the young *khan*, shewing that he was uneasy at our protracted absence, and complaining of the difficulty of finding subsistence in the country. I made advances for the purchase of grain and hire of camels, and wrote to the Hindoos at Zeedee, Kozdar, and Baughwanna, to prepare supplies.

Here, a Persian letter was received by my Brahooe interpreter, Moolla Mahomed, from the *moonshee* of Lieutenant Hammersley, stating that I was ordered to join my regiment at Candahar, and that that officer was appointed to Kelat. Letters reached me also to the same effect. This information was industriously circulated in the camp, and the chiefs waited upon me to know if it was true. I was forced to acknowledge that it was Lord Auckland's order, and, after much discussion, they determined that an appeal to Mr. Ross Bell should be made against it by the *khan* and all his chiefs.

We resumed our journey on the 16th, and arrived at the young *khan's* camp on the 20th. The deputies accompanied me to Meer Nasseer Khan, to whom I presented the letter and compliments of Mr. Bell, and proposed that Meer Khamal Khan, to whom I said Mr. Bell had more particularly addressed himself, not only as the highest in rank of the deputies, but as the *khan's* relation, should relate all that had occurred at the interview with the political agent. The *meer*, who was in the best possible humour at his reception at Baugh, detailed with eager delight the attentions paid to the deputies; their being allowed to enter the camp and *durbar* with their arms; the assurances that his alienated lands should be restored, and the money levied by the *naib* Mahomed Hussein refunded; not forgetting the ball-shooting matches with the Burra Sahib.

On giving to the young *khan* "Ross Bell's hand," the *meer* dwelt with enthusiasm upon every kind expression he could call to mind as coming from the Sahib-e-Kelan, whose refusal to release the son of Meer Boheer and the Zheree prisoners taken at Kotroo he justified with consummate tact. He appealed to Meer Khan Mahomed and the *darogah*, who confirmed his statement, and the *khan* testified his gratification at the recital.

We commenced our march towards Quetta on the 21st of March, and reached Zeedee, where the *khan's* mother was, next day. Here I was seized with fever and ague, but was obliged to examine into claims instituted by the Hindoos at this place, for grain supplied to the camp in my absence, and to negotiate for the restoration of articles of value belonging to the *khan* and his mother, which had been pledged to relieve their pressing distress. Matters were not adjusted so as to allow of our departure until the 24th. When I took leave of the young *khan's* mother, she gave her son (of whom she was dotingly fond, he being her only child) to my protection. "Take him," she said, weeping; "he is yours; if you are kind to him, an orphan, God will be kind to you; place him upon his martyred father's throne, and the Ahmedzyes will bless you, and the Brahooe and Belooche will remember you in their prayers."

Upon the march, it soon became evident that Rheimdad had commenced his intrigues. He had assumed all the airs of office at Zeedee, took a prominent part in everything, and was obviously plotting the downfall of the *darogah*. His object was to prevent the meeting between the *khan* and Mr. Bell; with this aim, anonymous letters were written to and received by the *khan*, dissuading him from proceeding further, and attempts were made to insinuate suspicions of me. Letters were dropped in the camp, stating that I was leading the *khan* into captivity; that Shah Newaz Khan was to be placed upon the throne of Kelat; that a great battle had been fought at Candahar, in which General Nott's army had been routed and dispersed, the general and a few *sepoys* having been seen flying towards Cabool!

The silly people into whose hands these mischievous inventions fell, whilst they believed them, characteristically concealed them from my knowledge; and the first indication I had that there was something wrong was by receiving a request that we should halt. I remonstrated, but in vain. As soon as it was dark, the *sirdars* met, and a stormy debate took place. The opposition, headed by Rheimdad, denounced me, and even the reasonable party were alarmed. Moolla Nasseer Oolla was sent for, and endeavoured to reason them into sense and tranquillity; but high words again ensued, and although the *khan* declared that he would believe me sooner than Brahooe or Belooche, the *durbar* broke up in a panic.

The following morning early, the *khan* came to my tent, expressing a hope that I should not be displeased at what had occurred, and Darogah Gool Mahomed (who had been infected by the panic) followed, who apologized in the name of the camp. I replied that, so long as they chose to place reliance upon information contained in letters without seals, and to keep that information from me, they would be at the mercy of every mischievous and ill-disposed person; and strove to dispel their suspicions by assuring them that their interests and ours were identical.

On the 31st, Meer Khamal Khan and Meer Esah Khan, who had not been summoned to the late *durbar*, rode up to my tent, fully armed and equipped, in a state of much excitement. They informed me that they had absented themselves from the *durbar* because men of no rank now engrossed the ear of the *khan*, and consequently their honour was not safe, inasmuch as they were pledged to accompany him and me to Mr. Ross Bell, and declared that they and their followers were ready to move. I applauded their conduct in adhering to the contract with the Company, and pacified them, saying I would go to the *khan* and settle a day to march.

In the course of this conversation, whilst they were exposing the characters and conduct of the opposition chiefs, the circumstance of the *shikaree*, Mallooke, being hired to assassinate me at Zheree was first disclosed. I spoke to the young *khan* respecting the complaint made by his best friends, the Sirdars Khamal Khan and Esah Khan, of the want of respect towards them, and the danger of throwing himself into the hands of Rheimdad and the other *khanezadehs* (slave-born), telling him I was well aware that persons not *sirdars* were dissuading him from going to Quetta, and entreated him to discard all such dangerous advisers and to pay no regard to secret and anonymous communications. The *khan* was much embarrassed, but assured me that he relied upon me, and was ready to move. I made up the breach between the *khan* and the two *sirdars*, and, the grain disbursements and other arrangements being completed, the march was resumed on the 1st April.

The *khan*, who had been attacked by fever on the 30th *ult.*, was much reduced and very weak on reaching Zingeerah, on the 3rd April, and on the next day I found we must halt at Sohrab. I had sent to the Hindoos to purchase grain, but reports being spread that the Brahooes would be allowed to plunder, the Hindoos ran to the hills. It appeared that Meer Azim Khan had made a *chupao* on Sohrab some months ago, and carried off their grain, so that their apprehensions were not groundless.

During the halt, Gool Mahomed brought me the draft of a letter from the *khan* to Mr. Ross Bell, of which I approved, suggesting, however, the use of milder terms when speaking of their grievances, namely, the capture of Kelat and "martyrdom"' of Mehrab Khan; the non-payment of the money promised for the passage of the Bolan; the *chupao* at Kotroo; the capture of Beejar Khan, and the seizure and hanging of the Kaukers at Quetta. My suggestions were adopted; the letter was brought to me fairly written, and I said it was quite unobjectionable; but when the question of its transmission was discussed, it was never mentioned to me that Rheimdad (who appears to have extorted a promise to that effect from the *khan*) was to be the bearer. I proposed, for reasons which I stated, that Meer Esah Khan should convey the letter to Mr. Bell, which suggestion was immediately assented to, and I wrote introductory letters bespeaking attention to the *meer* and his followers on his route.

On the 6th April, having sent off the baggage as usual, I waited some time for the *khan* to recommence our march, when Kallee Khan, a *duffadar* of irregular horse, who lived between Mr. Bell's camp and the *khan's*, came and informed me that the whole night had been spent in the *khan's* camp in *durbar*, respecting some papers from Kelat, Rheimdad having been very busy in the matter. I sent Moolla Nasseer Oolla to the *khan*, to say, if he was not ready, I would go gently forward. The *moolla*, on his way, called upon the *darogah*, whom he found in great grief. He said that letters had been received from Kelat, which declared that I was taking the *khan* into captivity, and Rheimdad had carried them to the *khan*, in consequence of which several of the *sirdars* had resolved that it was dangerous for him to proceed. Moolla Nasseer Oolla, with much difficulty, persuaded the *darogah* to accompany him to Rheimdad's quarters.

The ex-*naib* had gone to the *khan's*, whither they followed him, and discussed the subject of the "letters without seals," which Moolla Nasseer Oolla did not scruple to say were written or concocted in the camp. Finding it impossible to change the resolution of Rheimdad and his party, the *moolla* left, and was soon after joined by Rheimdad, with a body of *sepoys*, and Fakeer Mahomed Beezenjow, of Nal, who accompanied him to the place where I was waiting his return. As soon as I saw Rheimdad approaching, I concluded matters had gone wrong, it being Gool Mahomed's office to bring me messages; and the ill-concealed delight which gleamed in the countenance of Rheimdad fortified my conclusion. "The *khan*," he said, "presents compliments, and has sent me to inform you he will go no further, and begs you will return to Kelat."

I replied, "Well, the *khan* is his own master; I will go and take leave of him, when I shall learn the truth from his own lips." Passing through the crowd, who reluctantly gave way, I walked quietly to the compound where the *khan* lodged, which was crowded with people, armed, and in a state of great ferment. I inquired for the room in which the *khan* was, and finding he did not come to the door to meet me, I looked in and saw that he was held back by Rheimdad's people, the *khan's* usual personal, guards having been removed.

On entering the room, I perceived two of Rheimdad's servants standing near the *khan*, with fierce looks, grasping, in a menacing attitude, the hilts of their swords, whilst the countenances of all around wore an expression of strong emotion. Not appearing to notice this, I took the young *khan* by the hand, and tears stood in his eyes when I said I had come to learn from him whether he really intended to go no farther, and wished me to leave his camp. He replied, without hesitation, in a firm and decisive manner, that he wished to go with me, but the *durbar* would not allow him; that letters had been received which affirmed that he was to be seized at Kelat or Shawl Kote; that our own *sepoys* had said so, and that Shah Newaz was to be replaced upon the throne. I told him that his principal chiefs had not been present when this resolution was formed, the Sirdars Meer Boheer, Meer Khamal Khan, and Meer Esah Khan having been absent, and I proposed that a *durbar* should be called when they should have returned.

Atta Khan (who was intoxicated with *b'hang* at the time) and Fakeer Mahomed interposed, saying the affair was settled, and the *khan* would go no further; adding, "Take leave and go; no one is angry with you, but go; you have always spoken truth; but Ross Bell has ordered it, who is the higher authority, and the Lord Sahib has removed our friend," meaning me, "and sent Hasly Sahib," meaning Lieutenant Hammersley, "who is our enemy."

I asked to see the letters they referred to, which they admitted came from Kelat; but this they refused, on the pretext that I would hang the writer, and I could get nothing from them but a reiteration of their resolution that the *khan* should not go further, and of their advice that I should return to Kelat. I appealed to the multitude, declaring I had nothing but the *khan's* welfare at heart, and asked whether I had ever been untrue to my engagements. I called upon Gool Mahomed, as the *darogah*, to advise his master. "I am humbled in the dust," was the old man's answer. Meer Esah Khan had now returned, and I addressed him, reminding him how he had boasted of the influence and bravery of his tribe. He replied that he was but one, and it was useless for him to speak.

"Better leave these people," he said; "they are mad." Before I took leave of the *khan*, I made a last effort to inspire him with spirit and energy to act for himself. He repeated that he wished to go with me.

"Who then," I asked, "should prevent you?"

Atta Mahomed said, "The *durbar* resolve he shall not go."

I asked him if he was the sovereign, and the *khan*, whether he wore a sword and shield to look at. Cries of "Rise! Take leave? Go to Kelat!" which had been heard at intervals, in a subdued voice, were now uttered loudly by most of the assembly. The agitation increased, and Meer Esah Khan, as well as my two *vakeels*, earnestly recommended me to take leave. Holding up my hand for silence, I declared I was the friend of the *khan* and of the Brahooes, and asked, if I left them, who would shew him the path to his father's throne? I implored them to wait until the absent *sirdars* returned that day; but after two hours spent in entreaties and expostulations on my part, and the reiteration of "Rise and go," from the people present, accompanied by a disclaimer of all anger or dissatisfaction towards me.

I shook hands with the young *khan*, and proceeded deliberately to the door, Meer Esah Khan placing himself behind me, and Moolla Nasseer Oolla and my Brahoe interpreter (who was almost expiring with fright) on either side. I walked very slowly through the crowd, towards the orchard, where my horses and camels were waiting for me, and where I told the *sirdar* and the *moolla* I would stay to take leave of Meer Khamal Khan, who was expected before evening.

They both answered at once, "No, mount immediately," Esah Khan offering to go with me. As they insisted upon my moving without delay, I requested Esah Khan to remain and explain to Meer Khamal Khan the cause of my departure, and to tell him that not a shadow of blame was to be attributed to the *khan*, who, in the presence of the principal *sirdars*, had been compelled to act as he did by bad advice. Promising to wait at Rodenjoh for a communication from the *sirdars*, I mounted and rode to Soormasing, intending to halt there for the night; but Moolla Nasseer Oolla and others begged me to proceed to Kelat, declaring that, from all they had heard and seen, they feared the Brahooes would make a *chupao* during the night.

I observed that, if they desired to destroy us, they had had better opportunities; but the *moolla* urging that, if anything befell me, he and his family would be dishonoured and ruined, I placed myself under the guidance of the *moolla's* son (the *moolla* himself and the servants remaining for the night at Rodenjoh), and with two attendants, one of them a deer-stalker, who knew the country, we deserted the road, and by a direct line reached Kelat about ten at night.

I subsequently heard, and have no doubt of the fact, that Rheimdad declared, that if the *darogah*, the *moolla*, and I resisted the retrograde movement of the *khan*, we should all be cut up upon the spot; and Meer Esah Khan assured me, that menacing gestures and signs were frequently made in *durbar*, by drawing fingers across the throat, and that whispers were circulated of "Kill the *Feringhee!*" I was likewise informed by Kallee Khan (who was ordered to leave the Brahooe camp and go to the English), that when the young *khan* learned I was gone, he cried bitterly, declaring he was ruined, and for some time refused to mount; and that he sent the *darogah* and Rheimdad to beg me not to desert him.

Although my negotiations with the *khan* were thus suspended by the temporary success of Rheimdad's intrigues, I did not consider they were broken off (as I informed Mr. Ross Bell), and I awaited at Kelat an opportunity to renew them.

The day after my return to this place, walking with Major Clarkson, commanding the 42nd Bengal Native Infantry and the garrison of Kelat, I related to him the remark made by Mahomed Nasseer Khan, in the mock *durbar*, that "even our own *sepoys*, at Kelat, had said he was to be seized." Major Clarkson doubted the truth of the statement, and I gave him the name of one of his own non-commissioned officers (which I had learned from one of the *khan's* servants), a Mussulman, as one of the parties to whom the report was attributed. Soon after, the major remarked, as a man approached us, "This is the very person you spoke of."

With Major Clarkson's permission, I questioned the man, who admitted that he had said in the *bazar*, to the Bullattees (people of the country), by way of joke, "that, when the *khan* came in, his regiment was to seize him!"

In my report of these transactions to Mr. Ross Bell, I traced the causes of the temporary failure of the negotiations to the letters written from Kelat,—no doubt by agents of Rheimdad and those who desired the return of Shah Newaz Khan,—believed by ignorant men, who had some reason for distrust, and were fortified in it by the conduct of the Government in announcing that I was to be replaced by Lieutenant Hammersley, towards whom they felt a dislike. This distrust, I observed, was not the growth of a day; it dated from the time when Shah Newaz Khan was allowed to cross the Indus in the train of Shah Shooja-ool-Moolk, which was one of the principal grievances complained of by the young *khan*.

Shah Shooja owed his life to the late Mehrab Khan, who, when the *shah*, in his flight from Affghanistan, neared Kelat, his pursuers close upon him and his cattle failing, marched out to his succour, drove his pursuers back, conveyed the *shah* into Kelat, fed and clothed him, and, when he desired to depart, filled his purse and escorted him to the Indus. In spite of this, Shah Shooja was suffered to bring the *khan's* deadliest foe in his train. Such a return might engender suspicion and distrust in men of more enlightened understandings than these rude and savage tribes; and when, on the fall of Mehrab Khan, we placed not his son, but Shah Newaz Khan, upon the throne, their belief in the treachery of the English became inveterate.

The impression amongst them was, that Mehrab Khan was sacrificed or "martyred;" that Shah Newaz Khan was brought across the Indus expressly to be placed upon the throne of Kelat; that Mehrab Khan's officers were bought over by Shah Shooja and Shah Newaz Khan, whilst the latter was residing under the protection of the British flag, and this impression was confirmed by the understanding that Shah Newaz Khan, after his expulsion from Kelat, was still maintained, west of the Indus, on liberal allowances paid by the British government.

Under the circumstances, I pressed Mr. Ross Bell to give the young *khan* a meeting at Kelat, which could be managed so as not to wear the aspect of improper concession, and when he was once there, and upon his throne, no silly *cabal* on the part of his chiefs could interrupt the negotiations; nothing would or could be refused, and no durbar could dictate to the *khan*.

On the 9th of April, a horseman arrived from the *khan*, with a verbal message, that Meer Khamal Khan had met him in his retrograde movement, and rescued him from the thraldom of Rheimdad, whom the *khan* had turned out of his camp with ignominy; adding, that the *sirdars*, Meer Khamal Khan, Meer Esah Khan, and Meer Boheer, would wait upon me immediately. Nothing could be more gratifying than this intelligence, which shewed, moreover, the influence I had acquired in the *khan's* camp. Meer Khamal Khan, who arrived on the afternoon of the 10th, confirmed the accounts I had received, and the next day I had letters from the *khan*, Gool Mahomed, and the Akoon Mahomed Sudeeq.

It appears that, when Rheimdad was turned out of the camp, he went to Meer Mahomed Azim Khan, at Zheree, and endeavoured to raise the country; but Azim was too prudent or too cunning to enter into the ex-*naib's* desperate schemes. Baulked in this design, he seized Dewan Ramoo, who, finding that the *khan*, to whose cause he was devoted, was in bad hands, had left the camp and come to Zheree. Ramoo was brought to Rheimdad's house, and 7,000 *rupees* were demanded of him. The *dewan* pleaded, as well he might, poverty; he was pinioned and placed in confinement.

Next day, Meer Azim Khan, hearing of the *dewan's* ill-treatment, armed some of his people and proceeded to Rheimdad's house, released Dewan Ramoo, and abusing Rheimdad, desired him to leave Zheree, which he was compelled to do, and after vain attempts to excite the adjoining population of Gud'h, he retired eventually to Moostung, where I found him, a few days after this (April 15th), comfortably encamped in the next garden to that occupied by Lieutenant Wallace, the assistant political agent.

Meer Boheer Khan arrived at Kelat on the 11th, and I arranged that he, Meer Khamal Khan, and Syud Faizil Shah, instead of proceeding with me to Mr. Bell, should return with all expedition to Baughwanna, whither the *khan* had moved, to prevent evil-disposed persons from persuading him to leave that place, and to be ready to accompany him to Kelat, if, upon considering my representations, Mr. Bell should invite the *khan* to proceed thither. I had resolved to go to Mr. Bell at Quetta, in order to obviate the effect which might be produced upon his mind by disingenuous suggestions respecting the motive of the *khan's* retrograde movement.[6]

I reached Quetta on the 17th of April, and my statements convinced Mr. Ross Bell that the khan's movement had been compulsory, and he therefore wrote to him to say that the whole affair was satisfactorily explained, and that he hoped he would proceed to Quetta without delay, under the assurances contained in his former letters. I returned to Kelat on the 22nd.

I forwarded the letters from Mr. Bell, with one of my own to the *khan*, to Meer Khamal Khan, Meer Esah Khan, and the Akoon Mahomed Sudeeq, at Baughwanna, begging the *sirdars* to lose no time in joining me at Kelat. Some disturbance appeared at this moment to have occurred at Baughwanna, for the Darogah Gool Mahomed had been at Sohrab, Zheree, and Gud'h; but the Beebee Ganjan, who had been at Sohrab when the *darogah* was there, on her arrival at Kelat,

---

6. My surmises were not without foundation. I afterwards received a caricature, representing the *khan* going off in high glee, whilst I was beseeching him, as "my son," not to leave "his father."

denied, "by the beard of the prophet," that she knew anything of him or his whereabouts.

This appeared to me so strange, that I drew Mr. Ross Bell's attention to the circumstance, and on the same day (24th of April) I received a letter from that gentleman, with an extract of one from Captain Bean, the political agent at Quetta, reporting the departure of Gool Mahomed from Baughwanna, "in the direction of Kharan," which he considered to be fraught with some mischievous intent, and which caused Captain Bean to "feel somewhat anxious regarding the safety of Kelat," though, in fact, Gool Mahomed was in the very opposite direction to Kharan, whilst, with upwards of 800 bayonets, the garrison of Kelat could have held the fortress against any force which the Brahooes or Belooches could have brought against it. Equally groundless was a report sent from Moostung, that the *darogah* was within eleven miles of that place, with a large force, intent upon surprising the weak detachment there. Such statements (denoting a lack of authentic information), however absurd they may now appear, tended very materially to disturb our camp, and to enable evil-minded people to perplex and neutralize my arrangements.

On the 25th of April, I wrote to Mr. Ross Bell, at Quetta, relieving his mind of all apprehension as to the danger of Kelat, and on the following day I had a letter from him (written before he had received mine), directing me to quit Kelat, and proceed to Moostung, on the evening of the 2nd of May, or morning of the 3rd, if the young *khan* did not join me before that time; and if he came, accompanied by Gool Mahomed and Rheimdad, he was to be told that it was necessary he should discard these two individuals from about his person prior to his arrival at Quetta, as they would not be acknowledged, or indeed permitted to come to that place under a safe-conduct. Mr. Bell observed that "the conduct of Rheimdad is what might have been expected:" whereas, as I have before stated, this man was released by Mr. Bell without my knowledge, and I wrote to him immediately that it was "a mistake."

Oh the 30th of April, receiving no letters from Baughwanna, I sent Moolla Nasseer Oolla thither, resolving to remain at Kelat until he should return with tidings of the *khan's* intentions. The next day, a man, named Kunder Bux, called upon me, and, stating he had come from Baughwanna, requested a private audience. He informed me, with a great parade of secrecy, that he was the chief spy of Mr. Ross Bell, who had sent him to Baughwanna, to ascertain what the *khan* and his chiefs meditated, and assured me they were a set of rascals, and had not the slightest intention to come to Kelat. He wound up his statement by declaring that he had lamed his horse by the rapidity of his journey, and requesting a supply of money, which I declined to give, being dissatisfied with his replies, and struck with the improbability of his story. On the following day, I received a letter purporting to come from the *khan*, which I knew to be a forgery.

Moolla Nasseer Oolla returned on the 2nd of May, with letters from the khan (having met his *kasid*), who, in consequence of information that Lieutenant Hammersley was coming to Kelat, with more troops, and that the Kotroo force was preparing to move, had gone to Muskye; but unaccompanied by a single chief. I sent the letters to Mr. Bell, pointing out to him that the departure of the *khan* for Muskye was a measure, not of hostility, but of natural precaution for his personal safety. My construction of the act was confirmed by letters brought on the 3rd, by Meer Esah Khan, from Meer Khamal Khan, addressed to Mr. Bell and myself, which stated that they had heard of operations meditated against them, and Meer Esah Khan had consequently been deputed to explain to Mr. Bell, that the khan had moved to Muskye until an explanation should be received respecting the military preparations, which were in fact making on both sides of Kelat.

In conversation with Sirdar Esah Khan, the communication made to me by Kunder Bux was mentioned, and it turned out that this identical man had been to the *durbar* at Baughwanna, telling them that he was Mr. Ross Bell's head spy, but, being a follower of the prophet, he would not betray them to the *Feringhees*, and gave them notice that it would be dangerous for them to go to Kelat or Quetta, for that he knew it was the intention of the *Sahib-loge* to seize the *khan* and his followers. At this moment, the *khan* and *sirdars* were ready to move to Kelat; but, after questioning Kunder Bux and another man from Kotroo, who affirmed that preparations were making there for the movement of the British troops, it was considered necessary to place the *khan* out of danger.

The facts, of the march of Her Majesty's 41st Foot to Moostung, and the arrival of a company of the 43rd Bengal Native Infantry, with two guns, at Kelat, from Quetta, coupled with the preparations making at Kotroo for the withdrawal of the force to Baugh, lent an appearance of confirmation to the representations of these men, that the English were about to attack the *khan's* camp. The resolution of the *durbar* was, therefore, very natural and prudent; and, accordingly, instead of moving to Kelat, the *khan* proceeded to Muskye, and the minor chiefs separated, each returning to his home.

Invitations had been sent to Meer Azim Khan, Sirdar Meer Taj Mahomed, the chiefs of Zheree, Punderan, and Nechara, to meet me at Kelat; but as they could not assemble there before the 9th or 10th of May, on the 5th Meer Esah Khan determined to write to Mr. Bell respecting Kunder Bux, and he accordingly drew up a statement of what had passed at the *durbar* at Baughwanna, requesting that the man might be secured, and confronted with him on his arrival at Quetta.

On the 10th, Prince Meer Mahomed Azim Khan, Sirdar Meer Taj Mahomed and his mother. Sirdar Meer Boheer Khan, and the Zheree, Punderan, and Nechara chiefs, arrived at Kelat, and on the 13th we commenced our march to Quetta. The very next day, on our arrival at Girannee, an incident occurred which shewed how frail were the materials to which I must trust for the accomplishment of my mission. A messenger arrived with letters from Lieutenant Wallace, Naib Mahomed Hussein, his native assistant, and Beebee Ganjan, and from the verbal statements of the horseman who brought these letters (as I afterwards found), upon the strength of the ordinary concluding paragraph of the *naib's* letter,—"I send this by a man you may trust, believe all he tells you,"—Meer Azim Khan took it into his head that he was to be exalted to the *khanship* of Kelat!

His partisans actually performed "*mobarik*," that is, saluted him as *khan*, and he made liberal promises of *naibships*. The *sirdars* and I, who were located a mile distant from Azim Khan and his party, did not hear of this farce until our arrival at Mungochur, next day, I called for the letters, in which I found nothing objectionable, and pacified the *sirdars* by assuring them that so important a measure could not have been decided upon without my being informed of it. Upon our approach to Moostung, on the 16th, we were met by Naib Mahomed Hussein, with a very large mounted *sowaree*. I acquainted the *naib* with the result of his message by the horseman. He denied that he had sent any message that could have had such a result, and said the horseman was a servant of the Beebee Ganjan.

This amiable lady had proposed herself, Azim Khan, and Naib Mahomed Hussein, as a regency for the *khanat*. I had received intelligence on our journey that Rheimdad was living at Moostung, and I asked the *naib* whether he was his guest. He disclaimed all intercourse with him, and gave him a bad character, I went immediately to Lieutenant

Wallace, who assured me that he had given Rheimdad no inducement whatever to visit Moostung. I proposed to him that he should give me six horsemen, that I might send Rheimdad down to Mr. Bell, at Quetta; but he said he had none to spare from district duty. I could not help observing that a crowd of horsemen had attended his native assistant, Mahomed Hussein. I wrote immediately to Brigadier England, commanding the troops at Moostung, for a guard to receive charge of a prisoner; the guard was sent, and Rheimdad, who (as I before stated) was residing in the next garden to Lieutenant Wallace, was consigned to the custody of the brigadier (though allowed every indulgence), to await the orders of Mr. Ross Bell.

We recommenced our journey on the 19th, and reached Quetta on the 21st. Next day, a *durbar* was held, at which Mr. Ross Bell assured the prince and *sirdars* that he had never employed Kunder Bux, who was afterwards produced, confronted with Meer Esah Khan and myself, and fully convicted.

On the 25th May, Sirdar Meer Esah Khan returned to the *khan* with assurances from Mr. Bell that he had been deceived by Kunder Bux, and had misunderstood the object of our military movements, and an invitation that he would join me at Kelat. The day after he had left, the news that Shah Newaz Khan had reached Dadur, on his way to Quetta, spread consternation in our camp. I had not been informed that he had been actually sent for, and I endeavoured to tranquillize the *sirdars* by stating that Shah Newaz Khan had disagreed with the *ameers* of Scinde, and was coming to Quetta merely to make arrangements respecting his future place of residence. The alarm which this incident excited, however, induced Mr. Bell to send off letters instantly, directing that Shah Newaz Khan should halt at Dadur. Meer Esah Khan had learned his approach, and had halted until he heard from me that the movement of Shah Newaz Khan would in no way interfere with the interests of Meer Nasseer Khan, and I despatched one of the *khan's* most trusted servants with a letter to his master containing the same assurance.

On the 1st June, the prince and chiefs having taken leave in *durbar*, we departed from Quetta, and arrived at Kelat on the 8th. Three days after, I despatched Moolla Nasseer Oolla and Dewan Bamoo to accompany the young *khan* to Kelat, having received positive instructions not to leave Kelat myself for this purpose. A *kasid* had arrived the previous evening from the *khan*, but his letter had been taken from him, and he had a deep sword-cut on the head. He informed me that the *khan* was unwell at Muskye, but that he waited only for the *moolla* and the *dewan* to commence his march to join me.

On the 19th, I received a letter from Mr. Bell, enclosing the copy of one from Major Gore Browne (transmitted through Brigadier England), stating that Darogah Gool Mahomed had passed me to the eastward and was not ten miles from the post of Moostung. I knew this to be impossible, and immediately wrote to this effect to Mr. Bell, assuring him that the *darogah* was quietly located at Baughwanna; nevertheless, on this loose and false information, he issued orders to Lieutenant Wallace, at Moostung, to seize the *darogah*. I felt that, had such an order got abroad, it would infallibly arrest the progress of the *khan*, and I despatched a *kasid* to Mr. Bell, entreating him to adopt no measures against Gool Mahomed, who would never embark in hostile designs whilst his wife and children were within my reach at Sohrab.

These circumstances prove not only how ill-informed were the British authorities at Shawl and Moostung as to the movements of the chiefs,—in fact, many of the "political" were made the dupes of their native *omlah*; but that there were individuals interested in widening the breach between the *khan* and the British authorities, who found the propagation of these groundless rumours the most effectual means of accomplishing their mischievous intents. Moostung was farmed by the *moonshee* of the assistant political agent of Kelat, residing at that place, and Shawl yielded a handsome emolument to the establishment there, and these places, as well as Kelat itself, would probably slip from their hands if I succeeded in inducing the young *khan* to come in.

On the 21st June, letters from Moolla Nasseer Oolla and Dewan Ramoo informed me that the *khan* was preparing to leave Muskye. Letters also came from Darogah Gool Mahomed, at Sohrab, whither he had been carried in a *kujawa* (owing to an attack of ague) from Baughwanna, requesting my permission to come to Kelat, to consult with me on matters of moment connected with the *khan's* approach, as soon as his ague would permit him to travel, and I granted the request.

The frequent reports, which reached Kelat, that I was to be recalled, and Lieutenant Hammersley or Lieutenant Wallace sent to replace me, caused me so much embarrassment, that I remonstrated by letters with Mr. Ross Bell on the danger attending such a measure, if meditated, and begged he would leave me undisturbed to complete the service he had committed to me. The country was quiet; the city of Kelat was daily improving, and I added that a change, for which there was no immediate necessity, might replunge affairs into confusion.

Accounts were received on the 25th from Baughwanna, where the *khan* was, that he had been seized with ague, and that there had been high words between Meer Khamal Khan and Dewan Ramoo: the latter was for proceeding directly to Kelat, the farmer for delay. The *dewan* prevailed. Another question was agitated at Baughwanna; namely, whether the *khan* should be married before or after his return from Quetta, and (his betrothed being present) it was decided that the marriage should take place forthwith. Moolla Nasseer Oolla subsequently told me that, when the former question was debated in *durbar*, the *khan* said, "I shall go to Colonel Stacy at Kelat; he has never deceived me; he has been my friend. If he seize me, as you say he will, I would rather be his prisoner than anybody else's, and I may be seized today or tomorrow; but I never will believe the colonel will break his word."

After the *durbar*, the *khan* ordered preparations to be made for the journey, and he told Nasseer Oolla that he had another reason for going, which he had not disclosed to the *durbar*. "If," said he, "I go upon the invitation of the colonel, and he restores me to my throne, he will never remind me of the boon; but if I now delay going, and afterwards proceed to Kelat by advice of one of my chiefs, that person will assume the merit of having restored me, and claim villages for himself and his family, grain for his relations, &c., which would get me a bad name." This reason, if not a shrewd one, is characteristic of the Brahooe principles of policy.

On the 26th, further notice reached me of Mr. Bell's intentions to send another officer to relieve me at Kelat, and I again wrote, strongly remonstrating against such a measure at the present crisis. A letter from Mr. Bell came on the 28th, disapproving in decided terms of my having allowed Darogah Gool Mahomed an interview, and ordering me not to remain at Kelat after the 28th. Mr. Bell, who had relinquished all hope of the *khan's* coming in, also spoke of establishing a provisional government, and mentioned (whilst he highly commended my exertions) that Lieutenant Hammersley, having been appointed by the Government to take charge of Kelat, was to proceed thither as soon as possible.

Intelligence arrived on the 30th from the *moolla* and *dewan*, that the young *khan* had been married to the daughter of Mehnaj Bee-bee, one of the widows of Sirdar Meer Reshid Khan, and that they were to commence their march this day, though illness prevailed at

Baughwanna, scarcely a man being free from fever or ague. Meanwhile, frequent *kasids* were passing between Shah Newaz Khan and Meer Khamal Khan, whose sister (when a widow) the former had married; and I reported the fact, as I had done before, to Mr. Bell.

On the 3rd July, letters came from the *khan* and Akoon Mahomed Sudeeq, to the address of Mr. Bell, and, having his authority to do so, I opened and read them, previously to forwarding them. They both contained assurances of their intention to join me without delay. On the 4th, Darogah Gool Mahomed was brought to Kelat in a *kujawa*, so ill that I was called up in the middle of the night to prescribe for him.

The next day I received a public letter from Mr. Ross Bell, dated 3rd July, enclosing one he had addressed to Lieutenant Hammersley, requesting me to make over charge of Kelat to that officer. The instructions to the lieutenant were, that he should lose no time in relieving me of the charge; that detailed instructions should be communicated, and that in the mean time he would exercise a careful watch over the native authorities of the district, and collect and record information regarding the movements of Nasseer Khan and Darogah Gool Mahomed, as well as the proceedings of the various Jhalawan chiefs.

In his letter to me (which acknowledged mine of the 30th June), Mr. Bell expressed much regret that I had not started for Quetta, and, referring to information which had reached him concerning the intrigues of Gool Mahomed, he observed he could no longer delay taking steps for the immediate administration of Kelat.

I immediately wrote to Mr. Bell, and, adverting to the letters I had forwarded to him from the *khan* and the *akoon*, on the same day he had penned the orders now received, expressed confidence that, on reading them, he would cancel the orders, and detain Lieutenant Hammersley at Quetta. It was very evident that Mr. Bell had felt the force of my letters of the 29th and 30th June, from the last paragraph of his private letter of the 3rd July:

> Were it possible Meer Mahomed Nasseer Khan now entertains any serious intention of joining you, he must have actually done so long before Lieutenant Hammersley can reach Kelat, a circumstance which would, of course, render it unnecessary to proceed with any new arrangements, pending a reference to Government.

I remained in a state of anxious suspense until the 8th, when I received an express from Mr. Ross Bell, written immediately on his reception of the *khan's*, the *akoon's* and the *dewan's* letters, which I had despatched on the 3rd. He courteously replied to their communications, cancelled the order for Lieutenant Hammersley to proceed to Kelat, and congratulated me upon my near prospect of ultimate success.

Another express from Mr. Bell, written on the same day, followed in a few hours, informing me that rumours were afloat of treachery on the part of the *khan*, warning me to be on my guard, and transmitting instructions to the officer commanding the garrison, to be upon the alert. Even at the last hour, the mind of the political agent appears to have been poisoned by the suspicions which these unfounded rumours infused into it. There was no ground for the slightest apprehension of treachery, though I took every precaution against it; the *khan* had only fourteen horsemen with him at Muskye, and, since his arrival at Baughwanna, I had always notice of the strength of his party.

From this time until the 20th of July, letters came almost daily from the *khan's* camp with intelligence of their progress, notwithstanding that almost every person, including the *khan* himself, had become ill with fever and ague, which appeared in the city and garrison of Kelat, and the villages around. On that day, I had a letter and message from the *khan*, stating that he was very weak, and that, instead of residing at the Charbagh, in Kelat (as I had proposed), he should prefer encamping at Babawallee, and begging me to join him at Sohrab: adding that I had cured him of ague once before. The truth is, that rumours were still industriously circulated that the *khan* would be seized, and the Brahooes had an idea that my presence was their only security. I promised, in reply, to meet the *khan* at Rodenjoh.

Accordingly, I rode out to that place on the 24th, and found the *khan* in a miserable state of debility, having had the fever and ague upon him for forty-five days. I had brought medicines, and persuaded him to place himself in my hands. The next day, we set off for Kelat, the *khan* being placed upon a camel, and we were forced to make six halts, in the sixteen miles, in order to rest and refresh him. I begged him to remain for the night at a place half-way; but he refused, and it was dark before we reached Kelat, when I had the pleasure of beholding the successful result of my long, tedious, and toilsome exertions.

As soon as the customary presents were got into the camp, I left the *khan* and drew up a report to Mr. Ross Bell, and as it records nothing of a secret or political character, I may be pardoned for inserting it, premising that the hurry in which it was written must be the excuse for its imperfect composition.

Kelat, 25th July, 1841.

Sir,—I have the honour to report that Meer Mahomed Nasseer Khan is with me, the guest of the Honourable Company. He arrived at Rodenjoh yesterday, and sent on to give me notice of his approach; also praying I would join him, which I did, and rode with him to Kelat. The young man is very weak, and much pulled down by his late illness.

Thus has been accomplished the wishes of the Government, without the loss of a single life; the deeply-rooted distrust of the tribes towards the English, and their vindictive feelings against us, changed to an anxious desire to ally themselves to the Honourable Company: and all has been brought, about at an expenditure of less than 20,000 *rupees*. By far the greater part of this sum is chargeable (if such should be the wish of Government) to the Kelat state, as money advanced to enable the young *khan* to disband his army, and for subsistence for himself, chiefs, and followers, during the time I was negotiating with him.

I cannot express the pleasure I feel on the young *khan's* arrival; a weight of responsibility is removed from my shoulders, which was a constant and most painful source of distressing anxiety. I never contemplated the disapprobation of the Government even had I failed, because, from the day I threw myself unattended amongst these strange people, from the moment I opened negotiations with the young *khan* at Zheree, on the 5th February last, up to the present moment, not a *roan* of any tribe has been in arms against us. Twice were the negotiations suspended, *viz*., first, by the villainy of Rheimdad, and secondly, by the rascality of the prisoner, Kunder Bux, a *moonshee* of the Bombay headquarters; still not a man appeared in arms against us; on the contrary, a renewal of negotiations was each time immediately sought for by a deputation of some of the senior chiefs of the *durbar*.

On my first going amongst these people, in the early part of February last, the feeling against our countrymen was most inveterately hostile; they were still smarting under the remembrance of their discomfiture at Kotroo, and the first discussion in *durbar*, on the object of my visit, was consequently of rather a stormy nature. But the arguments quietly offered to their consideration softened down these angry feelings, and the result of temper and conciliation has not only, I trust, led to the present happy occurrence, *viz.*, the coming in of the *khan*; but calmed their angry feelings against us, and left in their place a favourable impression on the minds of both the Brahooe and Belooche tribes, of the sterling value of our national character.

I have periled my life, and suffered many privations, the last seven months; but I was a volunteer for the duty, as well as volunteer for the Army of the Indus. If, in the fortunate accomplishment of the task assigned me, I have merited your approbation, I shall forget the dangers, troubles, and losses I have encountered, in the pleasurable contemplation of the success of my exertions.

I cannot in justice close this hurried report without bringing to your favourable notice the highly praiseworthy conduct of Moolla Nasseer Oolla, Babee, my *vakeel*: from the moment he joined me, on the 11th December, 1840, he has never slackened his persevering and valuable exertions in carrying out the orders of Government. I therefore hope, after inquiry, you may be able to recommend him for some mark of approbation from the Government.

The scale of allowances for the establishment under me was drawn out at a moment when my exertions had been foiled for a time by those two villains, Rheimdad and Kunder Bux, and I feared at such a moment to solicit for Moolla Nasseer Oolla a monthly allowance such as I felt his eminent and unwearied services deserved. I would now presume to suggest that, instead of 100 *rupees per mensem*, Moolla Nasseer Oolla, Babee, should be allowed at least 200 *rupees per mensem*, from the time of his accepting the Company's employ.

I have the honour to be, Sir,
Your most obedient servant,
L. R. Stacy, Lt. col. on special duty.

A copy of this letter I transmitted to the secretary to the Government of India, and received the following reply:—

To Lieutenant-Colonel Stacy, on special duty.

Sir,—I have the honour to acknowledge the receipt of your despatch, dated the 25th *ultimo*, and of its enclosure, reporting the arrival at Kelat of Nasseer Khan, and your intention to accompany him to Quetta. In reply, I am directed to inform you, that the Governor-General in Council considers you entitled to great credit for the zeal and perseverance which you have exhibited in the performance of the duty assigned you, and it is his Lordship in Council's pleasure, that you continue for the present in charge of Nasseer Khan, regarding whom no specific orders will be issued till Government is apprised of the sentiments of Major Outram, who has been appointed Mr. Bell's successor to the charge of our political relations in that quarter, and you will be pleased to place yourself in immediate communication with that officer.

I have, &c.

T. H. Maddock,

Secretary to the Government of India.

Fort William, 30th August, 1841.

On the 27th July, the *khan*, who was decidedly improving, rode to the Charbagh, and returned to join the officers of the garrison and me at a ball-shooting match. On this day, I made arrangements for moving with him towards Quetta, and we commenced our march on the 29th, the *khan* being in high spirits, though still weak, in consequence of which the journey subjected him to much fatigue. We rode into Moostung on the 1st August.

The report, that I was to proceed to Candahar inmiediately after my arrival with the young *khan* at Quetta, was revived. He came to my tent upon this subject; but I could only reply, as before, that my remaining with him rested wholly with the Governor-General. He felt the difficulty of his position, young and inexperienced, surrounded by men whose counsels had ruined his father, and without a single friend in whom he could implicitly confide; under the influence of these feelings, he spontaneously drew up a letter to Mr. Ross Bell, which he sent by his *moonshee.* In this letter, the *khan* said:

I have heard that, in a few days. Colonel Stacy is to be removed from me. You know the minds of my subjects; they are all made happy by the humanity and kindness of Colonel Stacy, because he is both sensible and good. From the time my father was killed, my affairs were in a bad state until Colonel Stacy came to Kelat; since then everything has gone well, because the colonel has been to me as a father. The road by Beila to Soonmea-

51

nee was shut; *cafilahs* and travellers could not pass by it; whereas, at present, through the exertions of Colonel Stacy, they pass and repass without danger of molestation, which makes everyone happy. I hope through your friendship I may not be deprived of Colonel Stacy, for by his means I hope to get my affairs put in proper order, and I am well aware that, in any other gentleman, I should not find such a friend as he is.

The same evening, I received a letter express from Captain Wallace, conveying the melancholy intelligence of the death of Mr. Ross Bell on the 31st July, and stating that he had assumed the superintendence of Upper Scinde until the arrival of Major Outram. The communication authorized me to assure the *khan* that no change would take place in the views of the British authorities regarding him, and urged me not to relax my exertions, hitherto so successful, in perfecting the important and difficult work I had in hand.

As it was inexpedient that the *khan* should learn this event from any other person, I requested him to come to me alone. It was a charming moonlight night, and I ordered carpets to be spread under some trees, a short distance from my tent. When he arrived, and every other person had retired, I communicated to him the death of Mr. Ross Bell, and requested to know his wishes. Without a moment's hesitation, he replied, "You are my father, and I am your son; whatever you advise I will do."

I told him that his alliance with the Company could alone secure his throne and his happiness; that he had seen the folly and the danger of Brahooe councils, and advised him to trust implicitly to the Company. He declared his resolution to unite himself to the Company upon their own terms. Thereupon, I proposed that he should convene a *durbar* immediately; he readily assented, and a summons was despatched to the chiefs, who were soon assembled. At the request of the *khan*, I explained the cause of their meeting so suddenly, and at such an hour, and added that, as the *khan* was young, it was their duty to advise him faiths fully, to the best of their experience and ability. It gratified me to find that their reliance on British integrity led the whole *durbar* at once to counsel the *khan* that he should trust to the generosity of the Company, and follow my advice, as his father and his friend. "All the chiefs, both of Jhalawan and Sarrawan, look to you," said they, addressing me; "if you are kind to him, an orphan, your name will be great."

Next day, I received a communication from Captain Wallace, enclosing letters to the *khan* from himself and Captain Bean, in delivering which I was requested to repeat the assurance of their kindest regard for his interests, and to add that, in Major Outram, he would find a warm advocate with the Government of India. In Captain Wallace's letter to me, he said that he had written to the *khan* to disabuse his mind of the idea that I was ordered to Candahar; "it would be utter ruin, at this crisis, even to talk of such a thing: you and you only can manage matters." These were some of the handsome and friendly expressions used by Captain Wallace, in which Captain Bean concurred.

During the ensuing month, nothing occurred at Kelat worthy of notice. Unremitted attention was required on my part to keep the *khan* amused, and to separate him from evil associates and advisers. No opportunity was lost of destroying the influence of Darogah Gool Mahomed, though in a quiet and inoffensive manner. This person, during the latter years of Mehrab Khan's life, had contrived to possess himself of every appointment in the *khanat*, which he bestowed upon his favourites. Soon after his arrival at Kelat, he professed to be very sanguine of the *wuzeerat*, notwithstanding the many broad hints I had thrown out, that a man of great ability was required to fill so important a post as that of *wuzeer* to so young a prince.

At a subsequent time, he affected to regard my hints as to his incompetency for the situation as jocular, and endeavoured to assume a kind of advocacy of the *khan*, asking what country he was to get, what money he was to have, &c., which I repressed in a civil manner, requesting him to take no unnecessary trouble in such matters, which would be arranged between the British agent and the *khan*. Captain Wallace and I succeeded in inducing Sirdar Mahomed Khan, Sheerwannee, the only remaining absent chief, to come in. Immediately after the *khan's* arrival at Kelat, this *sirdar*, who, as before mentioned, had been mixed up with the affair of Lieutenant Loveday's murder, requested to see me, and we had a long conversation, in the course of which he gave an account of the destruction of the lieutenant's *moonshee*, and the party of *sepoys* under his orders, which accorded precisely with the published statement.

The *sirdar*, by my desire, wrote a petition to Mr. Ross Bell, and I told him he might, pending his orders, remain under my guarantee of safety at Nechara. In my report to Mr. Bell, I was obliged, in justice to Mahomed Khan, to say that, in my conversation with him, he solemnly declared that whoever told me what I informed him had been reported to Mr. Bell,—namely, the details given me respecting Lieutenant Loveday's death by Darogah Gool Mahomed, at Rodenjoh, on the 25th of January,—was a slanderer. The three persons who were present when the *darogah* gave me the particulars, namely, Esah Khan, Moolla Nasseer Oolla, and Moolla Mahomed, were fortunately in the room when I mentioned the fact to the *sirdar*.

During this interval, likewise, I submitted to the Governor-General (Lord Auckland) and the envoy and minister to Cabool (the late Sir William Macnaghten) the circumstances attending my successful negotiations with the *khan* and Brahooe chiefs, and the position in which I was placed on the death of Mr, Ross Bell; suggesting to both the expediency, upon public grounds, considering the influence I had acquired over the young *khan* and his *sirdars*, that I should be suffered to remain at Kelat, lest (as I foresaw) the affairs should fall into disorder. His Lordship, in his reply, spoke in very kind and laudatory terms of my "enterprise and determination," and congratulated me on the success which had attended my efforts; but seemed to misapprehend my position, which was not that of an acting political agent, but a field officer of the army on "special duty."

"On the 3rd September, I received a letter from Major Outram, reporting his arrival at Quetta, and of his having taken charge of the agency of Upper Scinde, and enclosing a letter to the *khan*, inviting him to Quetta. I accordingly accompanied him thither, and the young *khan* was kindly received by Major Outram, who congratulated me on the success of my measures, and the unremitted zeal with which I had prosecuted the very difficult and embarrassing negotiations which had been confided to me. At the subsequent *durbar*, the major assured the young *khan* of the favourable feelings of the Government towards him, and, on his side, the *khan* declared he appreciated the friendship of the Company, and desired to enrol himself amongst the number of their dependants, to live under the shadow of their flag, and to accept whatever terms they offered him. A salute of twenty-one guns from the lines, repeated in camp, announced the *khan's* acknowledgment of the Company's paramount power, and his alliance with the British Government.

We remained at Quetta until the 14th, during which the *khan* and his attendants were highly gratified by the spectacle of our camp and *sepoys*, and especially by a review which Brigadier England ordered for the young *khan*, whose delight and astonishment at the movements of the Bombay Horse Artillery were boundless. The *khan* and the Brahooe chiefs were unable adequately to express their sentiments of admiration.

Accompanied by Major Outram, we reached Kelat on the 26th September, and the 20th *Shaban*, A. H. 1257, answering to the 6th October, 1841, was fixed upon as an auspicious epoch for the installation of the *khan*. Accordingly, on that day, Meer Mahomed Nasseer Khan, son of the ill-advised and ill-fated Mehrab Khan,—who, with all his failings, was an admirer of the English,[7]—was placed upon the throne of his ancestors.

The hour of four p.m. was appointed for the ceremony. I proceeded to the palace about half all hour before that time. Major Outram and every British officer off duty being present, after the usual compliments, the proceedings commenced, and were conducted in strict accordance with Brahooe customs by Major Outram, assisted by Brigadier England and myself. A close-fitting vest, called by the Brahooes *Futtooee*, was first handed to the *khan*, and put upon him by the *kismutgars*, and then the *kummerbund*. Major Outram then presented the sword. A rich *kimkob chogah* was next thrown over his shoulders, when the major led him to his chair. The *khan* being seated, the first fold of the turban, binding the *jeggah* to the cap, was made by Major Outram, the second by the brigadier, and the third by me.

The turban completed, Major Outram shook hands with his Highness, and offered his congratulations (*Moobarik*); he was followed by the brigadier and myself. Every British officer present, rising, then came forward, shook hands with the young prince, and offered *Moobarik*. The chiefs and officers of state then rose, and coming to the front of the carpet on which the *khan's* chair was placed, offered their *Moobarik*. To the surprise of all present, the *Moobarik* of every one of the natives was offered to me: "*Moobarik Khan Sahib! Moobarik Colonel Sahib!*" resounded on all sides.

I was highly gratified at this unexpected tribute of respect and esteem, the first and only instance of the kind recorded in any Asiatic court; and Major Outram, Brigadier England, and every British officer who witnessed the scene, appeared to feel satisfaction and pride at so unusual a mark of honour being conferred upon one of their countrymen. At the conclusion of the ceremony, a royal salute was

---

7. Meer Mehrab Khan was in *durbar* when a *kasid* brought the intelligence that the English army had crossed the Indus, and was encamped upon its right bank. The *khan* immediately stood up in open *durbar*, and invoked success upon the British arms!

fired from the citadel.

During the proceeding, the young *khan* exhibited great command over his feelings; the only instance in which his sensibility in the least overpowered him was when Major Outram and the British officers shook hands with him and saluted him as "Khan of Kelat;" tears were then observed to glisten in his eyes; but it was only a momentary triumph of natural emotion, which was instantly subdued.

Shortly after the installation, as a complement to the ceremony, according to Brahooe etiquette, Major Outram and the British officers accompanied his highness in a ride round the city.

In the evening, the Jhalawans and Sarrawans performed their national dance (*chap*) round a large fire. It is graceful and imposing, though, like all native dances, there is little variety in it, the dancers moving very slowly in a circle to the music of kettledrums and brass clarionets.

Meer Mahomed Nasseer Khan is a young man, of straight, wiry build, but on a rather small scale. His features are handsome; his address is good, and he possesses a greater command of language than any native I have ever met with. He was educated under Darogah Gool Mahomed in the Brahooe accomplishments; namely, taught to read Persian (not to write it), to ride on horseback, to shoot with ball so accurately as to hit the object at the longest distance, and to hunt on foot as well as mounted. He is beloved and respected by Brahooes and Belooches as much as Meer Shah Newaz Khan was despised.

On the 13th October, Kaissoo, the man who put Lieutenant Loveday to death, and who had for a long time defied all our vigilance and activity, was brought in and made over for trial in the agency camp. He gave the following account of the transaction.

On the day of the battle at Dadur, he (Kaissoo) was on duty over the prisoner (Lieutenant Loveday), the other two men in charge of him, Moolladad and Kurreem Khan, being away, the former on business at Dadur, the latter with the troops. Upon the appearance of the English army, the *khan's* troops fled, and on the near approach of the English, he (Kaissoo) became alarmed. The camel on which Lieutenant Loveday rode had been driven off with the rest, and he (Kaissoo) came up to the lieutenant and said "I must kill you, because the *khan's* army has fled and the English are approaching."

Lieutenant Loveday asked if he had the *khan's* orders to kill him; he replied in the negative. The lieutenant then desired him to go and inquire the *khan's* orders, and he accordingly went in the direction of the flying troops, but not finding the *khan*, he returned, and told Lieutenant Loveday the *khan* had fled.

During this time, the English army was getting very near, and he again came up to Lieutenant Loveday, and said, as the English were close at hand, he could delay no longer, and must kill him. Lieutenant Loveday said nothing, but merely put his hand to his moustache. "Unable to wait any longer," Kaissoo added, "as the English army was close, I drew my sword, and killed my prisoner, and then fled with the rest of the people."

Major Outram and his party quitted Kelat for the Bolan on the 15th October, and three days after I accompanied the *khan* to the agent's camp in the Bolan, whence I proceeded to Dadur.

The day before we left Kelat, the *khan* led me into the women's apartments to take leave of his mother. I gave the best advice in my power to the old lady, who cried bitterly. When going away, I took the *khan's* hand and placed it in hers, saying, "At Zeedee, you gave me your son, then a homeless wanderer; I promised he should be my son until I restored him to his father's throne. I have redeemed my pledge, and now give him back to you: may his reign be long and happy!"

Thus was brought to a successful conclusion a ten months' tedious negotiation, prosecuted with anxious toil, not unaccompanied by personal risk, amidst vexations, perplexities, and disappointments, which would have subjected the best disciplined temper to the severest trials. The late Mr. Ross Bell well knew the difficulty and delicacy of the task when he judged it expedient to confide it to an old and experienced officer. Experience, indeed, can alone afford a true notion of the peculiar obstacles which beset the path of a negotiator amongst ignorant and semi-savage tribes, whose habitual craft, dissimulation, and suspicion were sharpened and aggravated by a sense, whether just or not, of perfidy and wrong experienced at our hands.

The character in which I appeared, subordinate to the political agent, whilst, to a certain extent, it limited and controlled my influence with the tribes, may also have exposed me to the jealousy of other British political functionaries, who conceived, though erroneously, that I was in a "false position," whereas I was in the proper position of a military officer on "special duty." To the ordinary embarrassments I encountered must be added those which were caused by the anonymous misrepresentations sent to the Brahooe *sirdars*, by natives in the receipt of British pay, at Quetta and elsewhere, interested (as I have before said) in preventing the return of the young *khan*, who thereby suffered unjustly the odium of being reluctant to come in and ally himself with the English.

Under these circumstances, I may honestly, and without presumption, claim some merit in having accomplished all, and more than all, I undertook to do; extricated Kelat affairs from an entangled and complicated web; saved the Indian Government from a protracted, inglorious, and expensive war; converted exasperated enemies into confiding friends, and made the *khanat* of Kelat one of the firmest and most useful allies of British India.

Nor must the simple but effectual means, to which I chiefly attribute my success, be overlooked, because they may furnish a lesson in analogous cases. At a time when these tribes were in a state of feverish excitement, I threw myself amongst them, unattended by a single *sepoy*, and thereby disarmed their suspicions, dissipated their fears, and conciliated their confidence. It required, it is true, some nerve to adopt and adhere to this policy; but the result vindicated its soundness. Upon every occasion, I experienced respect and forbearance, even at the mock *durbar* at Sohrab.

Kelat – From 13th October, 1841, to 6th March, 1842

Major Outram, the political agent for Scinde and Beloochistan, in his report to the Government of India, announcing the young *khan's* submission, invited "the acknowledgment so justly due to Lieutenant-Colonel Stacy, for the untiring zeal and indomitable courage with which he pursued his object to a successful termination." He further expressed in that report his personal obligations to me for the cheerful manner in which I at all times afforded him my aid, and for the valuable information contained in my letters to him. Mr. Secretary Maddock replied, by direction of the Governor-General in Council, "that the great zeal and unwearied perseverance of Lieutenant-Colonel Stacy, in the pursuit of an object of very difficult attainment, have been noticed with much satisfaction by the Government, and have entitled Colonel Stacy to its marked approbation."

Major Outram, moreover, pointed out the advantages that would accrue from my remaining with the young *khan* for the present, and therefore recommended that I should continue my services, on special duty, until my regiment, which was under orders to return to India by the Bolan, should pass Dadur or Baugh. The Government readily assented to this proposal.

The treaty with the Khan of Kelat having been completed, the remaining points for consideration were, first, the opening of the Bolan Pass; and, secondly, a treaty with the tribes inhabiting the range of hills from the mouth of the Bolan east to within twenty-five miles of Shikarpore. The most powerful and most intractable of these tribes was that of the Doda Murrees.

Major Outram requested me to give my immediate attention to the first point, and to exert my influence in accomplishing the second object after our arrival at Dadur.

The causes which led to the Bolan Pass being closed against us were the following:

1. The withholding from the Panazye Kaukers the annual tribute they received before our arrival from the valley of Shawl, by our civil authorities at Quetta.

2. The treatment of some Panazye Kaukers, who were enticed into Quetta by Jan Allee, the Government *moonshee*, and five of them afterwards hanged—a transaction which left an impression of perfidy on our part in the minds of the clan, and respecting which much correspondence took place between the Quetta authorities and the Government, not, I believe, to the satisfaction of the latter. The chief of the Panazye Kaukers, Meer Pokar Khan, and his youngest brother, accompanied the men thus inveigled, and the former was never afterwards held in any respect by the Kaukers, who set him aside and elected Meer Guffoor Khan, his younger brother, as their chief, under whose orders they committed outrages of which the English complained.

3. The taking Shah Buzzoorg, Panazye Kauker, into our service, by the political authorities at Quetta, as native commandant of a corps of Bolan Rangers. He was a man of no account in the clan, though a brave, and dashing soldier; and his withdrawal made the whole clan, excepting his associates, our enemies. This corps of Bolan Rangers was composed of the dregs and off-scourings of the country; half of them were allowed to be absent at a time, and they made use of this liberty to plunder *cafilahs* and murder in the pass, which was thereby virtually shut by these very men.

4. The haughty tone of the political officers at Quetta, and the terms they held out to the young *khan* and his adherents.

6. The oppression of the minor tribes inhabiting Moostung, who were driven to become freebooters in the Bolan by the tyranny of Gholam Hussein, Lieutenant Loveday's *moonshee*, who had been permitted to farm Moostung.

To all these provocations it must be added that the English, in the first instance, never paid the sum agreed upon for the safe passage of the Army of the Indus through the Bolan, though Darogah Gool Mahomed was sent by Meer Mehrab Khan to Quetta to receive it; a breach of engagement which was felt deeply and resented by the late Khan of Kelat.

In order to heal these wounds, and to bring all the matters of complaint to an amicable arrangement. Major Outram authorized me to open a communication with Meer Guffoor Khan, Panazye Kauker. Accordingly, I wrote to him through his priest and chief adviser, Sahibzadeh Ramatoola, requesting they would both meet me at Moostung; and stating that the Khan of Kelat was now seated upon the throne of his father; that the English and the *khan* were now one; that I was empowered to hear their grievances and settle their claims, and that they might be assured that the sincerity which had characterized all my proceedings should be observed towards them. The *khan* likewise wrote that he would be with me at Moostung, and desired their attendance.

It subsequently appeared that the letter, which officially announced the installation of the *khan*, had not at this time reached Meer Guffoor's camp. The intelligence had been communicated by the Kauker emissaries at Quetta; but this evidence was not deemed sufficiently authentic and secure; and, on our arrival at Moostung, a son of Ramatoola and five or six men from Meer Guffoor Khan came with letters from that chief and his holy adviser. Amongst the Brahooes, letters are little more than mere formal credentials; the last sentence of the letter is generally to this effect:

The bearer is a trustworthy man; he will tell you all that has passed; believe what he says.

These persons were feasted in the Brahooe fashion, and their letters were received in *durbar*. Next day, they were sent for, in order that the replies might be delivered to them, when the son of Ramatoola, because he had not been allowed to attend the discussion of the terms, and to sit on the same carpet with the *khan* and me, became moody and uncivil, which obliged me to reprove him, and he was dismissed in a very surly humour.

On the following day, the 22nd of October, we crossed the Moostung Hills, and encamped at the entrance of the Bolan Pass. The next morning we moved again, and reached Ser-e-ab, in the centre of the pass, where we were to have joined Major Outram; but want of fodder had obliged him to proceed further, and it was not until the 23rd that the camps united, and marched together through the pass to Dadur, not a shot being fired nor a soul seen in the pass.

In the circular sent by the Khan of Kelat to all his chiefs, announcing his installation, he strictly enjoined them, under the penalty of loss of lands, not to permit their people to maraud in the Bolan. In twenty days afterwards, the pass was clear of robbers.

Upon our arrival at Dadur, the settlement of the eastern boundary of Cutchee, from Tull to within a short distance of Shikarpore, demanded attention. This range of hills is inhabited by different tribes, all engaged in one pursuit—plunder. The road was infested by gangs of robbers, and murders were committed close to Dadur itself.

I first wrote to the Doda Marree chief. Sirdar Meer Mahomed Khan, informing him that the English and the *khan* had entered into bonds of mutual friendship; that the *khan* intended to visit Lheree, and I should accompany him; and, as it was desirable that the chiefs should follow the *khan's* example, I invited him to join the other chiefs there. The Doda Murree tribe were so prejudiced against the English, by reason of our imputed bad faith, that they had resolved never to be upon terms with us again; and it was not until my friends, the *sirdars* from the *khan's* camp, and the Syud Ameer Shah, had made them acquainted with my behaviour towards the Khan of Kelat, that the Murree chiefs would listen to the orders which the *khan* had issued for their attendance at Lheree.

Constant complaints having been received from the political authorities at Quetta of the inactivity of Naib Mahomed Sudeeq, who, like Ahmed Shah, at Moostung, was a creature of Shah Shooja-ool-Moolk, I proposed to Major Outram to send up Naib Rheimdad, who was still in confinement, as the only man of whom Meer Guffoor Khan and his Kaukers stood in awe. It was accordingly so determined by Major Outram, who wrote to Quetta proposing this arrangement, which was, however, at first, strongly opposed, notwithstanding that Mahomed Sudeeq had been suspected by the assistant political agent of tampering with Meer Guffoor Khan's party; but his conduct becoming daily more questionable, the release of Naib Rheimdad was solicited with equal earnestness, and the mode of doing it was left to me.

On the 16th December, I took the opportunity of Rheimdad's sending me a very submissive petition to consult the *khan* about his liberation; and upon his Highness telling me I might arrange it as I thought proper, I explained my plan of sending him to Quetta, which was highly satisfactory to the *khan*. The measure would, as Moolla Nasseer Oolla observed, balance the power of the two parties, that of the *wuzzeer* Moolla Mahomed Hussein, and the *darogah* Gool Mahomed. I sent for Rheimdad to my tent, and heard his defence, which was plain and plausible.

He acknowledged that he was guilty of having carried off the *khan*, which he had done in consequence of the many letters sent to the camp; he steadily refused to say whom he believed or suspected to be their authors, and he declared that even at Sohrab he had no intention of turning back until he heard that our own *sepoys* in Kelat had openly avowed the design of the English to seize his young master there, as Beejar Khan had been seized by Mr. Ross Bell; and that he argued with himself, "Why should the colonel, a follower of the Book (the Bible), feel so much interest and affection for one of a different creed?"

But, he added, now that he saw I was sincere, that I had adopted his master's orphan, shielded him from harm, and placed him upon his father's throne, he renounced his suspicions, and would join all Brahooes and Belooches in invoking blessings upon my head. I then told him that, if he wrote a solemn oath in the *State Koran* to serve the *khan* honestly and faithfully, I would add my forgiveness to his, and recommend him to Major Outram to be employed under the political agent at Quetta. He was highly pleased, and promised as liberally as Brahooes do on all occasions. Being admitted to the *khan's* presence, he expressed regret, and was pardoned; the next day, the political agent received Rheimdad, and informed him that he had been appointed to act under the assistant political agent at Quetta. He was accordingly ordered to take forty horse and escort Major Sotheby's detachment through the Bolan to Shawl Kote, which was done without molestation.

On the 28th November, Sahibzadeh Ramatoola arrived in the camp at Dadur, bringing with him Meer Burkodar, elder brother of Meer Guffoor Khan (a far superior man, and in greater esteem with the Kaukers), who was accompanied by four of the most influential of the Panazye Kaukers. Futteh Khan, son of Meer Azim Khan, chief of Sangan; Meer Esah Khan, chief of Mundye, with others of less repute, were of the party. Two days after, Meer Mahomed Khan of Lheree, came, with Dost Allee Khan, uncle of the Doda Murree chief, Meer Deen Mahomed. Much of this day (December 1st) was spent in my tent with Meer Burkodar and Ramatoola; at the close of the visit, it was settled that they should go to Lieutenant Hammersley, at Quetta, on a bond of security signed by Major Outram and myself, which was accordingly given.

The 3rd December was fixed for the hearing of the Murrees. They were the most pertinacious of men, and urged and re-urged all the instances, which they had got by rote, of our supposed bad faith, as well as other accusations, very skilfully prepared, which, though disproved by me, were not abandoned. The seizure of Beejar Khan was, as usual, put foremost in the list, and I honestly confess they had, in my opinion, ground for their charge against us in this matter.

The incidental circumstance of Captain Postans having, according to Brahooe customs, shaved off his beard and given it to Syud Ameer Shah, in expiation of an admitted breach of faith on his part, in sending Syud Ameer Shah with an invitation to Beejar Khan to come and visit him, and then delivering him over to the principal authority, was a malicious distortion of the truth. It is true that Captain Postans had shaved his beard about that time; but the rest (as proved by questioning Ameer Shah himself) was a deliberate falsehood. That Beejar Khan was seized, however, and thrown into prison, and that all his horses, camels, and equipments were sold by public auction, is a fact, and the sum of 1,000 *rupees* was subsequently given to him as an indemnification.

So thoroughly and obstinately were the Doda Murrees convinced of our want of sincerity and false dealings, that they had refused (as Captain Postans' Diary attested) to have any intercourse with us, or even to receive a letter from the English camp. It was consequently a task of vast difficulty to disabuse the minds of the Doda Murree chiefs, to, soothe their irritated feelings, and to justify or explain the acts charged against us. The *durbar* lasted for some hours, and I at length succeeded in overcoming their objections, and they consented to wait upon the *khan*. Much of my success I owed to the ability with which the young *khan* (who, in public as well as private, paid me the external marks of respect which, amongst the Brahooes, a son shews to his father) seconded my efforts. Further, both Brahooes and Belooches reposed unbounded confidence in my word, and the *khan's* followers were ready to vouch for its integrity.

These semi-savages were received in the evening by Major Outram, who declared he was ever ready to listen to their complaints and to redress their wrongs, and advised them to place confidence ill "the Colonel Sahib." They were feasted, received their despatches, and next morning started for the tents of Dost Allee in the hills east of Lheree. On the 6th the party from Meer Guffoor took leave, much pleased with their treatment, which had greatly abated their dislike of the English.

All matters having been adjusted touching the Bolan Pass, the restoration of Cutchee to the *khan*, and in the vicinity of Dadur, His Highness resolved to march to Baugh, to receive the *naib* of Cutchee, and thence to Lheree, where, it was arranged, the Murree deputation should be received. In the course of this journey, we were to conclude treaties, not only with the Murrees, but with the Booghtees, the Doomkees, the Jakranees, &c., tribes on the eastern range, with most of whom our name was in bad odour; indeed, the whole of Cutchee looked upon us as a faithless race.

We moved from Dadur on the 7th December, and reached Baugh on the 9th, where, to our surprise, we were joined by Meer Azim Khan and Beebee Ganjan. I was sitting with the *khan*, the *wuzzeer* (Moolla Mahomed Hussein), and some of the court, when the *meer* rode up to the tent, drunk, and conducted himself with great impropriety. When I reminded him of a letter I had received from him, in which he promised to abstain from strong drink, he burst into a laugh, made many excuses for this indulgence, and quoted Hafiz until we were weary. The next morning, the *wuzzeer* came to me, and observing that the *meer*, after I had quitted the *durbar* tent, had given his tongue great license against the *khan*, his family, and me, asked what should be done with him.

We knew well what had brought the *meer* and Beebee Ganjan through the snow from Kelat. The latter existed upon intrigue. In Mehrab Khan's time she possessed great sway over her infatuated husband, and grossly abused her power; since his fall, in order to sustain her influence, she had employed every artifice to prevent the coming in of the young khan; and now she was winding her web of intrigue round Meer Shah Newaz Khan, in conjunction with Meer Azim Khan, and endeavouring to detach such of the chiefs as were not well inclined to the young khan from his cause in favour of a son of Mehrab Khan by a slave concubine. I recommended that the *meer* should not be permitted to go with us to the frontier, and that, when we returned to Kelat, he should be placed under surveillance.

With respect to Beebee Ganjan, I proposed that she should be kept within the Meeree, or citadel of Kelat, and informed that it was unbecoming the widow of a *shaheed* husband to appear in public; that her followers should be reduced from 250 to 40, the customary number in the country; that the children of Mehrab Khan, by the concubine, should be taken from the charge of their mother and placed under the care of the *khan*, as to their support, education, and marriage, according to the customs of the Brahooes; but that no immediate step should be taken. These plans I had previously submitted to the khan, who approved of them.

On the same evening, Syud Ameer Shah, Meer Mahomed Khan, Lheree; Beejar Khan, Doomkee, Meer Beloche Khan, with their followers, and some: Doda Murrees, arrived from Dost Allee, in the Eastern Hills, and next day they were received in *durbar*. They brought letters, which expressed fears of meeting us at Lheree, asking security, &c. The two following days we had long discussions, the Murrees being most wearisome debaters. They left us in the evening.

We moved towards Lheree on the 13th (the *meer* willingly remaining at Baugh until our return), and after being forced to halt in sight of the place, to listen to a long tirade from some of the Murree clan about our breaches of faith, we reached our ground on the 14th. Amongst other charges made by the Murrees, they asserted that Captain French was then preparing a *chupao* at Seebee. It appears that Captain French either asked permission to join me at Lheree, or was desired by Major Outram to do so, to assist in the investigation of some cases in which he was concerned as assistant political agent at. Seebee, and to obtain information respecting other matters. It was, however, unfortunate that Captain French should have been permitted to make this journey before it had been mentioned to me, so that I might have prepared these people for it; and, but for the reputation I enjoyed amongst all the tribes, it might have caused the rupture of the negotiations.

On the 16th of December, Dost Allee and the Murrees arrived, halting under some trees, close to the fort, and about two hundred yards from our encampment. The *khan* was dressing when Meer Mahomed Khan, Lheree, came to my tent to notify Dost Allee's arrival. I sent him back with Moolla Nasseer Oolla to invite Dost Allee to my tent, until the *khan* was ready, and I learned afterwards that, although all his attendants voted against his going, Dost Allee insisted upon doing so, and one Kullunder, a Murree, who had attended some of the *durbars*, and was the most intractable of all, but who had been yesterday converted by my giving him my hand, at his request, and swearing, in their manner, to the sincerity of my intentions, declared that they were safe with the "Brahooe Colonel," one of the many *sobriquets* I had received. Dost Allee accordingly came, with Kullunder and two others, the rest staying behind.

Tea was brought, but Dost Allee would take none, begging that I would send to the *khan* to receive him and give him his *rooksut* (permission to depart), as, though he was willing to stay, the Murrees would not hear of it, having been informed by one of their people who had actually witnessed the "preparations," that Captain French was meditating a *chupao*. I proposed to send Kullunder to speak with his brethren and press them to remain; but Dost Allee replied, "Not a Murree will take the bridle out of his horse's mouth."

After a time, I repeated the proposal, Moolla Nasseer Oolla and the Brahooes ridiculing their fears, and extolling me as "the truth-speaking man." After much difficulty, Dost Allee consented to return to his followers and try to persuade them to remain until the evening or the following morning. They determined to see the *khan* before they gave me an answer. The interview with the *khan* took place about ten o'clock.

Dost Allee arrived at the *khan's* tent, and made his prostrations to him as his *dunnee* (master), kissing his hand, and the *khan* motioned him to be seated near him. Dost Allee then introduced about six of the most respectable of his followers by name, who were allowed to kiss the *khan's* hand. The rest stood in front, offering their *salaams*, but afterwards sat down. There never was seen so great a tumult in a *durbar*-tent, Dost Allee having little control over his people. He manifested much surprise, upon his entrance, at seeing me seated on the same carpet as the young *khan*, a distinction allowed to none but the nearest relations.

When the exchange of compliments was over (a very tedious ceremony amongst the Brahooes), the young *khan* gave a detailed account of past transactions,—the death of his father, the occupation of his country by the English, and, referring to my offices, he said, God had sent him a second father in the Colonel Sahib, and, placing his head on my arm, he said:

This is my father; this is the friend who, though I often did wrong, never forsook me, seeing I was young and wanted advice. Ask the Brahooes and Belooches whether he has ever swerved a hair from his word. He has come with me, that, as the English and I are one, so shall it be with the Murrees, that friendship may pervade the country.

He added, that I had authority to conclude any arrangement with them, on the part of the English, and the Murrees might rely upon the most scrupulous fulfilment of my promises. I never met with a man who won so much upon an auditory as the young *khan* did upon this occasion. His great command of language; his quick comprehension; his prompt and apt replies; his graceful figure, and Brahooe beauty, combined with the conviction that he was "*the* Ahmedzye," subdued all opposition, and his hearers left him delighted as well as convinced.

After the *durbar*, the *khan* and Dost Allee had a private consultation, at which Nasseer Oolla was present on my part. I knew that my absence would be more palatable to the Murree chief, and I had settled the terms with the young khan. The treaty was soon concluded; the Murrees were to renew their allegiance to the *khan*; one of the sons or a nephew of the chief was to be in attendance upon His Highness when he came down to Cutchee, with fourteen horsemen, and a village near Gundava was assigned for their support. The ceremony of announcing the treaty to the Murrees, and of entering it into the *Koran*, was fixed for the ensuing morning. I had an opportunity, after Dost Alice's interview with the *khan*, of an hour's conversation with the former in my tent, when I shewed him the groundlessness of the notions entertained by his people of English perfidy, and explained the severity with which breaches of faith were visited by our Government.

On the 17th the *durbar* assembled early; the treaty was read, and approved by all; it was then copied into the Koran by Moolla Mahomed Hussein, who, after passing it to the *khan* and Dost Allee, read it aloud, and this final reading was followed by a general expression of approbation. In about an hour, Dost Allee and his suite came to my tent to take leave. They seemed much pleased, spoke of the kind manner in which they had been treated, and were profuse of their promises. Before Dost Allee took leave of the *khan*, it was arranged that his son should immediately attend upon His Highness, joining him at Gundava.

In reporting to the Indian Government the results of the negotiations with the Kauker and Murree chiefs, Major Outram stated that, although the impression made upon the minds of the former; as to our breach of faith towards the Kaukers who were executed, had been removed, yet it was a great misfortune that a distinct and public avowal of the terms on which the prisoners were received from the chief was not made before executing them, since it would have precluded their mistaken belief of the participation of British officers in such treachery, which had led to the Kauker rebellion the preceding year. With respect to the Murrees, he said:

It will be observed with regret that, with these tribes also, we have borne the character for perfidy which had been attributed to us above the passes. However absurd the groundless 'beard' story alluded to in these papers really is, the belief in its truth was universal, but I trust has now been removed by Colonel Stacy's tact, in publicly confronting with the Murrees the *syud* who was said to have borne the pledge from Captain Postans, and who, if he had recourse to that imposition to gain credit with that gentleman by the success of his mission, was thus compelled to proclaim his own falsehood.

These cases are examples of the necessity for dealing direct with such ignorant people, which will, I trust, not be lost on my assistants, and especially will warn them, in every case of a criminal surrendering himself, personally to demand from the person the understanding on which he had been induced to give himself up, when, should any deceit by our underlings have been practised, the individual, however great his guilt, should be dismissed with sufficient law to enable him to return to the place from whence he was brought.

It is but justice to Colonel Stacy to say, that I owe the success of these arrangements almost entirely to the exertions of that gentleman, who so disinterestedly and cordially aids me in every measure calculated for the public good. As exemplifying his unwearied zeal, I annex extracts from that officer's private letters to myself, shewing the obstacles he has had to encounter, in consequence of the suspicions of our good faith which had unfortunately been engendered.

The reply of the Government acknowledged in very handsome terms my "ability, energy, and zeal."

Captain French and Lieutenant Forbes arrived on the 18th December, and on the 20th the right of the *khan* to the country of Mull was finally established, and Captain French reported accordingly.

On the following day, a *moonshee* from Major Outram's camp sent to Moolla Mahomed Hussein (the *wuzzeer*) the Loodiana native newspaper, containing unfavourable accounts of the English in Affghanistan. I communicated this to Major Outram, and next day, we heard of the withdrawal of our force from Killa Abdoolla. The attachment and confidence of the young *khan* were not shaken by this intelligence; he talked of charging the Affghans at my side, his eyes glistening with vivid emotion as he said it. Large supplies of wheat and *attah* were collected by me and sent to Dadur, and I received orders

69

to purchase camels.

A detachment was sent up the Bolan under Captain Woodburn, and fears were entertained that it would be attacked, as I had moved off. I wrote in reply that there was no ground for any alarm, and so it proved, for no molestation whatever was offered. The Kaukers would always have been stanch friends, had they been differently treated.

Having completed the treaties[1] with the senior tribes, and received the written pledges of those of minor rank, we marched from Lheree on the 1st January, 1842, and reached Baugh the next day, where I found a letter from the *khan's* mother, full of prayers for my welfare, and a very long one from Darogah Gool Mahomed, avowing his conviction that, when God willed the death of Mehrab Khan, he sent me to be a father to his son!

Everything having been settled at Baugh, we left it on the 8th, and, halting at a place called Nasseerabad, half-way to Gundava, an express from Darogah Gool Mahomed was received, with letters from Faiz Ahmed, Babee, containing a copy of the proclamation issued by the insurgents at Cabool, and details of various reports brought to Shorawuk respecting the state of affairs in Affghanistan. I watched narrowly the feelings of the camp throughout the day, but, although the news had transpired through the horsemen who had brought the express, I could not perceive the slightest indication of an unfavourable change.

The young *khan* came to my tent at dusk, and we had a long conversation on the subject of these disasters. I explained to him that treachery might occasion some temporary inconvenience to us, but that our resources were inexhaustible, and that all traitors would be eventually punished. The *khan* never evinced any distrust of the stability of our power, nor did I detect the slightest vacillation on the part of the Brahooes, who remarked, whenever the subject was mentioned, "We have made terms with the English, and we shall not be the first to break them."

We arrived at Gundava on the 9th, and on the 14th I received a letter from Major Outram (to whom I had communicated the letters just referred to), inquiring whether I could not move to Dadur without exciting suspicion, though it had been determined that Gundava should be the place of assembly for the chiefs at the signing of the treaty between the Company and the *khan*. On the 22nd January, the political agent communicated to me the intelligence of the mur-

1. See Appendix, No. 4.

der of our minister and envoy at Cabool, Sir William Macnaghten. Mr. Clerk, the Governor-General's agent on the northern frontier, in transmitting this sad intelligence to Major Outram, suggested to him "the great importance of applying every possible means for the maintenance and the strengthening of our positions in and above the passes on this side."[2]

When the letters were brought to me, Sirdar Meer Khamal Khan and Sirdar Meer Esah Khan (who were often my visitors) were sitting round the fire. I read the letters, folded them up and threw them on a shelf where I was in the habit of putting the newspapers; and their usual question, "What news?" I answered by adverting to some indifferent matters which they knew were in agitation.

I was deeply impressed with the serious responsibility of my situation at this unexpected and alarming crisis. I saw how much depended upon my exertions, and that, unless I succeeded in keeping the various tribes of the *khanat* of Kelat, split as they were into discordant factions, faithful to their engagements, and friendly to the English cause, and unless the Doda Murrees, the Boogtees, and the clans on the eastern frontier, adhered to the arrangements I had recently made with them, all communication between the Indus, and Dadur, Quetta and Candahar, must be cut off, and not a man of our forces above the parses, or even on the right bank of the Indus (for Hyderabad might be expected to let loose her swarms of Belooches upon the retreating army), was likely to return to India. Moolla Nasseer Oolla, whose tried honesty inspired me with implicit confidence in him, was in the habit of coming to me and chatting for an hour or two after dinner, and it was on these occasions that we discussed matters to which we did not desire others to be privy.

He came this evening as usual, and when the old man had settled himself by the fire to his satisfaction, leaned his back against the wall, his knees confined by his *loongee* passed across them and round his waist, I prepared him for the communication. Adverting to the high character I had received of him from Mr. Masson, to the success which had crowned our joint exertions, and the mark of approbation about to be bestowed upon him by my Government (the gift of a silver snuffbox, with a suitable inscription), I reminded him that I had never concealed anything from his knowledge, and I was now about to give him a still stronger proof of my sense of his integrity by disclosing the news brought by the last *dâk*.

2. Papers relating to Military Operations in Affghanistan, 1843, p. 102.

I then informed him of the murder of our minister and envoy at Cabool, who, having been induced to meet the Affghan chiefs, at a conference, had been treacherously shot. I desired him to think of the matter and to give me his honest opinion. The old man wished me to say what I deemed best to be done, and I explained to him my view of the position of the *khan*. He was now, I observed, but just seated upon the throne, and had to contend with a strong party, including the wives and brother of the late *khan*, his concubine and three illegitimate children; that Shah Newaz Khan (to whom the Ittazee *sirdar*, Meer Khamal Khan, had given his sister in marriage) was evidently in communication with that party; that all the Mhengals were dissatisfied, and no great reliance could be placed upon the chiefs of the Eastern frontier; that if one *sirdar* broke his allegiance, it might provoke a general insurrection, since the peasantry had enriched themselves so much during the last two years by plunder that the *sirdars* were scarcely able to restrain them, and if a single tribe raised the cry of a religious war, every Mussulman would enter into it with enthusiasm. I added that the *wuzzeer*, as he knew, could not be trusted, and that Beebee Ganjan and Meer Azim Khan, who were upon the spot, were unprincipled intriguers.

Under these circumstances, which the *moolla* was aware was the true state of the case, we agreed that the best course was to impart the tidings to the *khan*, and to be guided in our future proceedings by the manner in which he received the intelligence. The difficulty was to obtain a private interview with His Highness without exciting suspicion; but, fortunately, the *wuzzeer* and the *dewan* were obliged, next day, to go to a village, a few miles off, to settle revenue accounts with the *zemindars*, and, the *meer* being always drunk, we arranged that the *moolla* should apprize the *khan* of my wish to speak with him in private.

Accordingly, the following day, after this intimation, I waited upon the *khan*, who, after I had been seated a short time, inquired if I wished to look over the palace, observing, that if I did, he would accompany me. Divining his meaning at once, I rose, and, desiring all his attendants but the *shah ghazee* and two orderlies to remain below, he took me through all the apartments in the three stories, and at last to the roof, where was one of those seats to enjoy the air, so common on the roofs of the Brahooe palaces. The *khan* was fatigued; after gaining breath, he desired the *shah ghazee* to remain, observing that "the colonel and he would go and sit in the tower,"—a small tower in which his father was accustomed to sit in the evening to inhale the cool breezes from the mountains,—and that, when the *moolla* (who was fairly exhausted in scrambling up the broken steps) arrived, he was to come to us.

The young *khan* then led on, but made me ascend the tower first, saying, "This was the seat of the martyred *khan*, my father; God has made it yours; go on, I'll follow." The stairs were crazy and scarcely safe; but I resigned myself to the Fates, and we at length got beyond hearing.

In this position I gave the young *khan* an account of the treachery of the Affghans, the murder of our envoy, and the state of our affairs at Cabool, and asked him to tell me frankly what were his true sentiments and wishes. He replied, "I shall be guided entirely by you."

I observed that it would be now impossible for Major Outram to come down from Dadur with the treaty, and therefore proposed that we should move thither, where we might receive intelligence more quickly. The *khan* concurred in this opinion, as did the *moolla*, who now joined us, and the former, moreover, saw the propriety of not yet divulging the death of our envoy, which event, though of course the subject of reports, was not authentically known. It was announced that, business preventing the British political agent from being present at the assembly of chiefs at Gundava, he had begged the *khan* and sirdars to sign the treaty at Dadur. This proposal excited no suspicion and was readily adopted, an allowance being usually made to the chiefs, by way of subsistence, when in our camp.

We commenced our march on the 27th, the real extent of our disasters at Cabool being, in the meantime, known. Some difficulty was experienced in inducing Meer Azim Khan to accompany us, but my advice and expostulations overcame his repugnance. I, succeeded, likewise, in an object upon which I had been long intent, namely, that of repairing a breach between Sirdar Meer Khamal Khan and Sirdar Mahomed Khan. They both met at my tent, when, as agreed, I placed the band of each in the other's, and mirth and festivity reigned in our camp.

At Sunnee, a *kasid* arrived during the night of the 29th, from Kelat, sent by Darogah Gool Mahomed to the *khan*, but with no letter for the minister or me. Mahomed Hussein came to my tent before sunrise, when Meer Esah Khan was there, and evidently wished to speak with me alone; whereupon, leaving the tent upon some excuse, I motioned to him to follow, and he told me three letters had been received express from the *darogah*, and that the *khan* had sent them to

73

me. Pointing to the tent, I declined receiving them until we came to our ground.

When we had arrived there, the young *khan*, hearing I was not well, came and sat some time in conversation, but people being present whom it would not have been prudent to order away, I whispered that I would come to his tent after dinner. I went accordingly, and the servants being ordered to withdraw, the *khan* placed three Persian letters before me. The red ink[3] signature of Shahzadeh Sufter Jung was conspicuous upon one of them, which called upon the *khan* to join in the holy war, in order to expel the Christian dogs from the land of the Moslems, &c. The other two letters were from *sirdars* of the insurrectionary faction.

After the *khan* had read these letters to me, he said, "I have but one wish, to be guided by you. I have made a treaty with the Company; the Ahmedzye will not be the first to break it." I proposed that he should consult Major Outram before he replied to the letters, or, if delay was objectionable, that he should write back immediately that the time was not come to make war with the English, whose armies surrounded him, and were daily augmenting. The *khan* decided upon waiting to confer with Major Outram, but he gave me the letters, requesting that I would forward them by my *dâk*. The letter of the Shahzadeh bore his seal in red ink; of the chiefs' letters, one had seven seals, the other five. Fearing to lose these documents by the *dâk*, I kept them until I could deliver them to Major Outram.

At Noshera, Moolla Faiz Ahmed called upon me early in the morning of the 30th, and as soon as opportunity offered, he gave me three letters from Shahzadeh Sufter Jung and the *sirdars*, which had been sent to him at Shorawuk, where the people, he said, were disposed to join the insurgents: they were of the same tenor as those addressed to the *khan*. I commended the conduct of Moolla Faiz Ahmed, and promised to represent it to the political agent. He was one of the persons strongly recommended to me by Mr. Masson, and who had behaved well to Lieutenant Loveday.

We arrived at Dadur on the 31st of January, and the *khan* paid a visit to Major Outram, without ceremony, and received a hearty welcome; visits were also reciprocated between General England and

---

3. A king alone signs in red ink. Prince Sufter Jung, a son of Shah Shooja, who had at one time been governor of the province of Candahar, and had been dispossessed in favour of Shahzadeh Timour, fled from the city of Candahar, and joined the insurgents.

His Highness. On the 7th of February, Meer Shah Newaz Khan arrived, and the following day he visited the young *khan*. There was an evident ill-feeling between them, though I had done all in my power to prevent its exhibition in *durbar*.

It was necessary to keep the *khan* and his party amused; ball-shooting matches were most to their taste; these were accordingly resorted to, and, with hunting and shooting parties, disposed of the time so agreeably, that the Brahooes gave to Cabool affairs not more than a transient thought.

Some rumours of my leaving the *khan*, and the near approach of Captain Pontardent, brought the *khan* to my tent on the 18th, where, dismissing all the servants, he inquired whether the intelligence was true. At this moment, I had no idea of leaving him, for it was the belief in camp that the whole force was to return by the Bolan,[4] and I had proposed to join my regiment from Kelat, as it should pass down. I therefore informed the khan that there was yet no alteration in my intentions. On the 25th, Captain Pontardent arrived in camp, as assistant political agent in Scinde and Beloochistan, to be stationed with the *khan* at Kelat, when I should join my regiment.

Meanwhile, I had completed an arrangement for the maintenance of Meer Shah Newaz Khan. In the first instance, I objected to the recognition of any direct claim on his part upon the Khan of Kelat; but this was overruled, and I made the best adjustment I could, satisfactory, I believed, to both parties. The instrument was sealed, and copies given to the *khan*. Shah Newaz, and Major Outram. A few days afterwards, however. Shah Newaz raised some objections, after copies had been exchanged, and the subject was again discussed in my tent, with considerable warmth. Shah Newaz Khan is a vulgar, forward man; the young *khan* perfectly courteous and dignified.

It is much to be regretted that Shah Newaz Khan should have been

---

4. The letter of the Governor-General in Council to the Secret Committee, dated February 19th, 1842, says, "Having on the 31 at January received information in regard to the actual state of affairs at Candahar, we addressed Major Outram, instructing him to communicate with Major-General Nott, and to arrange in concert with Brigadier England, and if the condition of the tracts under his immediate charge should admit of it, for having the disposable part of the troops under the orders of that officer moved above the Bolan Pass as early as possible, in order that if Major-General Nott should decide upon withdrawing from Candahar, the troops in question might be marched forwards to the foot of the Kojuck Pass, on the Quetta side, so as to facilitate and support such withdrawal."—Papers relating to Military Operations in Affghanistan, 1843, p. 108.

brought hither by Shah Shooja-ool-Moolk (to whom he was related by marriage), no doubt with a view to his supplanting Meer Mehrab Khan on the throne of Kelat; but the step having been countenanced by some of our government functionaries, Shah Newaz Khan had some pretence to expect a maintenance when he was thrust out of Kelat. His allowance, however, should have been proportionate to the incomes of the Brahooe nobles, or to the poverty and dependence from which he had been raised; and he should have been sent west of the Indus, instead of being located on the confines of the Kelat territory, which enabled him to engage in a correspondence with Beebee Ganjan and Meer Khamal Khan, with a view to his acquisition of the *khanship* of Kelat. The *adnamahs* between the *khan* and Meer Shah Newaz Khan were at length finally exchanged on the 28th.

General England resolved, under instructions, to move up the Bolan Pass, as far as Quetta, and if possible to Candahar,[5] General Nott having refused to evacuate that city. The Government stood pledged to the khan that I should remain with him until my regiment passed Quetta, Dadur, or Baugh, on its way to the provinces, and the difficulty was to reconcile my moving up with General England with this engagement. It was arranged that the *khan* should be invited to Major Outram's tent the following day, and the circumstances of the case explained to him, and that a promise should be given that, on the return of the troops, I should rejoin His Highness at Kelat, or wherever he should be, and remain a month or two with him. This arrangement was carried into effect. The *khan* regretted my departure; but when he understood that I might, by remaining with him, lose not only the esteem of my friends and companions, but the honour of commanding my regiment in battle, he yielded a reluctant consent, upon the express understanding that I was to return to Kelat.

After the installation and other *killuts* had been presented to various chiefs, on the 7th of March I made over charge of the office to Captain Pontardent. In the afternoon I took a final leave of the *khan*, whom I allowed to attend me to a stream which divided the two camps, and there we parted, the Brahooe and Belooche chiefs overwhelming me with their valedictory expostulations, "Why did I leave them?"

Here I may close the second portion of my *Narrative*. During the period of five months which it embraces, my exertions had soothed the irritated Murree tribes, and extinguished in them that sense of

---

5. Papers relating to Military Operations in Affghanistan, p. 165.

our perfidy, which in savage nations keeps alive a rankling spirit of hostility; and induced the Booghtees, Doomkees, and other clans of the Eastern hills, to connect themselves with us and our ally by ties of friendship; the disturbed country of Cutchee was settled; the route of the Bolan Pass, the communication between Candahar and India, was reopened (a service, pronounced by the Duke of Wellington, in the House of Lords, to be of the greatest value and importance); the British character, through my means, was better understood and appreciated than heretofore amongst these wild and warlike nations, and I had (to use the words of one of my official superiors) "turned the Brahooes from the bitterest foes to the best friends of the British."

The state of the Bolan prior to this period is shewn in the following extract of a letter addressed to me by Major Boyd, Deputy Quarter Master General, Scinde Force, dated 17th May, 1843:

With reference to the state of the Bolan Pass, during the autumn of 1841, I can safely say, it was impossible to go through it without a strong guard, as it was in October I was employed in surveying the road leading into the Bolan from Kelat, and it was during this time that the Kaukers were so troublesome, and committing murders in the Pass.

The sudden outburst of the insurrection at Cabool, assuming the character of a religious war against the infidel English, added another unexpected and formidable element of disorder to the intrigues of the *khan's* enemies; yet the fidelity of the young prince and his principal *sirdars* was secured, and the Governor-General (Lord Ellenborough) in council, writing to the Secret Committee, on the 22nd March, 1842, was enabled to relieve the otherwise dark picture of Indian politics, by stating that:

The young Khan of Kelat and his chiefs remain firm in their allegiance, and none of the tribes of Cutchee and near the Bolan Pass have yet shewn symptoms of hostility consequent on the intelligence of our disasters at Cabool, and the combination of chiefs against us in the Candahar provinces.[6]

---

6. Papers, *ut antea*, p. 147.

March to Candahar – From 7th March, 1842, to 10th May, 1842

I was authorized to continue on special duty as far as Candahar, without interfering in any way with the district of Shawl. Major Outram officially acquainted Brigadier England that I was to act as his representative in all communications for the purpose of effecting amicable understanding, procuring supplies for the troops, intelligence, &c., on this side of the Kojuck.

I joined the Brigadier-General at Kundye, and we passed through the Bolan without any molestation or inconvenience, except the detention for two days at Seer-e-Bolan by a high wind. At this place, we received a letter from Lieutenant Hammersley, stating that, on the strength of the interview (see section 2) with Meer Burkodar, Panazye Kauker, on the 1st December, at the camp at Dadur, his brother, Meer Pokar Khan, had been induced to visit the political assistant at Quetta. By the horsemen who brought this letter, I was told that Lieutenant Hammersley had placed Pokar Khan under surveillance, but that this chief had made his escape, and fled to the hills.

The detachment reached Quetta on the 16th March without interruption. The escape of Pokar Khan made it prudent to adopt the precaution of crowning the heights; but no enemy appeared. The Naib Rheimdad rode out to meet me, and expressed much gratitude for the restoration of his master (the *khan*) and his slave (himself).

On the 21st I was informed that Mahomed Sudeeq, who was in the Pesheen valley, with a strong force, was bent upon hostilities when we should enter the Kojuck Pass; that some of his chiefs were very anxious to separate from him, and that, as soon as our army should enter the valley, they would come over to us on the first opportunity. As General England had resolved to move forward; I assured him, both verbally and in writing, that, unless Naib Rheimdad was allowed to accompany us as far as the foot of the Kojuck, we should not get a particle of information.

I had no authority in the Shawl district, and the assistant political agent objected to this man accompanying us. I then represented to General England in writing that it was necessary he should take guides from Shawl, as he might expect to find every village deserted, and to meet the enemy at Hykulzye,[1] and I made a last effort to persuade the general to take Rheimdad; but it failed. With much difficulty, I obtained permission from Lieutenant Hammersley that this man should accompany me to Koochlaq.

On the morning of the 24th March, we marched to this place, not a soul appearing in this part of the pass. During the day, I received a letter from Meer Nasseer Oolla Khan, of Hajee Khan's tribe, whom I invited, as well as the ex-*naib* of Pesheen, Sa'af Oolla Khan, Battuzye, another of Mahomed Sudeeq's party, to join me, giving them every assurance of protection and respect.

Early on the 25th, whilst standing outside my tent at Koochlaq, I observed a man with an ass-load of fowls go into the fort. He afterwards came to the spot where I was talking with Rheimdad, and said "The Patans are coming; they are close at hand, on the Hyderzye road." Walking down the south face of the fort, I examined the hills to the west with my telescope, and saw horsemen distinctly; I counted twenty-three, one, on a white horse, being conspicuous, and their numbers increased rapidly. I went instantly to the general's tent, and reported the enemy's picquet on the hill above the river. The general, who could scarcely credit the intelligence, despatched his *aide-de-camp*, who returned and reported them visible from the lines with the naked eye; whereupon the general ordered a troop of cavalry, twenty men of the horse artillery (to act as dragoons), and two six-pounders, to move immediately, and the two flank companies of Her Majesty's 41st to follow.

The cavalry moved off towards the enemy, a few of whom had crossed the river, looked at our camp, and, returning to their comrades, who had dismounted, were sitting enjoying the scene; and the rest of our party soon followed. The enemy waited until our cavalry turned to the right, towards the only fordable *ghat* of the river, when they mounted and disappeared. As soon as the enemy retired, the general

---

1. See Appendix, No. 5.

halted the guns and flank companies on this side of the river, about a mile from the ford. Our mounted party soon shewed, going over the hill on which the enemy had been located. At this time, about 100 foot were observed running from the western hills, whose retreat (as the flank companies had been halted) was a fortunate event for our mounted party, who came upon the rear of the picquet.

The enemy, finding their horses failing, pulled up, faced about, and charged down upon our party, fighting well; five were sabred, the rest escaped; on our side we had two wounded. A *kasid*, by whom I had sent the letters to Meer Nasseer Oolla Khan, and Meer Sa'af Oolla Khan, returned in the evening, stating that he had left them in a bush, after shewing them to one of their men; that both chiefs were anxious to leave Mahomed Sudeeq, but that their wives and families would be sacrificed if they should attempt to join me at this moment.

My anticipations respecting the impossibility of procuring information, if Naib Rheimdad was not allowed to accompany the force, were too surely realized. Syud Mahomed, who had promised to come to me at Hyderzye, which we reached on the 27th, appeared; but I could not extract any information from him, nor could my servants get a word from his attendants, beyond the fact that Mahomed Sudeeq had been at the village the day before and had gone they knew not where. The 27th passed, and still not the slightest information of the enemy could be obtained.

The 28th was a sad day for us; we were fairly beaten. We marched early about six miles from camp, and found the enemy capitally posted. Shortly after leaving camp, we saw horsemen on every hill to the left. I went myself to ascertain if the enemy were in force in the valley which lies behind. I had travelled that road once, when by myself, after leaving General Nott's force at Chummun for Quetta. I examined the valley minutely with my glass; only a few single men here and there, making for the enemy's intrenched position, were to be seen, and several small parties amongst the hills, all making for their headquarters.

The column was halted, whilst the general and his staff rode forward to examine the position of the enemy; and in a quarter of an hour, it was ordered to advance. On coming up to where the general was standing, Leslie's troop of horse artillery were ordered to form battery, and try the men on the hill on the left, which completely commanded the road. In the meantime, the general took the column to the right; the light battalion, under that gallant officer Major Apthorp, of the Bombay Native Infantry, was ordered to the front. I remained with the battery. Two guns were afterwards ordered to accompany the column. The enemy on the high hills, after standing about six or eight shrapnells, appeared resolved to storm the guns, which had been left unprotected, and were coming down in a dense crowd. The guns were beautifully served.

Captain Leslie ordered grape to be ready; Dr. Baxter and I were serving with the left gun. In the meanwhile he laid two guns, with round shot; the first went into the very centre of the body of men, and brought with it a heavy mass of earth; the second was fired with equal success, and the whole group were in the greatest consternation and distress, making every endeavour to regain the top of the hill. In this situation, several shrapnells were fired into them, at a slight elevation, with great effect. It was afterwards ascertained that the general had moved on the smaller hill; seeing which, the force on the hill to the left attempted to join their comrades, but were prevented, as has been shewn. A slight undulating ground, descending to the road between these two hills, hid the column from us. The firing became smart; it was evident that the light battalion was engaged.

Everything being settled on the left, I went off in the direction of the firing. Crossing the first ridge, I was astonished by seeing our men beaten back, and rallying in disorder. I passed Major Apthorp, wounded, and being led to the rear; I think Assistant-Surgeon Davidson Was with him. He was sensible when I passed. The light companies had rallied, and I walked on towards Her Majesty's 41st, on the extreme right. General England and his staff were dismounted, and standing in conversation, not far from where the light companies had rallied. I joined them. It was useless to stand and lament over what could not be recalled.

A retreat was determined upon. I observed to the general that the day might be retrieved, and offered to lead into the intrenched position with 100 men, properly supported; and I am confident that I should have succeeded. The men were in courage, and anxious to recover the bodies of their comrades. The general replied, he had not men. I proposed that the left hill should be attacked first, as it commanded the smaller one. The enemy were certainly in strength, and very bold; but our men burned with rage at seeing their comrades cut up before their eyes. I think I pressed my offer three times, the last time volunteering to lead with 80 men; but the general felt he had too few, and that the stake was too great; there were some *lacs* of *rupees* in the waggons.

After about a quarter of an hour, the general resolved to retreat, and wait at Quetta until the arrival of the detachment which was to have joined us here. I was asked for the nearest water, which I pointed out, and begged the general to remain until I should find a spot by which we could take the guns across the ravines on our right. A place was soon discovered, and the retreat commenced: it was evening before we reached Niah Bazaar.[2]

The serious character of this disaster, which I sincerely believe would have been prevented, if I had been allowed to employ the services of Rheimdad, may be appreciated by considering the effect which it produced upon the determination of the Governor-General. Lord Ellenborough, in his letter [3] to the Commander-in-Chief, dated "Benares, April 19th, 1842," expressed himself as follows:—

> The fall of the citadel of Ghuznee had removed the principal object for which it was expedient to retain the force under Major-General Nott in its advanced position of Candahar. The severe check experienced by Brigadier England's small corps on the 28th *ultimo*,—an event disastrous as it was unexpected,— and of which we have not yet information to enable us to calculate all the results,—has a tendency so to cripple the before limited means of movement and of action which were possessed by Major-General Nott, as to render it expedient to take immediate measures for the ultimate safety of that officer's corps, by withdrawing it, at the earliest practicable period, from its advanced position, into nearer communication with India. Under this impression, I have thought it right to transmit the inclosed instructions to Major-General Nott.

These instructions were, to evacuate the city of Candahar and retire to Quetta.

General Nott himself, writing to Mr. Maddock, from Candahar, on the 18th of April, said that the moral influence of this check "had been great throughout the country, and had added considerably to the difficulties of his position."

Our reverse appeared to have affected the whole detachment. Never was a camp put down which was calculated to give greater confidence to the enemy; it was of no form or shape; Her Majesty's 41st were huddled within the ruined walls of the fort of Old Bazaar,

---

2. See Appendix, No. 6.
3. Papers relating to Military Operations in Affghanistan, p. 224.

and the commissariat and native regiments were in no order at all. It rained heavily from 10 till past 11 p.m., when the full moon shone forth. I did not go to bed, and was standing at the door of my tent, when I saw Majors Wyllie, Boyd, and Davidson passing from that of the general, who had called several officers. I had not been summoned. Pointing to a string of camels, moving towards the *godown,* I asked them whether the men could have correctly understood their orders to load. Neither of the three officers (to whom I am well known, and whose merits are known to me) seemed inclined to reply: it appeared to be a secret.

This was not a time for scruples, and I observed it was evidently in contemplation to retreat immediately, and earnestly begged them to return to the general and represent to him that to attempt a retreat at that hour, the tents charged with rain, would expose the force to confusion, disorganization, and destruction, and pledged myself, if he would wait until day, I would shew him a road direct to Hyderzye. After a long conversation, the three staff, at my earnest request, returned and communicated what had passed between us to the general, who adopted my recommendation, and the camp enjoyed repose until sunrise.[4]

It was seven a.m., of the 29th, before we were ready to move off. Great was the loss we had sustained, which fell in much larger proportion upon the officers than upon the Government. I lost my tent, chair, table, &c. Our march in retreat the morning before was most orderly; that of this morning equally so, until we reached Hyderzye, when, upon its being discovered that we were not to halt there, considerable confusion ensued, and before we got to Koochlaq, the force was in disorder. At the Lora, near Hyderzye, two guns from the horse artillery were required to keep off the enemy. On arriving at the ground, in the evening of the 28th, I had pointed out the value of this position,[5] as not only giving us safety for the night, but offering every possible advantage for renewing the conflict with advantage in the morning.

We halted at Koochlaq on the 30th, where I found a letter awaiting me from Meer Guffoor Khan, Panazye Kauker. Koochlaq being under Lieutenant Hammersley, and my orders strictly forbidding me to interfere in any way with his arrangements, I was powerless.

At sunset, some officers saw (or thought they saw) a body of men moving along under the hills in front of the camp. I had accompa-

---

4. See Appendix, No. 7
.5. See Appendix, No. 7.

nied the general to shew him a spot of ground for his camp,—a fine open space, with plenty of water. Major Boyd, deputy quarter-master general, had only completed his arrangements for the camp, when an infantry orderly, sent from camp with a verbal message, informed the general in Hindoostanee, that "the *sahib* sent a *salaam* and said the enemy's army had crossed the river, and were moving direct upon the camp."

We, of course, made the best of our way back. The line had been turned out, but nothing could be seen; the troops remained under arms until eleven p.m., when a strong party of our cavalry returned, reporting that not a soul was to be seen in any direction. The general went round about twelve o'clock, to see if all were on the alert, and, as he had expressed a wish to speak to me, I waited his return, when he consulted me regarding the road, should the Moorzah Pass be occupied. I had travelled both roads, and assured the general that, if the first pass should be occupied, I would take him another road (which I knew perfectly), where the enemy could not offer opposition without paying dearly for it.

We marched the next morning, and found the Koochlaq or Moorzah Pass occupied, and therefore passed steadily on, leaving the entrance on our left, well out of shot, moving slowly (to give protection to all), and halted from time to time, to enable the baggage to be collected on our reverse flank. In this manner we reached the *ghat*, where a very high and rugged rock rises abruptly from the river, and consequently had to be crowned. The enemy had also quitted their first position, and were gathering in strength upon a high ridge of rocks, which connected the Koochlaq or Moorzah Pass with the Lora river. The head of the column had passed: I had shewn the best ford, this river abounding in quicksands.

The artillery had crossed; a company of native infantry had possession of the high rock over the river; the enemy could not see them, and were pushing on to secure it, dropping shots into any baggage, which, in order to shorten the distance to the *ghat*, ventured too near the hills. They appeared in such numbers, that it was deemed prudent to drive them off, particularly as the baggage was up and crowding, and there was but space for a single camel to pass down to the river at a time. Accordingly, a spot was selected, which offered a favourable ascent; two companies were to mount at the same time, so as to get the enemy between them, and cut off their retreat to the Moorzah Pass.

A company was also sent round the base of the hill rock on the river, to prevent the enemy from escaping by the plain. Thus hemmed in, they lost eighteen killed on the spot: the rest got away. We had only two men slightly wounded. About three p.m. we reached Quetta.

Whilst we remained here, I thought that, employed as I was, upon a special service, it would be no forward presumption on my part, but rather a manifestation of honest and commendable zeal, if I submitted to the Major-General the opinions which my experience and observations in these parts had enabled me to form respecting the course of action to be pursued by him, and the true policy of our government in the embarrassing position of affairs. Accordingly, I communicated in writing to Major-General England these opinions, which were to the following effect:

After pointing out the difficulties attending the procuring and conveying supplies between Quetta and Candahar, since the affair at Hykulzye, which had dispelled the illusion that we could obtain supplies in the Pesheen Valley, I observed that that affair, however unfortunate, had not been wholly without use, in shewing how imperfect were our means of information. The existence of a fortified position, which, it appeared, the enemy had been employed upon for the preceding two months, was utterly unknown to us, nor should we have learned that similar works had been prepared in the Kojuck, but for our advance on Hykulzye: our ignorance of this intrenched position proved no less our want of common information beyond our picquets, than the unanimity of the people around us.

I suggested that our greatest obstacle was our retaining the province of Shawl[6] for Shah Shooja, which prevented our availing ourselves of the Khan of Kelat's services, and that, were Shawl made over to the *khan*, and if his *wuzzeer*, or the *darogah*, or Naib Rheimdad, with Moolla Nasseer Oolla, Babee, were deputed by him to attend me with the force, the having men of their rank and talent to be the medium of communication with the enemy, would be the means of breaking the confederacy, and one party at least would be with us. We were pledged by treaty, I remarked, to assist the Khan of Kelat against foreign invasion; to do this, Shawl must be held by the *khan* or the English.

For the preceding three months, we had been openly attacked by the Doorannee tribes of Affghanistan. The restoration of Shawl to the Khan of Kelat would, therefore, be no breach of faith, for the Dooran-

---

6. Major Hough (*Narrative*, section 2) says, "This province was the gift of a king of Affghanistan to one of his nobles, for service performed, as a *shala*, or dowry, with his wife."

nees had released us from all engagements by their perfidy. By restoring Shawl Kote to the *khan*, his influence would fix the wavering Panazye Kaukers in our power. Koochlaq and the dependent villages (which are almost all *enamee*), instead of being a rendezvous for spies and marauders, would, under the *khan's* authority, be purged of such miscreants, and we should command, not merely sources of information, but a direct line of communication with Candahar; whilst the transfer of the district to the *khan* would secure his attachment and conciliate the good-feeling of the whole *khanat*.

I ventured further to suggest that, as open war had been declared against us by the Doorannees, the Barukzye party (that of Dost Mahomed Khan) should receive our support, which would detach them from the Saddoozyes, and dispose them to reward the Khan of Kelat, by making the Kojuck the natural divisional line of the two countries, and the boundary of the two states; and that, by such an arrangement, the British Government would go far to make the *khanat* of Kelat a substantive power, equal to its own defence, instead of being compelled to lean, as entitled by treaty to do, upon the military aid of our government.

The letter, which had reached me at Koochlaq from Meer Guffoor Khan, contained a proposal for a meeting. The messenger named two people (natives), whom Meer Guffoor Khan wished to be sent to his encampment as hostages during the time he remained at Quetta. These people readily consented, under my guarantee, and I went immediately to explain Guffoor's proposition to the general, before communicating it to the assistant political agent, and General England approved of it. He was aware of the view which Major Outram had taken of the claims of the Panazye Kaukers upon Shawl, when Meer Burkodar, on my invitation, visited the agency camp at Dadur, in November, 1841.(See section 2)

The interview sought by Meer Guffoor Khan appeared to me most desirable for two reasons; first, it would afford an opportunity of settling in a single day the claims advanced by the Panazye Kaukers to an annual payment from Shawl, the inhabitants of which province migrate in considerable numbers to Baugh and its vicinity, the Panazye Kaukers having received an annual payment, nominally for the protection of the valley, but in reality for abstaining from plunder: secondly, it would offer me a chance of being able to detach the Panazye Kaukers from the confederacy formed by Mahomed Sudeeq in the Pesheen Valley.

Accordingly, I sent Meer Guffoor Khan's letter to the assistant political agent, with one from myself. The reply I received was, that there were objections to the interview, which should be stated in writing to the general. These objections of the assistant political agent were communicated to me by Major-General England, and I returned them with a letter, in which I attempted to shew their fallacy. However, as I was interdicted by my instructions from all interference in the province of Shawl, I could carry the matter (as I informed the major-general) no further. The following day, more objections to Meer Guffoor's visit were urged by the assistant political agent; but they were not shewn to me, and I concluded that a negative had been put upon it.

On the 3rd April, plans of very extensive fortifications at Quetta were submitted by the engineer and approved of by Major-General England, and next day, half the troops were employed upon them or upon outworks, their labour not being suspended even on Sunday.[7] The troops moved inside the intrenchments on the 17th.

A Patan horseman from Candahar, who arrived on the 5th, declared that there had been a great battle, in which the English had lost many men, but the Affghans double the number; that 150 horsemen from Shorawuk had joined Mahomed Sudeeq with 138 camels carrying *attah*, and that Meer Guffoor Khan was in treaty with him. These three items of intelligence proved correct: Meer Guffoor gave the enemy upwards of 300 stout soldiers, who were opposed to us soon after.

I had a long visit from Syud Moobaruk Shah, who, after stating the great dislike which the Affghans entertained towards Shah Shooja-ool-Moolk, spoke in strong terms of the obstinacy of the English in still persisting to uphold him upon the throne, and to regard him and treat him as a friend.

Molladad, Kumberaree, who arrived from Moostung on the 16th, informed me that the people of Shorawuk had thrown off all allegiance to the *khan*, and declared for the insurgents. Travellers from Koochlaq reported that the enemy had retired from its vicinity, and

---

7. General Nott's opinion of these fortifications is expressed in his despatch to Major-General England, April 18th, 1842 (Papers relating to Military Operations in Affghanistan, p. 249): "You say that you are 'not aware if you know the localities of Quetta.' I know them well, and I hope I shall be excused when I express my surprise that the authorities of Quetta should for a moment have thought of throwing up breastworks and intrenching that straggling and wretched cantonment, when the town and citadel are so well calculated for every purpose which can render a post at all desirable in Shawl, and I am quite certain may be well defended by 500 men."

that Mahomed Sudeeq had gone to Killa Abdoolla to confer with Meer Saloo Khan. Further reports informed us, that these two chiefs had disagreed, and that Mahomed Sudeeq had gone to the Shahzadeh, Sufter Jung, whom he talked of following, and that Hubbeeb Oolla Akoonzadeh was to have charge, if Mahomed Sudeeq departed for Candahar. Mahomed Sudeeq had placed several chiefs in confinement on suspicion, and had exerted himself to the utmost to persuade the people to embrace the insurgent cause, but it was evidently not popular in the valley, and for sufficient reasons. The valley of Pesheen is inhabited principally by horse-breeders and cultivators, who had everything to lose and nothing to gain by adopting the cause of the insurgents, who had, moreover, disgusted them by taking their sheep without payment. Meer Guffoor Khan, Kauker, had not yet completed terms with Mahomed Sudeeq.

General Nott's letters having stated that he was in the utmost distress for money; that "money could not be borrowed;" that "the pay of the troops in Candahar was four months in arrear," and "there was not a *rupee* in the treasury;"[8] I contrived on the 22nd April to get a *hoondee* for 15,000 *rupees*, which I sent to the assistant political agent to forward, urging that, small as the sum was, it would relieve their dreadful distress, and might prevent the *shroffs* at Candahat, in some measure, from holding back, or asking higher premium, by shewing that funds could be supplied from below the pass. Much delay and a long correspondence ensued, the assistant political agent starting various difficulties, and appearing to think that General Nott and Major Rawlinson were not in such straits for money at Candahar as I supposed.

On the 23rd, Major-General England received orders from Major-General Nott to march a brigade from Quetta, so that it might reach the southern side of the Kojuck Pass on the 30th April, or the 1st May, General Nott promising to send forward a brigade from Candahar, consisting of three regiments of infantry, a troop of horse artillery, and a body of cavalry, which would be at Chummun, at the northern foot of the Kojuck, at that date. We were consequently ordered to march on the 26th. So confident had been the belief that the force would not move towards Candahar, that houses had been purchased, and everybody had settled down as if in a cantonment.

We reached Koochlaq on the 26th, and found the Moorzah Pass

---

8. Despatches to General England and to Mr. Maddock, 18th April, 1842.— Parliamentary Papers, pp. 247 and 249.

deserted. A servant of General England (a man of Her Majesty's 41st), coming by himself late in the evening, was murdered. As we proceeded on to Hyderzye, the next day, not a particle of intelligence could be had. Syud Bugheea, of this place, came to beg protection for his crop, and I conversed with him for more than two hours, trying him in every way, but could not extract the slightest information from him respecting matters in advance.

The only circumstances that came out were, that Sabash Khan and Nawab Khan, Meer Guffoor's nephew, had made a bargain for 300 Panazye Kaukers, who had accordingly joined Mahomed Sudeeq (and who fought against us the next day); and that Meer Guffoor Khan and the rest of the tribe were in the hills near Quetta, ready to profit by any disaster which might befall us.

The force marched early on the 28th towards Hykulzye, and had not proceeded two miles, before horsemen were seen by twos and threes on the hills on our left, and a few now and then on the right. The baggage was carefully kept together as we marched over the large plain, at the end of which was the enemy's position. They occupied the same ground as before, but the high hill on the left had been strengthened by two or three *sungahs*, a kind of screen formed of large stones piled one upon another, about two or three feet high.

As we approached the enemy, the baggage moved to the right, and, according to a plan previously arranged, the force was divided into three parties, one to attack the high hill on the left, under Major Simmons, Her Majesty's 41st; one, under Captain Woodburn, to storm the small hill, against which we had failed the same day last month, and the reserve, under Major Browne, Her Majesty's 41st.

As soon as all the parties had reached their respective positions, the artillery opened. The left party, having a much greater distance to move, started before the right. They advanced in excellent order, led by their gallant commander, and the Affghans moved to meet them; but were dispirited by the determined bearing of this party, and not one would advance beyond their last *sungah*.

As soon as the party on the left had gained the hill, the whole pushed forward with a "hurrah." The troops were as steady as on parade; the artillery practice was admirable; discipline and tactics were too much for the enemy, who turned and fled. Captain Delamain was let at them with the cavalry, but only succeeded in coming up with a few, and they shewed themselves game to the last. The sword, in my opinion, is not the weapon for a trooper in Asia; had our men been armed with lances, they would have killed many more and suffered less.[9]

As soon as the cavalry returned, the column moved on to the encamping-ground, having first collected the remains of the gallant fellows who had fallen in the last affair.

It appeared that Mahomed Sudeeq and Saloo Khan were jealous of each other. The latter was appealed to by the Pesheenees, who looked upon him as their head, against the conduct of Mahomed Sudeeq and his rabble, who took twenty sheep a day for their consumption and refused payment, although five camels laden with treasure had been sent down to Mahomed Sudeeq to defray expenses. Again, Saloo Khan was displeased that the other should assume authority over him. The day preceding the action, Saloo Khan was sent for by Mahomed Sudeeq to be at his post, but he made some excuse, and did not join until the next morning, after the action had commenced.

Subsequently, when I was treating with Saloo Khan, I heard that, in order to ruin Mahomed Sudeeq, he had discouraged the choice troops with him by telling them we had now brought two armies, and that it was folly to stand and be killed by guns. Saloo Khan had gone to the insurgents' camp near Candahar, to ask the command of the Pesheen valley, and some money to carry on the war, both of which requests were refused; and this disappointment, no doubt, inclined him to listen to my proposals of separating from the insurgents and joining our cause.

I had, for the last month, derived great assistance from the *sait'h* (or banker) Moorj Mull, a most respectable man, a partner in the largest banking house at Shikarpore, who accompanied Major Davidson, the deputy commissary-general. Embarked in a new service, not having an individual about me upon whom I could rely, it was fortunate that I secured the services of Moorj Mull, through whose servants I discovered, on the 29th, that Saloo Khan was not far off our present locality, the bank of the Lora. I had a letter carefully prepared, which I sent off to him in the charge of two horsemen, and in the evening I received a letter from Saloo Khan, written before mine had reached him, stating that the flight of the enemy had been owing to him; that he was a friend of the English, and that he desired an interview.

A few hours later, a reply to my letter came, much to the same effect as the previous communication, with the addition of an offer on the part of Moozum Khan and other chiefs to accompany him, and

9. Appendix, No. 8.

make terms, and a promise to re-establish the *dâks* immediately if I required it.

On the 30th, we reached Abdoolla-khan-ke-killa. I had sent off, in the morning, a reply to Saloo Khan, and afterwards despatched Hubbush Khan, with Mootee, a Hindoo, attached to Sait'h Mooij Mull, to accompany Saloo Khan to our camp. The following day we marched to Abdoolla Kareez; and in the afternoon, Moozum Khan, Raheem Khan, and Nasseer o-deen Khan, came to me with a letter from Meer Saloo Khan, to ascertain the terms I proposed. We sat in my tent for several hours, until the dinner prepared for them was reported to be ready, and then separated. The next morning they came to my tent and were very anxious for presents, as they asserted matters were settled. I replied, they required no consent and seal, and declined any *killuts*.

The force moved off a little before day broke. I was delayed some time by the unsatisfactory parting with the chiefs, and afterwards went to the ground occupied by Moorj Mull, to learn whether I could, if required, procure horsemen to convey a letter to Saloo Khan. I then rode to the head of the column, and joined General England before the low ground and stunted trees which mark the entrance of the defile leading to the Kojuck Pass. Having been over this pass four times before, each time in command, I was intimately acquainted with every turn.

I was riding with the horse artillery, when the halt sounded. I waited full half an hour, until, tired of the delay at such a moment, I went back to ascertain the cause, and met General England, with whom I was returning, when, at a spot near the head of the horse artillery, he dismounted, called for his chair, and sat down. I explained to him that we were entering the defile leading to the pass, and observed that the Candahar troops would rob us of our share of the credit of forcing the Kojuck if we delayed. The column was at this time well locked up. I continued to urge this for at least a quarter of an hour, and finding that the general did not think it expedient to move, I begged him to give me a *havildar's* party, and offered to go in advance, and ascertain whether the pass was occupied. This and every other proposition I made were refused.

Disappointed in the extreme, I went to the head of the horse artillery. Major Waddington, of the Engineers, hearing the halt, had returned from the head of the column, composed of Bombay native infantry, and joined General England, and, observing that the column was well up, begged him to proceed. The general still declined, and

Major Waddington left. He was passing to the head of the column, when we spoke to each other, and found that our communications with the general had been of the same tenure. We agreed to proceed on, and taking twelve men from the advance, we had scarcely got half a mile before we met some of the irregular cavalry of the Candabar force, who very composedly reported all clear for us. We could only say, "You will find the general a little further on." I accompanied Major Waddington to shew the gun-road, by the water-course, and, as we walked on, we found the Kojuck crowned by parties of the 2nd, 16th, and 38th regiments of Bengal Native Infantry, part of the force sent under Lieutenant-Colonel Wymer by General Nott, from Candahar.

General England's troops were much disappointed and vexed at being kept back, yet generously expressed no jealousy at the distinction won by their comrades. These fine fellows had been led forward by Colonel Wymer at daybreak to occupy the heights commanding the pass from Chummun to the western side, to secure General England's party a safe passage. I have never seen our *sepoys* to such advantage. It was impossible to climb the precipitous hills in pantaloons; this part of their dress had, therefore, been discarded, and the men were in their *doties*. As they shewed on every accessible point, they were the admiration of all. I can easily imagine how painful it must have been to the Bombay regiments to find the Candahar troops in foil possession of the pass before they were allowed to enter it.

On arriving at Chummun, I heard that the chiefs sent by Meer Saloo Khan were so indignant at my refusing them money and *killuts*, that they had agreed not to communicate my arrangement to him; whereupon, I procured two horsemen from Sait'h Moorj Mull (Hubbush Khan and his servant), and having Written a letter to Saloo Khan, fully explaining everything (not omitting an account of the conduct of the chiefs), I despatched it, promising the bearers a reward of thirty *rupees* if they executed their commission. My letter was read to Hubbush Khan, who was thus put in possession of its contents, lest some treacherous *moonshee* should read it to Saloo Khan otherwise than it was written.

We halted on the 3rd at Chummun Trees. This was a great relief to me, being perfectly exhausted, Besides enduring much anxiety of mind, I had scarcely been in bed since the 29th *ultimo*. Shore Dil Khan, son of Meer Guddoo Khan, killed in our service in the Ghilzie country, came to visit me this day.

The next day we halted at Chummun, on the 5th at Gulzye, and the

6th at Meel Munder (Mehel Manda), where I was much relieved by the return of my horsemen, accompanied by Meer Atta Oolla Khan, eldest brother of Meer Saloo Khan, who brought a most satisfactory letter from the latter, and stated that his brother would accompany me to Candahar, if I would guarantee him protection, and conclude with the authorities there the arrangement proposed by me. I treated Meer Atta Oolla Khan with respect, giving him quarters in my tent, and reported to General Nott the arrival of the *moolla*, for so Atta Oolla Khan had become.

We reached Tukt-e-Pool on the 7th May, and Deh Hajee on the 8th. On the preceding day, Meer Raheem Khan, Meer Nasseer-o-deen Khan, and Meer Noor-o-deen Khan, joined our camp, begging to be included in the arrangements; to which I agreed, and they were protected, housed, and fed by me until our arrival at Candahar, which we reached on the 10th May, 1842. I took the chiefs with me to General Nott, with whom I sat a short time. He wished me to make over the native correspondence, as well as the parties, to Major Rawlinson, which I accordingly did in person, and with this act I ceased to be on "special duty."

A few days afterwards, I called upon the general: Major Rawlinson was with him, explaining my arrangements. I said, "I hope the general approves of them;" and I received from General Nott a reply in the affirmative; and he signed them on the spot.

I may observe, in passing, that, on my arrival at Candahar, I asked General Nott whether he had received the 15,000 *rupees* for the draft I had sent from Quetta. He denied that he had received any draft from me, or from Quetta. On leaving the general, I visited Major Rawlinson, to inquire about this draft, and learned that it had only reached him along with us!

The result of this part of my "special service" was very satisfactory to me. I had a difficult, as well as a responsible office to execute, and was provided with no instructions for my guidance; nay, I am bound in justice to myself to say that information was even kept from me. I had, therefore, to think and act for myself, and, in respect to the arrangement with Saloo Khan, I acted counter to the express and recorded sentiments of Major-General England, who, on the 30th April, entered a written protest against them, most distinctly stating and declaring that he would be no party to any promise or treaty with Saloo Khan; that he knew little of his history, but believed he served with the enemy against us whilst taking our pay; that he deserved no mercy at our hands, and all he undertook was that he should have safe-conduct to Candahar, if, during the march, he conformed to the rules of the camp, and that, on his arrival at Candahar, he should be delivered over to the authorities at that place, to be dealt with as they might see fit. It is a sufficient justification of my perseverance in the arrangements against which Major-General England felt it to be his duty so formally to protest, that they were approved, confirmed, and adopted by General Nott.

When I returned to India, I found that these circumstances were altogether unknown. I wrote, therefore, to Major Rawlinson, who happened to be at Ferozepore, as follows:

Camp, 4th January, 1843.

My dear Rawlinson,

In conversing with Mr. Maddock, the day before yesterday, I said it had been my good fortune to reopen the road between Quetta and Candahar, in May 1842, when I brought up to the latter place the eldest brother of Saloo Khan, to conclude with General Nott the arrangements I had proposed to his brother Saloo, at Killa Abdoolla. I was present at General Nott's when you reported on it; but will you kindly write to me a letter, stating such was my good fortune, that I may shew it to Mr. Maddock?—Yours, &c.,

L.R. Stacy.

Major Rawlinson, Sec

I subjoin the reply:—

My dear Stacy,

In reply to your reference on the subject of the reopening of our communication between Candahar and Quetta, in May 1842, I can have no hesitation in bearing testimony to the value of your services on that occasion. It was, in fact, entirely owing to your exertions at Killa Abdoolla, and your bringing with you to Candahar Abdoolla Khan, the eldest brother of Saloo Khan, that we were able to make those arrangements with the Atchukzye tribe, which provided for the reopening of our *dâk* communication with India, and which maintained that communication regularly and uninterruptedly during the remainder of our stay at Candahar.

I think it was mainly owing to the character you had established, by your successful negotiations in Beloochistan, that Sa-

loo Khan was persuaded to entrust you with his proffer of submission, and to commit his brother to your care for the purpose
of concluding arrangements with us at Candahar; and I am thus
of opinion that you are fairly entitled to whatever credit is due
to the happy results of our arrangements with the Atchukzye.

Believe me, &c.,

J. C. Rawlinson.

Brigadier Stacy, &c.

Candahar to Cabool – From the 10th May, 1842, to the 18th September, 1842

Soon after the arrival of General England's Bombay detachment at Candahar, the following force, under Brigadier Wymer, was despatched to Kelat-e-Ghilzie, to bring away the garrison of that place, conformably to the orders of the Government:—Captain Leslie's troop of horse artillery; Captain Blood's four 9-pounders, horse-battery; 3rd Bombay Light Cavalry, Captain Delamain; detachment Christie's horse; detachment Haldane's horse; Her Majesty's 40th regiment; 2nd and 16th Bengal Grenadiers; 38th Bengal Light Infantry, and the Madras sappers and miners.

This detachment left Candahar on the 18th May. It was arranged in the enemy's camp that, as soon as Brigadier Wymer should be well on the road towards Kelat-e-Ghilzie, the Ghazees of the Ghilzie country should attack the garrison of that fort;[1] and, at the same time, the Ghazees under Prince Sufter Jung, Meer Ahmed Atta Khan, and other chiefs, were to attack Candahar.

I had been sent across the Urgundab River on the 12th May, with a force consisting of a troop of horse artillery, Christie's horse, Haldane's horse, and a brigade of infantry (the 42nd and 43rd regiments of Native Infantry and 5th Shah's Infantry), but with strict injunctions to protect the crops and property of the people generally; the object

---

1. In fact, Kelat-e-Ghilzie was attacked early in the morning of the 21st May, by a body of 4,000 Ghilzies, provided with scaling-ladders, who advanced to the assault in the most determined manner, but, after an hour's fighting, were repulsed by Captain Craigie, commanding the garrison, with much loss.—Despatch, No. 380; Papers relating to Military Operations in Affghanistan, p. 314.

of this march being solely to induce the Ghazees in that quarter to try their strength in the field. They retired before this force, and the detachment returned to Candahar, after going as low down as Neelah Karaize, on the morning of the 17th, as directed.

On the 27th and 28th May, the usual supplies daily brought to the town were nearly stopped. The Ghazees were seen moving on the hills both towards Babawullee and in the direction of Chilzeenah, and on the 29th, as soon as day broke, they were observed in parties between the cantonment, which was unoccupied, and the Babawullee Ghat.

Turner's troop of horse artillery, Tait's cavalry, the 42nd Native Infantry, and the Shah's 5th Infantry, had been encamped outside the town since the 23rd May. On the 26th, the 43rd Native Infantry were ordered to join this party, and I moved out with them, and took the command of the whole, as brigadier.

On the morning of the 29th May, a little before ten a.m., I received notice from General Nott, that the Ghazees were moving round towards my post, and he recommended that the party over the cattle at graze should be put on the alert. The party and camels were called in, and orders were at the same time sent to have the 42nd and 43rd regiments of Native Infantry ready, but not to fall them in without further orders. About a quarter of an hour after this, a third order came, directing me to march the 42nd and 43rd regiments of Native Infantry to the cantonment, there to pile arms and await further orders. A request, on my part, to be allowed to take the two horse-artillery guns, under Lieutenant Turner, and a *russalah* of cavalry, was granted. This compact little force was soon on the road; the 42nd had 356 bayonets, the 43rd 322; two complete companies from each regiment were on grazing guard duty, the rest on *godown* and various other details outside the city.

As soon as they had cleared the house and gardens (Royal Burial-ground) nearly facing the Eedgah (or northern) gate of Candahar, the enemy were seen in strong parties from the two hills close to the cantonment up to the Babawullee Pass. As the detachment approached the open country near the cantonment, the enemy were observed in great strength; they were assembling on the plain between the main *kareez*, or water-course, and Babawullee, with the Babawullee and Kotul-e-Moolieh Passes in their rear, and the Babawullee gun-road on their right. A pencil note was sent off to General Nott, giving notice of the strength of the enemy, their position, &c.

I took up a position near the barracks, facing the enemy, and directly opposite the only spot where the canal was passable for guns. A small deserted village on the right of the position, walled in and with only one entrance, was occupied by a company of the 42nd Native Infantry. As soon as I had selected my position, I sent Lieutenant Knox, brigade quarter-master, to acquaint General Nott that the enemy were rapidly forming; that, besides the two passes and the gun-road to Babawullee, they had possession of the Chilzeenah road, and had posted a force of from 1,000 to 1,200 men on the hill commanding it.

Captain Anderson arrived with two guns of Turner's troop, escorted by a party of an officer and thirty-four rank and file from the Bombay light infantry battalion, and another party, from the Bombay 25th Native Infantry, of an officer and thirty rank and file. Some of the enemy's horsemen rode to within range and fired into the column; some men also got behind the walls of an old house at the foot of the hill on the left, and, firing long shots into the 43rd, wounded three or four men before they were dislodged.

The two last guns were planted, commanding a road behind the barracks, and which could be approached by the enemy from the Chilzeenah road on our left. A note was received at this time from General Nott, saying that Cooper's troop of horse artillery, Her Majesty's 41st (352 bayonets), and the Poonah Horse, had marched to join me. This addition to the force soon arrived, and were placed in readiness to move as General Nott and his staff reached the ground. I made over the command, reported the arrangement of the force, and particularly drew the general's attention to the body of the enemy in possession of the hill on the left.

General Nott approved of the arrangement, and instantly ordered the light companies of the regiments under Brevet Captain Macpherson, 43rd Native Infantry, to drive the enemy off the hills on the left, supported by the remaining companies of the 43rd. These companies were soon in order, and on the word "Forward!" were off at the double, with a cheer that prognosticated success. Major Nash, commanding the 43rd Native Infantry, with the supports, moved on, inclining to the left, towards a road at the foot of the hill, beyond cantonments, and which led direct upon the Chilzeenah road. The *russalah* of Christie's irregular cavalry, under Lieutenant N. B. Chamberlain, was in attendance at this point.

No sooner had the light companies driven the enemy down the hill on the Chilzeenah road, than Lieutenant Chamberlain was upon them. The foot-men escaped over the garden-walls, which extend almost up to the canal in front of the cantonments, skirting the gun-road; but their cavalry soon got jammed in the Chilzeenah road, which, in the first part, runs between the village on a rising ground to the left and a long walled-in garden to the right, and afterwards is bounded by a deep canal on the left, the bridge over which, about a mile in advance, is not more than ten feet broad.

Many of the enemy, finding it impossible to escape, made a virtue of necessity, and, turning round, met Lieutenant Chamberlain and his men with considerable impetuosity. Lieutenant Chamberlain's horse was killed under him, and he himself received a severe wound in the thigh. His *naib russaldar* and five men were wounded at this point; but they left forty-two of the enemy dead on the spot. The light companies, and Major Nash, with the supports, and the two horse-artillery guns, posted in the rear of the column with the supports, soon came up, and scattered the enemy in every direction.

The greater part of the infantry gained the Babawullee gun-road, screened by the many gardens in this direction; the rest continued on the road to the lower *ghat* of the Urgundab by the Chilzeenah. The chiefs, seeing the distress of this party, attempted to call off General Nott's attention by advancing, and opening a sharp fire on the column; they maintained this fire for a short time, but it slackened as General Nott advanced, and ceased as our guns opened.

As soon as General Nott saw the light companies ready on the left, he moved forward also direct on the enemy. Major Rawlinson, with the Persian prince, Syud Azah Khan, and his *sowars*, about 100, and the horsemen attached to the Agency, were on the right, beyond the village occupied by the company of the 42nd, moving parallel with General Nott, their right thrown a little forward. Captain Anderson's guns soon began to play, advancing by sections with the infantry column.

The hill on the left was lost to the enemy from the moment our light companies moved on it. This evidently disconcerted their main body, and the steady advance of our main column, their right routed and their left threatened by Major Rawlinson and the Sheah prince, appeared to embarrass the chiefs. At this moment of consternation, a shot from one of our guns killed the *yaboo* (horse) of Shahzadeh Sufter Jung, standing close to the prince and the *sirdars*. A panic then appeared to seize them all, and in a moment they made off by the three remaining routes open to them; namely, the gun-road, the Babawullee and Kotul-e-Moolieh Passes.

Major Rawlinson and his party, on the first symptom of the enemy's indecision, made a very capital charge, and succeeded in killing several. Those who escaped by the Babawullee Pass, the road over which had been strongly fortified by a *sungah*, or breastwork of stones, leaving only a narrow pathway, planted a white flag, under which to conquer or die, and commenced a languid fire of *jezails*. General Nott still steadily led on the column, and it was resolved that the road and the pathway should be stormed simultaneously; that the 42nd, being exactly opposite the breastwork, should storm that, whilst Her Majesty's 41st foot moved direct upon the white flag.

At this moment, the column was close to the *bumbah* (arched-in reservoir). It was between two and three o'clock p.m.; the thermometer 137 degrees.[2] The men had been out since ten and eleven a.m.; the general, therefore, halted the column, to give them an opportunity to drink water. The guns in the meantime made some capital shots at the *sungah*, or stone breastwork, and dropped some shrapnells with admirable precision near the white flag.

The column moved on to the attack; Her Majesty's 41st inclining a little to the right, on the line of the pathway; the 42nd direct to the front. The enemy had not the heart to stand, and as the *ghat* was reached, those only first up had the satisfaction of seeing them in full flight, crossing the gardens bordering the river. Those of the enemy who fled by the gun-road were punished by a section of Anderson's guns, which played upon them until they were out of reach of even round shot.

Having gone over the *ghat*, with the two infantry regiments, Her Majesty's 41st and the 42nd Native Infantry, and finding the enemy had completely disappeared, I halted the men. Captain Polwhele arrived with orders from the general to send back Her Majesty's 41st regiment, and to take the 42nd Native Infantry back to camp by the gun-road.

Major Nash, with his party, except the cavalry, which had been called back, pushed the enemy on the left, and gave them no time to consider whether they should turn on the handful of men before whom they were flying like so many sheep. It was the distant booming of the two horse-artillery guns with this party, playing on the enemy, whilst they were descending to the river, and which we distinctly heard, that induced General Nott to send me home by the gun-road.

The general moved home with the troops as soon as Her Majesty's

2. At eleven o'clock a.m., two thermometers shewed 150°.

41st recrossed the *ghat*. I marched round by the gun-road, reaching my camp a little after 5 p. m.

On the road to camp, I received orders to bring the whole of my detachment and stores inside the city that evening; to enable me to do so, working parties, and cattle from both branches of the commissariat, were sent to bring in the grain, stores, &c. This was accomplished by 8 p. m., when the whole of the regiments and stores were within the walls of Candahar.

The same night, I received orders to march at 3 a. m. the following morning, the 30th May, with a detachment which would be placed under my command, consisting of Cooper's troop of horse artillery, the whole of the cavalry, the 5th Shah's Infantry, and the 2nd brigade of infantry. It was conjectured that the intention was to beat up the *sirdars'* quarters, in order that they should be perfectly convinced we were always ready to beat them in the field, even in the absence of half the force.

The several regiments met at the point of rendezvous at the hour named, and moved off quietly. I ordered the 42nd Native Infantry, under Major Clarkson, to move on the Babawullee Pass, with directions not to go beyond it, until the arrival there of the detachment by the gun-road, but simply to hold possession of the pass.

The parties met and proceeded about a mile onwards, and then halted, whilst a small body of horse, under Major Rawlinson, went to reconnoitre. From the top of the hill, under which the detachment was concealed, the enemy's force could be distinctly seen moving off across the plain on the opposite bank of the river. A party of their horsemen exchanged a few long shots with our party, and then, recrossing the river, joined the *sirdars*. At one time Major Rawlinson had hopes of decoying the enemy across, and the detachment moved on about a mile or mile and a half, to be ready for them. Some few horsemen did cross, but, finding the English at hand, returned after reconnoitring.

The affair of the 29th had the effect of breaking up the confederacy, of which Meer Mahomed, Mahomed Sudeeq, and Aktar Khan were the principals: Shahzadeh Sufter Jung was a mere puppet in their hands. Upon reaching the right bank of the Urgundab, on the night of the 29th, the *sirdars* and chiefs held a *durbar*, when very angry words passed, each charging the other with losing the battle by his cowardice. Even if my detachment had not been sent out on the 30th, it is supposed the enemy would have broken up for the time, and have waited some more favourable opportunity. The demonstration of the 30th, however, dispelled all doubt, and, as Major Rawlinson said, succeeded in fairly breaking up the enemy's camp.

No division order was issued on the subject of these two days' operations, but I received (with the commanding officers of regiments) a note[3] from the assistant adjutant-general of the force, desiring that the major-general's thanks should be communicated to the respective regiments.

The letters in which General Nott reported the operations of his force have been noticed in various quarters for their remarkable brevity, and the meagreness of their details. The following is a copy of the general's despatch to Mr. Maddock,[4] reporting these operations:—

Candahar, May 29, 1842.

Sir,

Aktar Khan, chief of Zamindawur, having assembled three thousand men, crossed the Helmund, and joined the rebel force under Prince Sufter Jung and Atta Mahomed, on the right bank of the Urghundab, taking advantage of the absence of Brigadier Wymer, who had been detached into the Ghilzie province with a large portion of my force, and nearly the whole of my cavalry. The enemy, under an impression that we had not a sufficient number of men to hold the city, and at the same time to attack them in the field, took possession of some steep rocky hills within a mile of the city walls.

I instantly moved out with the troops noted in the accompanying field return, leaving Major-General England, K. H., in command of the city. The Ghazees had about 8,000 in position, and 2,000 men guarding the Baba Wullee Pass, and roads leading to their camp. Our troops carried all their positions in gallant style, and drove them in confusion, and with great loss, across the Urghundab River.

I was ably assisted by Brigadier Stacy and every officer present. Major Rawlinson, political agent, with his accustomed zeal, was in the field, and gallantly led a small body of Persian and Af-

---

3. My dear Brigadier, The General begs you will intimate to the 42nd and 43rd regiments that he was much pleased with their conduct in the field on the 29th *ultimo*, against the enemy.

Yours, sincerely,

Brigadier Stacy.   T. Polwhele.

4. Papers relating to Military Operations in Affghanistan, p. 312.

fghan horse to the charge.

I enclose a list of killed and wounded.

I have, &c.,

W. Nott.

The Governor-General of India, having determined to withdraw the British force from Candahar, ultimately left it to the discretion of Major-General Nott to decide whether he would retire by the route of Quetta, or by Ghuznee and Cabool. In his "secret" letter to the major-general, dated "Allahabad, July 4th, 1842,"[5] Lord Ellenborough announced to him that nothing had occurred to induce him to change his first opinion, that the bringing back the armies then in Affghanistan at the earliest period at which their retirement could be effected, consistently with the health and efficiency of the troops, into positions where they might have easy and certain communications with India, was a measure commanded by considerations of political and military prudence; but the improved position of the Candahar army had induced him to leave to the option of the major-general the line by which he should withdraw it; at the same time, his Lordship pointed out what appeared to him to be the risk and dangers of the Ghuznee route. Major-General Nott replied to this letter (July 25th):

"Having looked at the difficulties in every point of view, and reflected on the advantages which would attend a successful accomplishment of such a move, and the moral influence it would have throughout Asia, I have come to a determination to retire a portion of the army under my command *via* Ghuznee and Cabool. I shall take with me, not a large, but a compact and well-tried force, on which I can rely. Your Lordship may rest assured that all prudence, and every military precaution, shall be observed; there shall be no unnecessary risk; and, if expedient, I will mask Ghuznee, and even Cabool; but, if an opportunity should offer, I will endeavour to strike a decisive blow for the honour of our arms."

Preparations were accordingly made for the immediate evacuation of Candahar, and the whole force marched on the 9th August, part under the command of Major-General Nott, for Ghuznee and Cabool; part under that of Major-General England, for Quetta, which was reached, with trifling loss, on the 26th August

The former column commenced its inarch in the following order:—Advance guard, 3rd Bombay Cavalry and Christie's irregu-

---

5. Papers, *ut antea*, p. 327.

lar horse: column, Captain Leslie's troop of horse artillery; Captain Blood's battery; Captain Anderson's troop of horse artillery; the 1st (Brigadier Wymer's) and 2nd (Brigadier Stacy's) brigades of infantry: rearguard, two companies of infantry from the 2nd brigade, and the whole of Haldane's horse. It reached Kelat-e-Ghilzie on the 17th August, and Mookoor on the 27th.

From Candahar to this place, 160 miles, not a shot was fired. The village of Mookoor was deserted, and the Affghans we saw perched on the hills were at first considered to be people who had fled from the village for safety. The picquets of the 1st brigade were within fire of these hills; indeed, a few shots rolled into the lines, and during the night there was a little firing by the enemy, whose long *jezails* enabled them to annoy us, whilst they were out of the reach of our muskets.

Early on the 28th, the troops marched from Mookoor in the following order:—Eight light companies. Captain White; the cavalry. Captain Delamain; the horse artillery. Captain Leslie and Captain Anderson; the 1st brigade of infantry, Brigadier Wymer; the 2nd brigade of infantry, Brigadier Stacy; *godown* and baggage; rearguard under Lieutenant-Colonel Lane.

As the column passed by the hills, a few long shots were dropped on them by the enemy. When day broke, we saw horsemen in small parties on our left, but keeping well under the hills. They were now joined by a body of both cavalry and infantry. Although they must have been from two and a half to three miles off, they approached firing their *jezails*. Lieut.-Colonel Lane, commanding the rearguard, sent notice of this party to Major-General Nott, who wished to get them between the cavalry of our rearguard (250 men, under Lieutenant Chamberlain) and a party which he desired Captain Delamain, commanding the cavalry, to detach immediately for that purpose.

Not knowing the nature of the ground, which towards the hills was full of very deep ravines, with precipitous banks, the major-general did not order any infantry with this party. Captain Delamain sent Captain Christie, with a party from his own regiment of irregular cavalry, and the detachment of the First Irregular Cavalry (two *russalahs*) under Captain Haldane and Lieutenant Travers. Captain Christie moved towards the enemy's left for about a mile, or a mile and a half, and was closing with the enemy, when our party came to the banks of a very deep *nullah*.

A footpath was soon discovered, by which the whole detachment had to file down; and form on the opposite bank. By the time our cavalry had crossed and formed, the foremost of the enemy had nearly reached the bottom of the bills. Captain Christie how led at a smart gallop, and very soon closed on the rear of the enemy, of whom upwards of fifty were slain by this party, and twelve by that under Lieutenant Chamberlain. Our loss in this affair was a *duffadar* and nine horses killed; Lieutenant Chamberlain and nine *sowars* wounded. The greater part of this loss was sustained from the enemy's footmen hidden in the ravines. The lieutenant was wounded in personal combat with one of the enemy's cavalry.

This affair did not delay the march of the column, which arrived at Oosman Khan-ke-kareez at 8 a.m. About 1 p. m., the grass-cutters of the cavalry were seen running towards camp, and as they approached were heard hallooing that the enemy's horse had come down and cut up several of their comrades. By some misunderstanding, the 3rd Bombay Cavalry bugle sounded to saddle. Captain Christie, who was coming in with the rearguard, moved off with the two *russalahs* of his own regiment and the cavalry of the rearguard, accompanied by some of the grass-cutters, to the fort, about three quarters of a mile from camp, behind which, they asserted, the enemy were hidden, and their comrades had been killed.

Captain Christie, with such men as were ready, went to the fort. There was no appearance of an enemy, except ten or twelve horsemen a long distance in advance to the left. After looking well about, Captain Christie resolved to take his party back to camp. Halfway between the fort and the camp, he fell in with two squadrons of the 3rd Bombay Cavalry, under Captain Delamain, to whom Captain Christie reported, that he had examined the country round about, and saw no indications of an enemy in the plains, but the few horsemen a long way off on the left. Captain Christie then rejoined his party, and finding Captain Delamain proceeded on, he rode back, and asked him if he should attend him. Captain Delamain considered it advisable that he should do so, and the detachment of Christie's and Haldane's horse joined.

Captain Delamain, after mounting, sent a verbal message to the general for instructions, and subsequently received a reply. He moved steadily on, and when abreast of the men seen by Captain Christie, a party, under Lieutenant Ravenscroft, were sent in pursuit of them. They came up with the enemy close under the hills, and cut up five of them; Lieutenant Ravenscroft and three of his men were wounded; the lieutenant subsequently died of his wounds. Captain Delamain proceeded to the end of the range of hills, turned to the left, and very shortly after bringing up his right shoulders, he saw Shums-ood-deen's army directly in front of him; the range of hills parallel to which Captain Delamain had moved separated the two camps.

The enemy's picquets had been seen on the top of these hills from the moment we reached our ground. Captain Delamain halted, and sent back an officer (Lieutenant Brett) to Major-General Nott for instructions. Shums-ood-deen's cavalry were calculated at from 5,000 to 6,000 men, and his infantry, which were on the hills, at 2,000. His cavalry advanced towards ours, and Captain Delamain retired at a walk, whilst the *jezailchees* on the hill moved quietly towards the comer of the hill round which Captain Delamain would have to pass. As their cavalry neared, they opened a destructive fire from their matchlocks, which wounded several, and were pressing us hard.

When our party reached the comer, the *jezailchees* harassed them considerably, and the enemy's cavalry were at the gallop, a large body being also intermixed with the *jezailchees*, who had possession of this point. There was no alternative; unless checked, they would have been upon our party. Captain Delamain, accordingly, resolved to charge those on the declivity of the hill. Our party halted, fronted, and a squadron, under Captain Bury, charged up the hill, the ascent of which was not very great. The enemy did not wait for them, but when about two-thirds of the way up, met our squadron with their whole force there collected. The crash of the collision was tremendous.

Our party was overwhelmed. For about a minute, the men plied their swords well, but the weight of hundreds, pressing on, forced them down, and they were driven back with fearful loss. Those who could disengage themselves fled do win the hill; the other squadron went about; Christie's and Haldane's horse did the same, and set off at the gallop; The dust rendered it impossible for the rear files to flee, and several horses fell. They went on at this rate for half or three quarters of a mile, before their officers could halt them.

This done, they again shewed front; but the enemy were content with the havoc they had made. Captain Bury, and Lieutenant and Brevet Captain Reeves, 3rd Bombay Light Cavalry, fell in the charge. The *subadar*-major was also killed; he was the oldest soldier in the regiment, wore a medal for Seringapatam, and had distinguished himself on several occasions.

There were also twenty-two troopers killed, and Lieutenant Mackenzie was wounded.[6]

The devoted gallantry of a *russaldar* of the 1st Cavalry, late Shah Shooja's force, upon this retreat; or rather flight, deserves notice, and I shall give the particulars in the words of Captain Christie himself:—

Wuzeer Khan, *russaldar*, 1st Cavalry, late Shah Shooja's force, was with me on the 28th August, in action with Shums-ood-deen Khan, and was the means of saving my life. In the retreat, the dust was so great that we could not see a yard before us. The enemy were pushing us very hard, and firing into us on all sides, when my charger fell headlong with me into an old *kareez*. Finding it impossible to extricate him, I climbed out, and ran on on foot, when I was perceived by Wuzeer Khan. He, it seems, in passing the *kareez*, saw my horse in it, and immediately concluded that I was killed, and commenced looking about for my body.

Soon after, he discovered me on foot, and, jumping off his horse, insisted on my immediately mounting and being off, as the only means of saving my life. This I declined doing, telling him, if I did so, that he would be inevitably cut up by the Ghazees, who were killing everyone they came across. He replied, 'Never mind me; I am a Mussulman, and have a much better chance of escaping than you have; if you stop another moment, you will certainly be sacrificed.' I then told him I would take his horse on one condition, *viz*. provided he would mount behind; but even this he would not hear of, again telling me, for God's sake, to be off, and that I might depend upon it he would succeed in effecting his escape.

Seeing that it was useless attempting to persuade him to get up, I (selfish as it may appear) rode off, and soon got to the other side of the *nullah*, when I found the cavalry once more forming up. Five minutes after, this fine soldier, to my great joy, came up and joined me, but not before he had been attacked by three of the enemy, two of whom he succeeded in killing. Such an act of devotion is seldom or ever heard of, and will, I am convinced, meet with its due reward from the British Government. He saw death almost certain before his eyes; notwithstanding which, he nobly preferred saving my life to his own. I beg to add, that this native officer has been recommended for the Order of Merit

6. The only report of this affair given in the parliamentary papers is contained in an extract of a letter (p. 390) from Captain Delamain to the Adjutant-General of the Army, dated at Cabool, September 28th, 1842.

for gallant conduct on a former occasion."

Upon Lieutenant Brett reporting the state of affairs to the major-general, Captain Leslie's horse artillery, with the 38th Light Infantry, was ordered to proceed as rapidly as possible to Captain Delamain's assistance. The first brigade of infantry, under Brigadier Wymer, with Captain Blood's 9-pounder battery, and Captain Anderson's 2nd troop of horse artillery, under Lieutenant Turner, conducted by the major-general, moved for the eastern side of the village or fort. I was sent with the 2nd brigade to the western side, with orders to proceed about half a mile or a mile in advance, and to support the advanced party, if I should find they required assistance.

When, therefore, I saw Captain Leslie and the 38th regiment Bengal Native Infantry had passed beyond the spot where the cavalry were drawn up, I detached the 43rd Light Infantry, with orders to keep them well in sight. The advanced party moved on to the scene of the recent action, from which the enemy had retired. They placed the bodies of their slain comrades in *doolies*, and returned to camp.

Major-General Nott, finding the gates of the fort shut, and several shots having been fired from it, desired the artillery officer to open upon them. The gates were shattered; the light companies rushed in, some entering by the gates, others, getting on their comrades' shoulders, climbed over the wall at a place where it was partially decayed. There were but few men in the fort, but they fought bravely, and it was half an hour before the last was killed; The women were placed under the protection of a guard, and the troops marched back to camp.

The force resumed its march (the enemy in great numbers moving parallel with us), and had reached its ground on the morning of the 30th, at Guine (or Goaine), all the forts in the neighbourhood being occupied by the Ghazees. A fort on the left of the camp fired a shot at us. It attracted particular attention, as the fort to appearance had very few men in it, and, with the force we had at our disposal, if properly applied, could not have stood half an hour. The major-general resolved to punish the garrison, and ordered the following detachment under his personal command to be ready to move out at 3 p.m.; namely, two 18-pounders, Lieutenant Cornish; a troop of Anderson's horse artillery. Captain Anderson; 3rd Bombay Cavalry, Captain Delamain; Christie's cavalry. Captain Christie; Her Majesty's 40th regiment. Major Hibbert; 16th regiment Native Infantry, Lieutenant-Colonel MacLaren; 38th regiment Native Infantry. Major Burney; Kelat-e-Ghilzie regiment, Captain Craigie. Her Majesty's 41st regiment. Major Browne, and the

42nd Light Infantry, were called for afterwards.

It was past three p.m. before the party was ready; when they quitted camp, they found the heavy guns (18-pounders) could not travel, the road was so bad, and it was four o'clock before they Were fairly on their march. The ground was very unequal, and broken into ravines. The 3rd Bombay Cavalry, the 16th Native Infantry, and the Khelate-Ghilzie regiment, the whole under Lieutenant-Colonel MacLaren, were posted to the left, with orders that, as soon as a breach was made, the infantry were to storm, and the cavalry to cut up every man who should attempt to escape.

The general moved to the left, followed by Christie's horse, Her Majesty's 40th regiment, and the 38th Native Infantry; and he subsequently ordered the 16th Native Infantry to join him. Anderson's guns opened on a flank tower, where some men shewed themselves; but after each shot, the enemy hurrahed, waved their swords round their heads in defiance, and returned the fire with their matchlocks. The 18-pounder practice was not effective, and, besides that, the object was changed after every few shot, and consequently no impression was made. Many shots passed through the fort, and others over it, nearly destroying some of our own cavalry.

The general, finding little progress was made, ordered up one of Blood's 9-pounder guns, Lieutenant Terry, under the protection of a company of Her Majesty's 40th regiment, to blow open the gate. The gun was run up to within fifty yards of the gate, and the very first shot went through it, but did not break it in. After a few discharges, it was found that they had no more round shot, and they therefore retired, but not before several men had been wounded.

Shums-ood-deen's army began about this time to shew a rapid succession of small bodies crossing the hills in front, and rather to the right. The dismounted branch kept more together this day than customary, and took up a position under cover of the low range of hills. The cavalry were as usual moving about, each chief taking his men where his own peculiar fancy led him, always keeping to the safe side. They very soon collected in considerable strength, threatening our right flank. Her Majesty's 41st, which had been left in camp, was sent for; and, though no instructions had been left me, having been watching with my telescope, from a mound on the left of the camp, the progress of events, I had quietly fell in the 42nd and 43rd regiments of Native Infantry, the only remaining regiments in camp. Leslie's troop of horse artillery also saddled, and stood ready for orders.

The 42nd regiment, Major Clarkson, was the next corps sent for, and, being fortunately ready, it moved out the moment the order was received. I arranged with Major Clarkson that, as the firing had been heavy and continuous, some ammunition should be sent to his post, and notice given by him to the commanding officers of regiments, that they might indent upon that quarter, instead of sending to camp.

Her Majesty's 41st regiment arrived in full time to share in the glory of the conflict. On reaching the major-general's detachment, Captain Nelson, acting assistant commissary-general, met them, with orders that they should form the supports. The light companies of Her Majesty's 40th and 41st, and the 16th and 38th regiments of Native Infantry, drove back the enemy's skirmishers, and General Nott then prepared to attack their main body.

The right of the line was thrown forward. The regiments moved on some way in quarter distance column, at deploying distance, Her Majesty's 41st being placed next to, and on the left of, Her Majesty's 40th, when orders were given to form line, light companies to the front. The line was formed, and advanced with a cheering "hurrah," when the enemy, who had kept up a brisk fire upon us from *jezails*, but fired wild and too high, broke and ran.

At this time, a message from Captain Delamain informed the general that a heavy body of cavalry threatened the left. Her Majesty's 41st was thereupon ordered to change position to the left, and move to Captain Delamain's assistance. Major Browne, their commander, was instantly in motion, and he soon came to the banks of a deep *nullah*, in which some of the enemy were snugly ensconced, plying long shots at the cavalry. They were immediately driven out. This was scarcely accomplished when Captain Polwhele, assistant adjutant-general, came with orders for Her Majesty's 41st regiment to rejoin the main column, as the enemy's cavalry had quitted the field. Before reaching it, however, another order was received for the regiment to return towards camp.

The steadiness and gallantry of the formation and advance of the line, with our skirmishers in front, won general admiration. The casualties of the enemy, it is supposed, were very few, as they would not wait the close, .and ran quickly. Their greatest loss was on the right, by the fire of the light companies. Two horse-artillery guns were brought into action by the enemy, and admirably served: one was, however, knocked off its carriage by a shot from one of our guns early in the action; the other limbered up, and made off at a tearing pace, when the line broke. Christie's horse had charged the runaways to the right; on their return, hearing that the gun had been taken off.

Captain Christie immediately pursued, with Lieutenant Chamberlain and two *russalahs* of his regiment, resolved to capture it. They soon discovered the tracks of the wheels, and pushing on at a good rate, saw, as they turned the corner of a hill, the gun and a body of cavalry escorting it. A shout gave the enemy notice of the proximity of our party; their cavalry set off at speed, and the drivers of the gun urged the horses to their utmost, but they soon flagged. Our men came up steadily, hand over hand, the drivers of the gun still exerting themselves to carry it off.

Lieutenant Chamberlain's first blow knocked off the driver of the near wheel horse; the traces of the leaders were cut, and the gun was captured. The man observed to be most active in taking off this gun, who rode the near wheeler, proved to be a drummer of the 27th regiment of Native Infantry, who had gone over to the enemy: he was sabred. With the aid of some rope, the harness was repaired; Captain Anderson slung the dismounted gun under one of his waggons, burning the carriage, and the captured gun and four of the gun-horses were brought into camp. The guns and carriages were ordered to be destroyed, and the horses and harness were sold by auction.

Whilst this was going on in advance, the general, finding the enemy completely discomfited and dispersed, ordered Brigadier Wymer to take the troops back to camp. The general and his staff had moved off, and Brigadier Wymer was following, when information was brought to Captain Anderson, who was still looking for the return of Captain Christie and his party, that the whole of the enemy's ammunition, tents, and baggage, had been discovered, separated from the field of battle by a low hill.

Captain Anderson begged the brigadier to halt until he could destroy the ammunition, but he declined, and the request was then carried on by Captain Anderson to the general, who gave an order to the brigadier for the troops to remain, whilst the tents and baggage of the enemy were burned and the ammunition destroyed. The quantity of the latter that which the enemy had taken from the 27th Native Infantry, at Ghuznee) was considerable. It was eight p.m. before the troops reached camp.

The killed and wounded in this action were comparatively few; but its effect dispirited the enemy as much as it exhilarated our camp. Such was the hurry in which they abandoned the field, that half of them threw away their sandals, in order to move the quicker.

The following division order was issued by Major-General Nott:—

Camp, Goaine, 31st August, 1842.

The Major-General commanding begs to offer his thanks to the whole of the officers and troops engaged in the action with the enemy yesterday. He is fully satisfied with their steady and gallant conduct, and will not fail to bring it to the notice of the Supreme Government.

General Nott's despatch to the Government is dated the same day; Brigadier Wymer's letter to the general is dated the succeeding day.[7] In both Captain (brigade-major) Scott is mentioned in very laudatory terms; but not a word is said of the capture of the gun, of the 41st Foot, or of the troops in camp, whom I had under arms, so that no sooner was an order brought for a regiment than it was in a condition to march off without the delay of a moment.

The force recommenced its march on the following day, September 1st. The affair at Guine (or Goaine) appeared to have so depressed the enemy that, up to the 5th, scarcely a shot was exchanged. The enemy's *videttes* were often seen at a distance, and the spots where some of their parties had bivouacked were discerned.

The Sheah Hazarees had joined us in great numbers immediately after our quitting Guine; they burned and destroyed everything as we passed along, to revenge themselves for the tyranny arid oppression they had suffered from Shums-ood-deen's people, who are Soonees. These Hazarees proved of great service to us, bringing the bullocks, sheep, goats, and fowls they carried off from the enemy's deserted forts and villages to our camp for sale at low prices.

The force encamped near Ghuznee on the 4th September, and on the 5th moved off early without the "general," or "assembly" sounding. As we approached Ghuznee, the road became extremely bad; the latter part was so intersected with ravines and deep water-courses, that it is astonishing how the horse artillery crossed them.

The order of march was as follows: the eight light companies. Captain White, Her Majesty's 40th Foot; the cavalry, Captain Delamain, 3rd Bombay Light Cavalry; Bombay horse artillery. Captain Leslie; Anderson's horse artillery, Captain Anderson; horsed 9-pounder battery, Captain Blood; 1st brigade infantry, Brigadier Wymer; 2nd

---

7. Appendix, No. 9.

brigade infantry, Brigadier Stacy; the rearguard was commanded by Lieutenant-Colonel MacLaren, 16th Native Infantry.

As we neared the enemy (day having broke long before), they appeared to great advantage, and in some order. Sultan Jan and Shums-ood-deen, and their immediate followers, were conspicuous by their gay attire and superior horses. Being drawn up on a gently rising ground, their strength appeared imposing, and their cavalry were very numerous: they seemed prepared and resolved to overwhelm our comparatively insignificant force. The horse were marshalled below; the ravines and water-courses were filled with *jezailchees*; but they fled before our men whenever they met. The only decent show of resistance was made by a party of matchlock-men behind a long line of old wall, on the Rosa road, where they stood pretty well, and did considerable execution, until they were driven from their post at the point of the bayonet by the light companies. The hills likewise swarmed with infantry, but there seemed to be no order amongst them; they appeared to act independently of each other, and were in constant motion.

The column passed to the right (east) of Ghuznee, and then turned to the left, at the garden called Sir John Keane's Garden. Major Sanders had been sent with the 16th Bengal Grenadiers and a party of horse to reconnoitre, and soon drew on him and his party a sharp fire from the water-courses. A party also shewed on our left, at a turn in the road. Two of the 9-pounders were left under Lieutenant Terry, and a company from the 43rd Native Infantry, under Captain Webster, and they were soon driven back. Captain Webster pushed forward a party of his men, and took possession of an old water-course, from which he completely commanded any advance in this direction. This party remained here until picked up by the rearguard.

The light companies were soon skirmishing with the enemy. The horse artillery was collected to the front, and Craigie's Kelat-e-Ghilzie regiment reinforced the 16th Bengal Grenadiers. The enemy appeared resolved to try us this day, and pressed the 16th and light companies, notwithstanding a sharp fire from Leslie's and Anderson's guns. One particularly good charge (for Affghans) was made on the 16th Native Infantry by the *élite* of the enemy's cavalry; but they were not well supported; their ranks evidently became thinner as they neared the bayonets. A volley, when about twenty or twenty-five paces distant, turned them to the right about; not more than six or eight men reached the bayonets, and they were soon dropped.

The first and second brigades of infantry pushed forward the light companies, and the 16th Bengal Grenadiers, supported by the horse artillery, had made the enemy turn, and they ascended the hills north of the city. Brigadier Wymer followed them with the first brigade directly in front; I led the second brigade to the left, inclining to the point of action. Both brigades reached the top of the hill simultaneously, but only in time to see the enemy in full retreat. The 16th Bengal Grenadiers and light companies gave the enemy no time to rally; they ascended the hills with them, the horse artillery throwing shells whenever an opportunity offered. The light companies and 16th Native Infantry continued to follow the enemy until they reached the village of Belall; the 2nd brigade held the heights next to this, and Brigadier Wymer's brigade those nearest Rosa.

A message was brought to me by Captain Ripley, D.P.M., and Captain Waterfield, A.D.C., from General Nott, desiring me to leave one regiment on the hill, and bring back the other two. This was immediately done. In passing the general, I went up to him, to receive his orders, and he asked me whether I had been on the heights. I answered in the affirmative, and the general remarked, there was heavy firing in the rear, and that he wished me to proceed immediately with such portion of my brigade as I chose to their assistance.

The heights were held by the 38th Native Infantry from the 1st brigade, and the 42nd from the 2nd brigade; the 16th also was left at Belall, where the 38th and 42nd Bengal Light Infantry afterwards joined them; and these regiments gave the working parties during the night.

After leaving the major-general, I rejoined the two remaining regiments of my brigade, namely, Her Majesty's 41st, and the 2nd Native Infantry. I desired Her Majesty's 41st to go to camp, and moved on with the 2nd Native Infantry. Abreast of the fort, Captain Leslie and his horse artillery were halted. Under cover of a garden-wall, close to the fort, was the light company of the Kelat-e-Ghilzie regiment. I sent word to the general of their location, and that I would bring them in before Leslie's battery moved. This was accordingly done: the company marched as the Ghuznee gun (Zubber Jung) threw a shot close to Captain Leslie's right gun. Previous to moving, two round shot were returned; the guns then limbered up, and moved out of range. I left a wing of the 2nd Native Infantry with them, and pushed on with the other towards the rearguard. The guns with the rearguard had ceased firing for some time, and about a mile from camp, from a mound of earth, the rearguard was distinctly seen coming on unmolested. The remaining wing of the 2nd was therefore sent to camp, and I followed as soon as the rearguard closed.

About two hours after all were in camp, the enemy made some good shots with Zubber Jung; the first was sent into the camp of Her Majesty's 41st, and was duly reported to the major-general, but he would not move the camp; a second fell in the lines of the 43rd Native Infantry, and a third in the lines of the 2nd Native Infantry, each being duly reported. After the third shot, an order was issued to strike the camp, and the force moved to a spot close to Rosa. Before the whole was clear off, eleven shots fell in camp: strange to say, a camel and a bullock were the only casualties.

Two guns of the 9-pounder battery were sent up to the hill above Belall, and three shots were fired, when the major-general stopped them. The first shot nearly struck the men around the great gun Zubber Jung; the second hit the parapet wall of the court-yard in which this gun was placed. There were but few sappers attached to this force; 200 *sepoys* from the 16th Bengal Grenadiers and 42nd Bengal Light Infantry were therefore told off for working parties during the night; and before morning they were ready to receive two 18-pounders, which left camp at 4 a.m. for this purpose, but which were sent back when, as day broke, it was discovered that the enemy had evacuated the fort.

From the fire of matchlocks from the fort on the Belall hill, the numbers within the fort must have been considerable. The fire was incessant, but harmless, from about 5 till 10 p.m. on the hill above Belall. As soon as it was ascertained that the fort was evacuated, the 16th Bengal Grenadiers were sent to take possession of it.

The despatch of Major-General Nott, which is given in the Appendix,[8] may be compared with the aforegoing more detailed account.

The fort, city, and citadel of this renowned place were doomed, and no pains or labour spared to level them with the ground. Major Sanders and his engineer department were most zealous in their endeavours to carry out Major-General Nott's orders, and on the 8th, many amateurs lent their assistance to complete the work of destruction. The mines were sprung between 4 p.m. and sunset; the citadel and town were then fired, and by 8 o'clock the whole place was in flames, and continued burning all night.

8. Appendix, No. 10.

On the 9th the force moved to Rosajah, about a mile north-east of Rosa, took off the far-famed Gates of Somnath from Mahmood's tomb, and piled them upon the 18-pounder spare carriage. No insult was offered to the presiding *moollas*, or to the tomb of Mahmood. On the 10th September, the force, with its spoils, commenced the first march towards India. It will be seen that we were not allowed to carry off our trophy without an attempt on the part of the Mahomedans to recover it, and wreak their vengeance upon the infidel captors.

On the 12th September, on approaching our ground at Sydabad, a few shot were sent amongst the quarter-masters and their party. The encamping-ground was very confined, and the camp pitched in a semicircle, conforming to a ridge of low hills. Officers commanding brigades, corps, and detachments were ordered to make arrangements for the protection of their own camps, several strong parties of the enemy having appeared on the highest hills. Three men of Her Majesty's 41st went to "fetch a walk" through some cornfields, when a party of the enemy, lying concealed, suddenly sprung up, attacked them, and killed two, the other escaping to camp.

The fort of Sydabad was that in which Captain Woodburn had been treacherously murdered;[9] it was, therefore, doomed to destruction. Mines were laid, the four bastions and gateway were blown up, and it was then fired. Some books and papers belonging to Captain Woodburn (including his will) and to other officers were found here.

As night approached, the greatest precautions were taken for the protection of the camp, as the enemy on the hills had increased considerably. The right of the camp (the 2nd brigade) was attacked very early; but the enemy found preparations had been made at all points for their reception, and did not return. I placed every sentry myself, and so complete were our arrangements, that, although the enemy were congregated on my flank, and tried almost all my flank picquets, I did not lose a man. Some attempts were then made upon the headquarters and the cavalry lines, but with little success; in an attack upon the left (1st brigade), we lost one European killed, and one and three natives wounded.

The next day, the force moved to Sheikabad. The enemy were much bolder; their numbers had greatly increased, and they were joined by

---

9. Captain J. Woodburn, 44th Native Infantry, commanding the 5th Shah's regiment, soon after the insurrection at Cabool, was on his way to that city from Ghuznee, with a detachment of 120 men, when he fell in with a body of the insurgents, and was enticed into this fort, where he and most of his men were killed.

about 1,200 Lohanees. As usual, they gave our quarter-masters and their party a few shot on their arrival on the ground. Near camp, within 100 yards of the road, on the slope of a hill, there was a small but high tower, with only one door, about eight feet from the base, in which three men were concealed, who suffered the column and some of the baggage to pass, and then opened their fire. Fortunately, a guard over some stores was passing at the time, and four men were sent up to the tower, who, by placing a musket inside, pointing upwards, brought down one of the assailants the first shot; a fire lighted below soon induced the other two to descend, one of whom was killed close to the door, the other shot in attempting to escape.

The enemy were strongly posted on the hills, on three sides of us, whilst small parties of from four to twenty men were prowling about, plying their *jezails* upon any who came within range. Our picquets were necessarily increased: three times were the front picquets fairly driven in, and as many times, after being reinforced, did they drive the enemy back, holding their position during the night against repeated attacks.

A little before sunset, about 1,600 or 2,000 men assembled on the hills on the left and rear of the camp. The 2nd brigade was on the left, and a picquet of eighty men were on its flank. Two guns, from Captain Blood's horse artillery, were sent to this picquet, under Lieutenant Brett. At the same time, a message was forwarded to me, through one of the staff, by Major-General Nott, requesting I would take a party of my men who might be ready, and drive off the enemy. Accordingly, I moved towards the hills with 120 of Her Majesty's 41st and about as many of the 42nd and 43rd Light Infantry regiments, who were ready accoutred; a second party of similar strength was to follow as soon as ready. I divided the party into two, giving the command of one to Brevet-Major Cochran, Her Majesty's 41st, and I conducted the other myself.

The parties were to go by two routes, and mount the hill occupied by the enemy. It was dark by the time the parties reached the hill; the enemy had fled and taken up a position on a range further back. Both parties pushed on in silence for the next range, which was particularly steep; the summit was gained, but the enemy had again retreated. I halted the men for a few minutes, to give them breath, and then faced about to return to camp; about two miles from which we fell in with the supports, and subsequently with a party of cavalry, which the major-general had sent to my assistance.

We reached camp about 9 p. m. About twelve at night, the enemy attacked the left picquets; the cavalry *patroles* were driven in; the officer on duty called in the advanced sentries, and Lieutenant Brett, having his guns all ready, gave the enemy two discharges, one quickly following the other, which had the desired effect, and with the exception of a shot now and then, the night passed quietly.

The force moved off from Sheikabad to Bin-e-Bedam, on the 14th September, in the usual order, except in the detail of the infantry of the rearguard; instead of a wing, in consequence of the increased numbers and boldness of the enemy, it had been augmented, the last two days, to a complete regiment, which this day was the 38th Native Infantry, commanded by Captain Burney.

The rearguard consisted of two guns from Anderson's horse artillery, under Lieutenant Frank Turner. 250 Christie's horse, under Lieutenant Chamberlain, and the 38th Native Infantry. The whole was commanded by Captain Burney. As soon, therefore, as the force moved, the necessary arrangements were made for the protection of the baggage. The enemy's strength appeared nearly equally divided; their detachment to the right and front of the old encamping-ground numbered about 2,500; that in the rear about 2,000; the former was strongest in cavalry; Lieutenant Pocklington and Lieutenant Ferguson, with about 200 men, were, therefore, placed on the left, between the baggage and a crescent-shaped range of hills, which had been the scene of contention the day before, and on which the enemy were now in force.

Lieutenant Nepean, with 100 men, was sent to reinforce the Lohanee guard, which consisted of a *subadar*, a *jemadar*, four *havildars*, four *naicks*, and eighty men, under a native officer selected for this particular duty. They were employed to watch over the Lohanees, to see that they did not take away the cattle when at graze, or the camels' loads, &c. The men opposed to me the day before were chiefly Lohanees. The guns, the cavalry, and the remainder of the infantry, formed the main body of the rearguard, ready to afford assistance in whatever direction it might be required.

The baggage, *godown*, &c. were moving off, the arrangements for their protection being completed, when a Lohanee camel-driver, belonging to the hired camels, fired off his matchlock. The enemy, who were seated upon a hill on the left, instantly rose, and descended, shouting and flourishing their swords. They collected at the bottom of the hill, and opened a very heavy but ill-directed fire upon the flankers, under Lieutenants Pocklington and Ferguson. They were coming on in such a dense body that the officer commanding the rearguard moved the guns down towards the party, with a reinforcement of 150 bayonets, which had the effect of sending the enemy back to the foot of the hills. It was afterwards discovered that the matchlock had been fired by the Lohanee in our camp as a signal to the enemy in what direction they were.

As the baggage and *godown* moved off, Lieutenant Pocklington's party marched parallel with it on the left flank. The ground being clear, the main body moved also. They were but a short time in motion before the two parties of the enemy united, and followed the rear, firing their *jezails*, and venting their abuse against the "Christian dogs." Fear of the guns kept their main body out of range for some time, though the chief who commanded them was distinctly observed riding about to the different groups, with some well-mounted followers, and three standard-bearers carrying white flags, apparently encouraging them. As the rearguard proceeded, they observed levies join those in the rear from the hills on the left, and by the time they reached camp, the numbers of this enemy were nearly doubled, or between 8,000 and 9,000.

About three miles from the old ground, the first serious attack was made, on the rearguard, as usual. They moved pretty smartly at first, the cavalry and infantry mixed up, more like a crowd than an army, shouting and bellowing like madmen. The balls from their long *jezails* began to tell, and, as they wore the appearance of a charge, the guns were unlimbered, and preparations were made to give them a warm reception. Finding that the column halted, and was ready to receive them, they shortened their pace, and pulled up at a distance of 500 or 600 yards. Our infantry moved right and left, out of the way of the guns, four shots from which, telling hard amongst them, sufficed to send the enemy flying in confusion, several horses being seen without riders.

The cavalry this day were of the greatest service. The main body of the force, led by the major-general, was never less than three miles a-head of the rearguard, and generally five miles. If the enemy had cut in between the general and the baggage, they would have had comparatively no force to oppose them, and might have caused us considerable loss. In consequence of this distance between the two bodies, our cavalry could not be permitted to charge when Turner's shrapnells made havoc and scattered confusion amongst the enemy; it was as much as the cavalry could do to keep the flanks clear.

The infantry flankers this day had constant work, and the guns were brought into play three times before we reached camp: it was, in short, one series of skirmishing all the way, yet not a camel was taken off. Captain Burney brought his detachment into camp about 2 p. m. Great credit was awarded him by his comrades for his conduct in not only keeping off the enemy, but in giving such excellent protection to the baggage. It may be remarked that not once between Candahar and Cabool was there any flank guard for the baggage.

As we neared the encamping-ground at Ben-e-Bedam, on the 14th, the enemy's cavalry were distinctly seen drawn up with as much regularity as Affghan manoeuvres admit, their right resting upon a very high and precipitous hill, and their left upon a deep *nullah*, with a shallow running stream, the banks in most places perpendicular. The hill above was completely covered with their *jezailchees*; the *nullah* concealed a second party, and a third, of infantry, were hidden behind the cavalry. There was such an indication of a real intention to dispute our progress; the position of the enemy was so strong; there was so much wild hallooing and frantic gesticulation, that the general prepared for work. Leslie's troop of horse artillery was the first to open, and every shot told admirably.

The enemy were immediately in confusion; the horse went about, taking a direction between the two ranges of hills, and never pulled bridle until they were well out of shot; about a mile in advance they separated into two parties, one going across the valley to the right, whilst the other moved through the pass, to the left, which lies at the end of this range of hills, leading to Maidan. The *jezailchees* concealed behind the cavalry scrambled up the rocks with the agility of monkeys; those in the *nullah* scudded across the open ground between that and the hills, whilst those upon the hills moved towards these two parties, to cover their retreat;

As soon as the enemy broke. General Nott moved on. The 2nd brigade of infantry and the troop of horse artillery, under my command, were ordered to cross the *nullah* and move parallel with the rest of the force. The firing from the hills was incessant. General Nott had ordered Captain White, with the eight light companies, to disperse the jezailchees, the hill in their possession almost commanding the encamping-ground. After a momentary survey of the position, Leslie's horse artillery and Blood's 9-pounders were directed to shell the enemy on the heights, whilst our most gallant light companies stormed in face of the hottest fire. They succeeded in taking the heights which commanded the road, but there was one high peak, isolated from that occupied by our men, still in possession of the enemy.

The cavalry, with Leslie's troop of Bombay horse artillery, were sent down the valley to disperse the body of horsemen which had separated from their comrades, and, moving to the right across the valley, had baited. They would not wait for the horse artillery; Major Delamain, therefore, tried them with cavalry only. Leaving the guns, our cavalry broke into the gallop, and moved steadily towards the enemy, who immediately dispersed in different directions. Our men consequently pulled up, and returned to camp.

One of Captain Blood's waggons having upset under the high hill, the enemy kept up a constant dropping fire upon the party employed in setting it to rights, and, seeing the troops move into camp, they grew bold, and came some way down the hill. The grenadier company of the 43rd Native Infantry were sent out, and drove them up again.

The camp was kept on the alert all day. Captain Burney, commanding the rearguard, succeeded in bringing everything safe into camp; but the enemy received such an accession of numbers, that the 18-pounders were ordered to be got ready at 4 p. m. to clear the front and left of the 2nd brigade, whilst some light guns were moved to the right of the front of the camp, to accompany a small force which was to drive the enemy From a position they had taken up, from whence (as I represented to the general) they would have allowed us no rest. The moment the enemy saw our party move from camp, they retired.

The practice of the 18-pounders was very good; but day closed, and we had the enemy on three sides; they sent down parties who annoyed us terribly, getting behind pieces of rock and firing into our camp. Our advanced sentries were posted in the *nullah*, and could fire at the enemy whilst screened from a return fire; but their *jezailchees* ensconced themselves behind cover of some sort, so that our men could not punish or check them. At 9 p.m., the enemy commenced descending the hill in a body, by a winding path, opposite the centre of my brigade, yelling, as usual, like savages. A white flag, which bad been carried about in a restless manner during the whole day, was seen, and glimpses were occasionally caught of a mass of people round it. The moon was behind the hill.

When evening closed, it was supposed that their attack would be in this direction, for the only other road down the hill was in front of

Anderson's troop of horse artillery; the 18-pounders were, therefore, loaded and laid for the open spot where the road for fifteen or twenty yards was destitute of any cover. As the white flag reached this spot, one of the 18-pounders was fired. The wild yells, which had hitherto been kept up, suddenly ceased; a profound silence followed; the *jezailchees* abstained from firing, and, strange to say, not another shot was heard from either side during the whole night.

Various explanations were given the following day of this unexpected issue of the threatened attack; the most probable related that the leader of the enemy's party, a bigoted *moolla*, had persuaded the people to make a night assault upon our camp; that he was heading them with the white flag in his hand, and had halted at the spot before mentioned to see that his men were well locked up, when our 18-pounder sent its shot into the midst of them, killing the *moolla* and many others, and the rest of the party, prudently determining that the hour was not a propitious one, retired for the night.

The very brief report of this affair by Major-General Nott is contained in the general despatch, relating to the 14th and 15th September, given in the Appendix,[10] and may be compared with the aforegoing detailed account. The second brigade is not even mentioned in the report.

The force marched on the 15th September from Ben-e-Bedam to Maidan. Shortly after moving off the ground, Major Nash, commanding the rearguard, sent to the general to say that the enemy were very strong both in horse and foot, and that the 43rd native infantry had not more than 500 bayonets. The general ordered a reinforcement of 100 men to be sent from my brigade; Captain Meares, 42nd Native Infantry, commanded this party.

After leaving the camp. General Nott moved to the left, under the hills, as if to take the road direct down the valley, despatching Lieutenant-Colonel Lane, with the 2nd Native Infantry, to the left, to occupy the hills commanding the *ghat* leading to Maidan. The enemy had parties on the hills from our very camp. Three batteries, of two guns each, about three quarters of a mile apart, opened upon some of the heaviest bodies, whilst the column moved steadily on.

As soon as the head of the column was in a line with the *ghat*, General Nott wheeled to the left and moved down directly upon it. An old castle, of great strength, on a high rock, in the very bed of the river, held out some time; but our artillery officers found a suitable

10. Appendix, No. 11.

spot, and opened their guns upon it. Captain White and the light companies made a sweep right and left to get at the enemy as soon as the shot should make a road in or drive them out; but they deserted the castle and joined their friends on some extremely high hills in their rear. These were stormed and taken, not without loss. The enemy not only kept up a sharp fire on our men whilst they were ascending, but pushed large stones over the sides of the hills, which, rolling down with fearful violence, carried everything before them. Both sides of the *ghat* were soon in our possession, and the column passed over it to Maidan without further resistance. Maidan was the finest valley we marched through during the campaign.

The rearguard on the 16th consisted of two guns from the 9-pounder horsed battery, under Lieutenant Terry, a part of the 1st Irregular Cavalry, with Captain Haldane and Lieutenant Travers, and the 43rd Native Infantry (less the light company), under Major Nash, who, as senior officer, commanded the rearguard.

The enemy were on the alert on all sides; their greatest strength was on the right and front of the camp (the second brigade), and they were strong on the hills to the rear of the camp; but Major Nash, having placed a company, under Lieutenant Holroyd, in the *nullah* which skirted the road, they could not come down. As soon as day broke. Major Nash made his arrangements; the guns, which had only to be wheeled round the cavalry, were divided and placed on the flanks, and the 43rd moved up to the guns, the point threatened by the enemy.

The attack commenced by some *jezailchees* attempting to gain a position on the rear and left, and it was necessary to drive them back. Lieutenant Trotter, with another company of the 43rd, was detached on this duty, and drove off the enemy, but not until some shots were exchanged, occasioning loss on both sides.

The strong party on the right and front left the low hill and marshalled on the plain, the white flag being present, moving rapidly in every direction. Before General Nott marched, he desired Major Nash to send small parties through the camp to enforce the loading of the cattle with greater alacrity; a very proper measure, for the enemy appeared resolved to make an attempt upon the baggage, *godown*, gates, &c. Before all the baggage had moved off. Major Nash was forced to check the main body of the enemy by a few shot from the 9-pounders, which caused them to fall back. The baggage being put in motion, the two flanking companies were called in, and the rearguard moved off, the cavalry leading, divided right and left; the 43rd, the guns, with three companies, on the right, under Captain Webster; two on the left, under Lieutenants Trotter and Holroyd, and one company in rear of the guns.

About a quarter of a mile from the old camp, the enemy made their first attack on both flanks. This was one of the most creditable exhibitions of bravery on their part. They came steadily on, and not a man turned until their proximity allowed our muskets to tell. At this time, Lieutenants Trotter and Holroyd charged the enemy very successfully on their flanks, when they turned and fled. It was in vain for our men to follow; they, therefore, contented themselves with firing into the retreating body as long as they were within shot. These two companies suffered considerably. The right flankers also not only held their own, but drove back their assailants with much loss.

Baffled in this attempt, the enemy essayed to get up a charge upon the column. As soon as the demonstration acquired the aspect of a resolution, the guns were got ready, screened by the rear company. When Lieutenant Terry judged they were within proper distance, the company filed right and left, and the guns opened. The first shot bore a cruel testimony to Lieutenant Terry's eminent skill and experience; it burst in front of the enemy, committing dreadful havoc. The second was equally successful, bursting amongst the enemy, who had turned on receiving the first. Unfortunately, the discharge of this shot broke the axle of the carriage: without any stir, the right gun was advanced a few paces, whilst a company of *sepoys*, placed before the broken one, concealed our misfortune from the immediate notice of the enemy; but when they halted, and faced us again, it was soon evident that they concluded something was wrong, for preparations were made for a renewed attack.

Captain Mathews having volunteered to carry a message to the general, he was despatched to report that the enemy were strong and bold; that it was utterly impossible to stop the baggage; that a gun had broken down, and not a man could be spared, and that Major Nash, therefore, begged that the broken gun might be replaced, and some reinforcement sent to protect the baggage.

Meanwhile, Lieutenant Terry divided his attention between the disabled gun and the enemy, giving them a round shot or a shrapnel from the front gun, now and then, as anybody of them approached. The disabled gun was taken off its carriage, and slung under a waggon; the wheels and carriage were packed on camels, and, in two hours, all moved on, followed by parties of *jezailchees* on three sides, who occasionally sent in a long shot.

Upon the report of Captain Mathews, General Nott ordered down two 9-pounders immediately, under the escort of some of Captain Christie's cavalry, and two companies of the 42nd Native Infantry. They met the main body of the rearguard about half-way, joined, and moved with them. When the rearguard were crossing the *ghat*, looking into the beautiful valley of Maidan, the enemy's force united, and attempted to obstruct our ascent. On a favourable spot, some way up, the guns were placed in position for the last time this day, and a few shot drove the enemy far off. The rearguard were not molested further.

Great credit was given to Major Nash and his gallant detachment for this day's work. No order was issued on the subject, but General Nott said he should take care to bring it to the favourable notice of Government. No official report of the affair has been published beyond that contained in the despatch before alluded to.[11]

The force arrived at its camp, within five miles of Cabool, on the 17th September, 1842.

---

11. Appendix, No. 11.

SECTION 5

Cabool – From the 18th September to the 8th October, 1842

General Pollock, having resolved to punish Ameenoolla Khan and his party, and at the same time disperse the force in Kohistan, before he turned his back upon Cabool, directed the assembly of a force under Major-General McCaskill, for operations in the Kohistan-e-Cabool. For this purpose, he placed at the major-general's disposal, from his own force, two squadrons of Her Majesty's 3rd Light Dragoons, one squadron of Bengal Light Cavalry, Brigadier Tulloch's brigade (less the 60th Native Infantry), and Captain Broadfoot's sappers and miners. General Nott sent a force, under my command, as brigadier, to co-operate with that of Major-General McCaskill, consisting of two 18-pounder battering-guns, Captain Blood's 9-pounder horsed battery. Captain Christie's corps of irregular cavalry, and the second brigade of General Nott's force, composed of Her Majesty's 41st Foot, and the 42nd and 43rd Bengal Native Infantry; the 2nd Native Infantry, belonging to this brigade, being left in the Bala Hissar, Cabool.

On the 26th September, these two detachments joined at Kho-ja Kawash, and, under the command of Major-General McCaskill, marched to near Zimmarree, on the 27th, and encamped within four miles of Istaliff on the morning of the 28th.

In the evening of that day, the major-general, accompanied by Major Sanders and the general staff, with a reconnoitring party, went down to the left of the enemy's position to ascertain the nature of the country and to gain information as to their strength and position. The enemy's skirmishers, concealed in the ravines and water-courses, tried long shots, as usual, and the firing latterly became brisk, but at such long distances, that little damage was done on either side. The return of our party to camp was evidently looked upon as a retreat, and we afterwards found that the enemy really so considered it, and made a feast to celebrate their success!

Istaliff is a place of such great strength, that it was settled at Cabool that we must lose a vast number of men in its capture, and this being the general opinion, every precaution was taken, not merely to guard against a reverse, but to obtain the place with as small a sacrifice of life as possible. Brigadiers and officers commanding the cavalry and artillery, with the general and staff, were ordered to meet at 8 p.m. at the assistant adjutant-general's tent, to receive instructions for the attack on the following morning. Opinions were invited, and some discussion of the mode of attack took place. The plan first submitted was abandoned, and the right of the enemy was fixed upon as the point of attack, instead of the left.

On the morning of the 29th, the "general" sounded at 5 a. m., and the "assembly" at a quarter before six. The two columns of attack were thus composed:—right column, under Brigadier Tulloch,—mountain train. Captain Backhouse; sappers and miners. Captain Broadfoot; Her Majesty's 9th Foot, Lieutenant-Colonel Taylor, K.H.; 26th Bengal Native Infantry. Major Huish:—Left column, under my command,—two 18-pounders, Lieutenant Cornish; Blood's 9-pounder horse-battery; Her Majesty's 41st Foot, Major Browne; 42nd Native Infantry. Major Clarkson; 43rd Native Infantry, Major Nash. Major Simmons, Her Majesty's 41st, commanded the rearguard, consisting of two squadrons of Her Majesty's 3rd Dragoons, and one squadron 1st Light Cavalry, under Major Lockwood, as senior officer, and a wing of Her Majesty's 41st Foot, under Brevet-Major Cochran. Captain Christie, with his corps of irregular cavalry, gave protection to the baggage.

We moved nearly along the whole of the enemy's line, concealed from right to left behind orchard-walls; the right column receiving at intervals a long shot from the *jezailchees*. The gardens round the fort of Istaliff form nearly a semicircle. When General McCaskill, after advancing about a mile and a half, turned gently to the right, and found the enemy's *jezailchees* reached his column, he ordered two of Blood's 9-pounder guns from the left column, and drove them back, the enemy, as they were forced back, retiring one and all upon the village of Emillah, which was crowded with men, hurrahing, dancing, and waving their swords in defiance.

The two columns had moved steadily on without interruption. As we neared the village, the light companies were thrown out to drive back the enemy's skirmishers, and shortly after, observing that the enemy had left several openings in the walls, the word was given,. "Forward!" The Light Companies of Her Majesty's 9th and the 26th Native Infantry, followed by the columns, pushed gallantly on, under a very heavy fire. The left column had to make a detour of some distance to gain the right of the village before the light companies of Her Majesty's 41st and the 42nd and 43rd Native Infantry received the word "Forward!" when they were off at the double. Each regiment gave two companies as supports. The remaining part of the column had to move considerably to the left of all, as the ground would not admit of the guns travelling direct in the line of action; besides that a very strong body of cavalry were posted a quarter of a mile beyond it» on the enemy's outward flank.

The attack on the village of Emillah was as bold in its character as it was spirited in its execution. The two columns, one being from General Pollock's army, and the other from General Nott's, displayed a spirit of chivalrous emulation throughout the day. The right column certainly not only reached, but entered, the village before the left, which, however, had thereby harder work, for the enemy were driven upon the left column. They suffered severely at this spot from the cross fire of the two columns, more so than at any place or in any action during the campaign, and being crowded within walls, they could not readily escape.

The village of Emillah being taken and fired, both columns brought up their left shoulders. The village was a mile beyond the gardens of Old Istaliff, which ground we had necessarily to retrace; I had entered in front; the right column on the flank. The right column made a quarter circle, and pushed after the flying enemy over hills and through orchards and gardens, without giving them time to breathe, passing considerably to the right of the old castle of Istaliff, and crossing the stream which runs at the foot of Istaliff, this column entered the town at the south-east corner, in two divisions, in parallel lines. The people in the town must have lost courage from our first vigorous attack upon Emillah.

We had been delayed at this village about half an hour, which allowed time for a man to carry the intelligence of its storm and capture to the town of Istaliff; and the scene which presented itself on our approach to it was singular and picturesque. The footpath which leads from the back of Istaliff, winding over the range of hills dividing Kohistan-e-Cabool from Toorkistan, was thronged with women, wending their way along the zigzag tracks which ran by the scarped sides of the hills, their snow-white dresses, in which they were shrouded from head to foot, giving them the appearance of a vast cavalcade of nuns.[12] Ameenoolla and his party, so full of vaunt and vapour the night before, were amongst the first to fly.

After the left column had completed the attack on the fortified village of Emillah, a very respectable body of the enemy, composed of both horse and foot, still shewed on their (the enemy's) extreme right. To leave them unmolested, and in possession of so commanding a position, menacing the rear of the left column particularly, should it move on without dispersing them, would have been highly imprudent, and moreover it was impossible to take the guns much farther, as the hills and gardens which lie between this and Old Istaliff are scarcely passable for camels, and we could not afford to leave even a wing to guard the guns, the enemy being ten to one, with a fortification to fight behind. I therefore ordered on the guns. The four 9-pounders of Blood's horsed battery were soon within range of the enemy, escorted by two companies of the 43rd Native Infantry.

Whilst the brigade, in the meantime, moved on gently towards the town, I watched on the left the movements of the enemy from the top of the first hill. The 18-pounders coming steadily on, and being near at hand, the 9-pounders opened. The first shot fell short, which drew a shout from the enemy, who brandished their swords; but the second was sent amongst them, creating confusion, and they fell back just under the brow of the hill, whilst some of the horsemen took post on another hill about 150 or 200 yards in the rear, at which distance it was found that the 9-pounders could not master them, though the excellent practice of Blood's guns dropped the shot so close over the summit of the nearest hill, under which the enemy had taken shelter, that they retreated again, and joined their companions on the hill in the rear. By this time, the 18-pounders were in position and opened; they fired but three rounds, but the practice was so excellent, that each shot told, and the enemy scampered off, never to be seen again, at least that day.

The two companies of the 43rd Native Infantry were directed to remain with the guns, and the brigade then pushed on at the double. The Light Companies of Her Majesty's 41st and the 42nd and 43rd Native Infantry had reached the first enclosure as the column

12. The long white veil (called *boorku*), worn by the Affghan women when abroad, completely envelops the person (holes being made for seeing and breathing), giving them, as Major Havelock says, the appearance of "walking mummies."

crowned the top of the last hill; Lieutenant Evans, with Her Majesty's 41st Light Company, on the left; Captain Macpherson and Lieutenant Trotter, with the 43rd, in the centre, and Lieutenant Woollen, with the 42nd, on the right. The 2nd brigade had made up their ground as they climbed over the first enclosure. Her Majesty's 9th, under Lieutenant-Colonel Taylor, and the 26th Native Infantry, under Major Huish, were on the right.

To preserve order over such ground was utterly impracticable, and the greatest care was necessary to prevent our suffering from our own fire; so densely crowded were the graperies and masses of fruit-trees. The enemy, outflanked by the right column, and flying towards the town, fell in great numbers. Their fire was too high, and when we got into an enclosure, and they had fired their matchlocks, they ran; our men, who were particularly cool and steady this day, never gave the enemy time to reload. Considering that the Kohistanees were under a cross-fire from the village of Emillah to the old castle of Istaliff, it is not astonishing that so many of them fell.

When the two columns entered the town of Istaliff, the firing had almost ceased, but all were pushing for the fort on the summit. About two-thirds up, the heads of the two columns met in the part of the town where the streets crossed: the right led by Lieutenant-Colonel Taylor, commanding Her Majesty's 9th, and the left by Major Browne, Her Majesty's 41st.

One gun was found abandoned by the enemy as the 2nd brigade passed Old Istaliff; another was seen on a spur below, as we reached the summit of Istaliff, still manned by the enemy. The Light Companies of Her Majesty's 9th and the 43rd Native Infantry made off at the double to charge this gun, and so equal was the race, that men of both companies claimed the merit of its capture. In the general's despatch, the honour was awarded to an officer of Her Majesty's 9th Foot, simply from the fact that Captain Macpherson, commanding the Light Company of the 43rd Native Infantry, belonged to my brigade, and being left after the action to take up a position at Old Istaliff, and watch the enemy during the night, I could not send in any report, and Brigadier Tulloch made no mention of any people of the 2nd brigade being there. Brigadier Tulloch, with Her Majesty's 9th and a party of the 26th Native Infantry, went down to the spur on which the last gun was captured. From this point Lieutenant Mayne, deputy assistant quarter-master-general, rode back to General McCaskill, reporting the total defeat of the enemy, and the capture of the town of Istaliff.

Some loiterers appearing on the hills at the back of the town, Captain Backhouse ascended the first range, with his mountain train, and completed the day's work by sending a few shot after them.

On reaching the summit of the town, I fixed on a courtyard, with a large *chibootra* outside, as headquarters, where all women and children were conducted, and placed in safety. Small parties from each regiment were despatched for this purpose in every direction, and from 100 to 150 women and children were collected: only one woman was killed and another wounded during the day. It was with one of these parties that Lieutenant Evans was killed, and one of his men. He was standing with his men, when an Affghan reported that some women and children were in a house below the principal mosque.

Lieutenant Evans, who had successfully conducted several of these helpless parties, again volunteered his services, and went with six or eight men of Her Majesty's 41st to bring them up. Upon approaching the house, he was shot dead. This occurrence being reported to me, I requested Captain and Brevet-Major Cochran to proceed towards the house and surround it, but not to allow the men to expose themselves; and I immediately sent off to Captain Backhouse, requesting he would hasten on with a gun. He soon arrived with the gun, and played on the door, but without effect, the doorway having been built up with mud and stones.

At this period I received orders to fire the city, and afterwards take up a position, with my brigade, for the night, as near the town as possible, I immediately ordered parties to fire every house, in the first place, round that which was still firing upon our men. Of the four Affghans who defended this house, three escaped by a drain, the fourth was killed by a shot the moment he shewed himself.

Khan Shereen Khan came from General McCaskill's camp, and afforded me much assistance in collecting the women and children, and about three o'clock, these poor people were conducted to a fortified garden, close to the foot of the town, which had been spared, as belonging to a relation of Khan Shereen Khan. The women and children were sent down under an escort, commanded by an European officer. As soon as the escort returned, I called in all the fatigue parties, and moved to the castle of Old Istaliff. Her Majesty's 41st and the 42nd Native Infantry were put in possession of the castle, whilst the 43rd were placed on a hill which commanded the road between the town and camp. These regiments had nothing to eat during the whole day (except fruit, of which there was a great profusion, of the very best quality), until 9 p.m. They had no great coats, and they had the prospect of a cold, bleak night.

The 2nd brigade was relieved the next day at 10 a.m. On the 30th, a party under the orders of Major Sanders was sent to complete the destruction of the town, and before night it was one blaze, and continued burning the whole of that night and part of the next day.

The report of this action by Major-General McCaskill to General Pollock, dated the 30th September, is given in the Appendix.[13] Having heard it asserted, on the 3rd October, that the town of Istaliff had been taken by the 26th Native Infantry and the 9th Queen's, I immediately addressed Major-General McCaskill, who forwarded, on the 6th October, a second improved report,[14] in which he stated that my report of the part borne by the 2nd brigade did not reach him till the 2nd October. But it was impossible to send in a report earlier than I did. My brigade was left to guard General McCaskill's camp from a surprise. At Old Istaliff I was relieved on the 30th September at 10 a.m. In the afternoon of that day I was asked for a report of my share of the battle, which I promised to send.

The next day I marched to Istagateh, which I reached at 3 p.m., and at four set out to rescue Major Nash from a handful of men. The following day I marched to Charikar, which I reached about noon, and at 3 p.m. went out with a detachment to destroy Apywar. In this way was the "working" brigade (for by this name the 2nd brigade was known) employed at this time. As I have already mentioned, the heads of the columns met in a cross-street in the town, where an incident occurred which, though trivial, may be mentioned as evidence of the fact. Colonel Taylor, of Her Majesty's 9th, was so winded that he could not speak. I was with Her Majesty's 41st, and, thinking he was wounded, I asked him if he was hit; he shook his head, and I gave him an apple, telling him to swallow the juice only, and in a moment he was restored. Her Majesty's 9th and the 26th Native Infantry bore the brunt below, at Emillah.

---

13. Appendix, No. 12.
14. *Ibid.* No. 13.

Cabool to India – From 12th October to 22nd December, 1842

The British forces[1] evacuated the city of Cabool on the 12th October, 1842, and, under the command of Major-General Pollock, marched towards Hindoostan. Major-General Sir R. Sale was detached with the 1st and 2nd brigades, the mountain train, the 1st Light Cavalry, the 3rd Irregular Cavalry, and Christie's Horse, over the Gospund Durrah Pass, to turn that of Khoord Cabool, in consequence of which movement the principal defile was passed without molestation. The force reached Bootkak on the 13th and Khoord Cabool on the 14th. On the following morning, it commenced its march from the Khoord Cabool Pass over the Huft Kotul to Tazeen. The rearguard, commanded by Captain Leeson, 42nd Native Infantry, consisted of two guns; from Captain Leslie's troop of Bombay Horse Artillery, under Lieutenant Brett; 200 irregular cavalry, under Lieutenant Cham-

---

1. 1st Division.—Four guns 3rd troop 1st brigade, horse artillery; No. 6 light field battery, two 18-pounders and detail E. artillery; mountain train; Her Majesty's 3rd Light Dragoons; four *risssalahs* 3rd Irregular Cavalry; one squadron 1st Light Cavalry; Her Majesty's 9th foot; Her Majesty's 18th Light Infantry; 26th Native Infantry; 35th Light Infantry; 5th company sappers and miners; Broadfoot's sappers; *jezailchees*; *bildars*; Sikh contingent.

2nd Division.—Two guns 3rd troop 2nd brigade horse artillery; Captain Blood's battery of 9-pounders; two squadrons 1st Light Cavalry: Her Majesty's 31st Foot; 2nd regiment Native Infantry; 6th *ditto*; wing 33rd Native Infantry; wing 60th *ditto*.

General Nott's force.—One troop Bombay horse artillery; one troop (late) Shah Shooja's horse; detachment foot artillery; 3rd regiment Bombay Light Cavalry; detachment 1st Irregular Cavalry; Haldane's horse; Christie's horse; detachment sappers and miners; detachment Madras sappers and miners'; Her Majesty's 40th Foot; 16th Native Infantry; 38th Native Infantry; 3rd (late) Shah Shooja's Infantry; Her Majesty's 41st Foot; 2nd Native Infantry; 42nd Native Infantry; 43rd Native Infantry.— Parl. Papers, 1843, p. 421.

berlain; and the 42nd Native Infantry.

This march over the Huft Kotul, fourteen miles of most difficult ground, I regarded as one of the most distressing marches we made. The column pushed on in extreme haste. We passed the bodies of five *sepoys* at the first dip down towards the pass which leads to the narrow valley at the head of which lies Tazeen. As we traversed this most difficult spot, no precautionary measures were taken, though the mangled bodies and remnants of baggage, medical stores, &c., bore witness that the Affghans had taken advantage of the favourable ground but the day before. When the column was about half way through the pass, an order was received, about 3 p, m., for the two brigades to send back 100 men each to the head of the pass.

Accordingly, 50 men from the Kelat-e-Ghilzie corps, and 100 men from the 43rd light infantry, were sent back. They had a little skirmishing by the way, and on nearing the rearguard it was difficult to pass the baggage, for the Affghans were on every hill, and constantly firing into the baggage line, which caused such a rush, that loads were knocked off, cattle and men thrown down, whilst the approach of night furnished an additional motive to hasten on. The column reached camp at Tazeen at half-past 4 p. m.

The rearguard had not got off the ground until eight that morning (the 15th), and they were no sooner clear of the hill on the right of the camp, and round which the road lay, than they saw horsemen in small parties on their right, evidently watching their movements. A company had been sent on to the Tunghee, in case the column should have left it unguarded, which proved to be the case; the company was therefore posted on a hill on the right, commanding it completely. The entrance to the Tunghee Pass was blocked up with cattle and baggage; the rearguard was consequently forced to halt. Several pretty strong bodies of men were observed moving in advance to the right of the road, evidently with the intention of attacking the rearguard at the entrance of the pass.

Soon after the rearguard recommenced its march, the horsemen, finding we had taken possession of the heights of the Tunghee, moved across to our rear, following at first quietly, keeping out of reach of shot; but they afterwards neared, and fired long shots into the column, so that it became necessary to open the guns upon them.

The rearguard made slow progress, and were often forced to halt. When they reached the top of the Huft Kotul, they observed the pass crammed with the cattle and baggage, and perceiving that it would be useless to proceed. Captain Leeson sent the cavalry to look out on the right, and directed two companies to move in advance and secure the heights. Whilst they were halted here, the enemy collected in great numbers, approaching as close as they dared; a few shots were fired into the column, and it was deemed advisable, before entering the defile, to drive them as far off as possible. Accordingly, Lieutenant Terry dropped some shrapnells amongst them, and closed the practice with a couple of round shot.

At 3 p.m., we first heard firing in the pass, and at five, we commenced descending. The cavalry were at this point ordered into camp, being no longer of any service. About half a mile from the watercourse at the drop into the pass, we were forced to halt again; the enemy grew so bold that it was found necessary to crown the heights with parties.

It was twilight as we began descending into the pass. Those in charge of the heights were ordered to drop down and form in the rear, as the rearguard column came abreast of their position. The column had scarcely reached the bottom of the pass, before the enemy, who had been driven off by the artillery, collected again, and rushed to the heights from which our crowning parties had descended, and poured in a heavy fire. A party of the enemy had taken possession of a small hill, which could only be seen as the column reached the watercourse; passing this, they commanded us completely. A company of the 42nd Native Infantry, being nearest, was ordered to drive them off, and this duty was most satisfactorily performed.

The body of the enemy, who had halted at the top of the hill, and fired into the rearguard as it reached the bottom, were encouraging each other to descend. They had evidently a thorough conviction of the risk of coming too close. However, they at length mustered sufficient resolution, and as the last half of the column was disappearing to the left, they rushed down the road, yelling and brandishing their swords as usual. The rear companies went about, and stood ready to receive them, whilst the guns opened, and punished the enemy severely, causing them to run back, when they were immediately exposed to a cross fire from the company of the 42nd Native Infantry, who, after disposing of the party holding the small hill, got a few shots at the retiring body running back to the head of the pass. Close to the water-course was met a reinforcement of 200 bayonets (100 from each brigade), sent back to the assistance of the rearguard by General Nott.

Although the heights were in our possession, right and left, the ridge of hills being by no means continuous, every break afforded shelter to an enemy, and now the heights on the right, and now those on the left, had to be taken; on one side there would be broken ground, ravines, &c.; on the other a gorge, or dry water-course, which was sure to conceal some of the enemy, who so frightened the followers, and the *surwans* (camel-drivers), in particular, that the greatest exertions were required to keep them with their cattle. When a camel was wounded, it not only caused a stoppage in the line, but raised such an uproar that the scene was indescribable. The company, which had been sent ahead, was constantly occupied in driving small parties off the hill before the cattle and baggage could pass on.

As the rearguard got into the pass, the battle began. The corner of the first hill on the left being turned, and a *havildar, naik*, and sixteen men being placed on a height which commanded the gun-road, the first two picquets were recalled as the column was ready to move on. When these two picquets were called down, there was not a man of the enemy to be seen (at that late hour they could only be discerned by watching for the light of their matchlocks), and the baggage having got a little on, the order to move was given.

It was, of course, darker in the hollow than above. We were scrambling on at a swift pace, the advanced party challenging our picquets on the heights: stray shots were continually exchanged; the enemy fired at the baggage or into the column, and our men sent a bullet at every match that was seen glowing, as the *jezailchees* moved along the hills. Our party was well together, all on the alert and expecting an attack, but none certainly expected to be attacked, and vigorously too, on three points at the same time. The detail of killed and wounded,[2] will shew that, although it was night, the enemy could find the direction of the column.

The rear party of the enemy were easily disposed of, but those to the right and left stood; a steady volley or two, where the matches shewed thickest, drove them higher up; but they still plied their *jezails*, and it was found necessary to dislodge them before the column could proceed. Four companies of the 42nd Native Infantry were told off for this duty, and they succeeded in driving the enemy from the heights and maintaining themselves there. The Affghans must have suffered severely, for they were not met again in respectable force.

---

2. Total, 12 men, 3 horses, killed; 3 officers, 9 non-commissioned officers, 37 men, 10 horses, wounded.

Arrangements were made against a second attack; attention was given to the baggage, many *surwans* having deserted their camels and several camels being wounded; servants and amateurs had likewise been hit, and, amidst the darkness and the rush to get forward, little could be done to assist them. The advance company protected the baggage in their vicinity, but it was judged expedient to keep possession of the position then held, in order to insure the safety of the baggage. During the attack, the ammunition-camels of the detachment (which had been placed between the advance and the column) contrived to get away, and it was necessary to send forward to camp for ammunition, and also for *doolies*, the killed and severely wounded far exceeding the means of carriage. Lieutenant Holroyd, 43rd Light Infantry, volunteered to carry a message to General Nott, and Captain Leeson desired him simply to give a statement of their present position, their total ignorance of the distance they had still to travel, or the nature of the ground, and to request that ammunition and *doolies* might be sent immediately. This young officer had to run the gauntlet, but reached General Nott in safety, and was ordered to return immediately with the reinforcement.

The cattle, baggage, &o. having moved on, and no sign of an enemy appearing, the rearguard prepared to follow, and the parties on the heights were called down, when the fire on the column was immediately reopened, and the heights were instantly reoccupied. Captain Leeson resolved to wait where he was until the *doolies* arrived,

The reinforcement, consisting of a wing of Her Majesty's 40th and two companies of Her Majesty's 41st, arrived at about 9 p.m., with the *doolies* and ammunition. Firing had ceased since the last reoccupation of the heights; the picquets were called in, and they moved into camp without further opposition about ten o'clock.

No order was issued, and no notice was taken of this severe affair, beyond General Nott's very meagre letter to Captain Ponsonby, the assistant adjutant general.[3]

General Nott's force moved to Seh Baba on the 16th October, to Kutta Sung on the 17th, and to Jugdulluk on the 18th. In the march through the. Jugdulluk Pass to Soorkab, on the 19th, the famous sandal-wood gates of the temple of Somnath had well nigh relapsed into the hands of the "Faithful."

By field-force orders, issued on the 18th, the "general" beat at 3 a.m. on the following morning, and the "assembly" at 4 a.m., and the

---

3. Appendix, No. 14.

force was to have moved in the following order:—Eight light companies, Captain White; the cavalry; the general and staff; the general and staff baggage; the horse artillery (Leslie's and Blood's); the two brigades of infantry; the gates; the baggage, *godown*, &c.; the rearguard. The "assembly," however, was not heard by my brigade (the 2nd), and it was consequently nearly light before I moved off; and very fortunate it was, as it turned out, that the second brigade was thus delayed.

The camp at Jugdulluk had been pitched in one line, the extreme of the left close to the entrance into the pass, and but this one road to it; the ground swampy in many places, stony, and irregular; indeed, it may be pronounced the worst encamping-ground between Cabool and Peshawer. The 2nd brigade was placed on the extreme right So soon as it was ascertained that the force had moved, I marched the brigade off. The pass was so crowded with baggage, cattle, &c., that it was utterly impossible for us to pass them in this state; a party was, therefore, pushed ahead by single files, accompanied by the provost-sergeant and his orderlies, with directions to form across the road, at the first point where the pass was very narrow, and there to stop the baggage. This done, the 2nd brigade passed by files to the opening left for it, and then formed column.

When nearly at the head of the pass, there was a halt, occasioned by the steepness of the ascent. I went forward to ascertain the cause, and found, at the head of the pass, that the infantry column had moved on more than an hour before, and that not a single man had been left on the heights, on either flank, for the protection of the Soranath Gates, baggage, *godown*, &c. I immediately sent back an order to Major Nash, commanding the 43rd Native Infantry, leading the column, to take possession of the large conical hill, about a mile from the outlet of the pass, and to detach parties on commanding heights, on both sides, to communicate with the picquets of the rearguard, with which it was calculated Major Simmons, with his acknowledged discrimination, would crown the heights previously to entering the pass with the rearguard.

Major Nash's orders were, that, as Major Simmons's parties came in sight, he was to move on, with his in advance, but always keeping up a communication with the rear. Captain Anderson, who was attending to the getting up of the last two guns of his 2nd troop *Shah's* horse artillery, did not wait for orders, but volunteered to stop with the remaining two guns, if I should consider it advisable. His services were immediately accepted, and the two guns were immediately placed in position to command the high ground on the right of the pass. The Jugdulluk Pass is extremely narrow;[4] the hills forming its sides are not very high, but are covered with holly-trees. Whilst these arrangements were in progress, a company of the 38th Native Infantry, under a *subadar*, which had been sent back by General Nott to the head of the pass, were placed by me under Captain Anderson's orders, to remain by the guns.

Matters were only just settled, and I was proceeding in charge of Leslie's and Turner's troops of horse artillery, with but the 42nd Native Infantry (Her Majesty's 41st being on rearguard duty, the 2nd Native Infantry lent to General Pollock, and the 43rd Native Infantry in charge of the heights of the pass), when the enemy were discovered on the right of a *nullah*, moving round to the pass. Two guns of Captain Leslie's troop were immediately opened upon them, and drove them up the hills; but, being screened by the holly-bushes, they could be seen only as they passed between the intervals.

The 2nd brigade found at this point Captain Leslie's horse artillery, Blood's battery; Captain Anderson's troop of horse artillery, under Lieutenant Turner, without a single file of infantry. I, therefore, sent off a horseman with a note to General Nott, describing the state of affairs at this juncture. It should be mentioned that, notwithstanding the 43rd Native Infantry had been distributed along the heights, the enemy made several attempts upon the baggage, though without success. The road turned to the left at the bottom of the hill, and ran along a water-course, with high mountains on the left, and low undulating hills on the right.

I resolved to leave a party here, and sent Brigade-Major Dixon to Major Clarkson, with orders to move in rear of the guns with his regi-

---

4. Major Hough (*Narrative*, section 7) gives the following description of the Jugdulluk Pass:—"The road lay first three miles E. over some steep spurs, or hillocks, running down to the Kutta-Sung. Then the valley widens, and you pass a *chokee* on the left. At four miles, enter the gorge of the Puree-Duree (Fairy Valley) Pass, taking a direction to the S. The pass is the bed of the Jugdulluk River. It is about three miles and a half in extent. It is very narrow and stony, with an ascent. The pass winds several times almost at right angles. The average width is about forty or fifty yards; but there are three places where it is less than ten feet,—indeed, only six feet; so that, if any animal fell, the road would be stopped till it should be removed. The almost perpendicular cliffs, on both sides, appear as if threatening the destruction of the traveller. A small party of armed men could stop the passage of any force which had entered it. This difficult pass is, in some respects, not unlike the defile of the 'Valley of Hell,' between Neustadt and Fribourg."

ment (the 42nd Native Infantry), and to leave an experienced officer, with eighty rank and file, at this spot. Captain Dalyell was selected for this duty. I had no sooner moved on, than the enemy neared this post, in considerable numbers. Their first attempt was on the baggage from the hill on the left. They subsequently repeated this attempt several times, but were always driven back by small parties sent to oppose them. Finding Captain Dalyell's party too much for them at this point, they assembled, in greater force, upon another high hill on the left, a little in advance, and from thence opened a dropping fire upon the baggage as it passed.

The parties which had kept the enemy in check on the first hill were too weak to cope with their increased numbers on the second hill. Captain Dalyell, therefore, collected and took the whole of his party along the bottom of the ravine, and stormed the height successfully, driving the Affghans down the other side, and killing several. Captain Dalyell was himself severely wounded, whilst leading the storm of this hill, about half-way up, by a ball which passed through the wrist-joint; but he never halted, or for a moment relaxed his exertions.

The orders given to Captain Dalyell were of a similar nature to those sent to Major Nash, namely, to move on with his men, as he should see the 43rd, under Major Nash, approaching; but Captain Dalyell considered the possession of this last hill of the utmost importance for covering the baggage, and, therefore, instead of moving on, he remained until Major Nash came up with the 43rd Native Infantry, when he represented to him the advantage of holding this hill, which had been secured with so little loss, and might not be so cheaply retaken. Major Nash, however, declined to relieve the party of Captain Dalyell, who thereupon resolved to remain until Major Simmons should come up. He was not only in very great pain at this time, but faint and weak from loss of blood, and Captain Matthews, 43rd Native Infantry, volunteered to take the command of Captain Dalyell's party of the 42nd, to which Major Nash assented, and passed on.

The rearguard this day was commanded by Major Simmons, Her Majesty's 41st, and consisted of two horse-artillery guns, under Lieutenant Brett, from Captain Leslie's troop; a squadron of the 3rd Light Cavalry, and a party from Christie's horse, the whole under Lieutenant Taylor, 3rd Bombay Cavalry; Her Majesty's 41st Foot, under Captain and Brevet-Major Cochran, together with all the picquets, and quarter and rearguards of regiments, of the day before, except the left flank picquet, which was furnished from the 1st brigade: this was directed to join. Major Simmons had to await the bursting of the two 18-pounders, which were destroyed at this place, and it was nearly 8 a.m. before the ground was sufficiently clear of baggage to allow of this being done.

Driven back from the hills forming the Jugdulluk Pass by the several companies of the 43rd Native Infantry, the enemy were in considerable force in the rear, and were silently waiting Major Simmons's moving off to determine their next attack.

When the baggage was clear off the ground, and the guns were burst. Major Simmons commenced withdrawing the picquets. It was most difficult ground, and any mistake or hurry would have entailed considerable loss. The enemy followed closely, the greater number making for the hills on the right. Only one *sepoy* was wounded in withdrawing the picquets. Major Simmons moved with strong flanking parties crowning the heights, and two companies in rear of the guns, through the pass, without losing a single load, and having only one officer and five *sepoys* wounded. The holly-bushes concealed the enemy, and gave them opportunities of firing and getting off before they could be punished. On Major Simmons's flankers joining those of the 43rd, the latter advanced, and at the head of the pass, Major Nash collected his regiment, and then moved on as usual in column.

Major Simmons's next move was no easy task, the enemy hanging in large numbers on his rear. At the head of the pass he found Captain Anderson, with his two guns and the escort of the company, 38th native infantry, left there by me. These were sent on, and the guns placed in position, about 500 or 600 yards in advance, to enable the two guns of the rearguard and the parties on both sides of the pass to be withdrawn without loss. General Pollock's force had suffered severely at this point, and the dead bodies lying in the road shewed the necessity of precaution.

All being ready in advance, our men descended right and left, under cover of Captain Anderson's guns, which did great execution; for the enemy, unaware of the precautionary measures which had been adopted, rushed up the hill in a body, hoping to cut up our small parties before they could run in on the main body. This, being expected, was prepared for accordingly; the guns opened on the enemy with great effect, and our several parties joined the column without losing a man. Whilst this was passing, a report from ahead stated that the baggage was attacked near the post of the 42nd Native Infantry, commanded in the first instance by Captain Dalyell and afterwards by Captain Matthews. Captain Taylor was immediately sent off with the cavalry to its assistance, a duty which was very successfully performed, some of the cattle being recovered and many of the enemy being killed by the cavalry.

It appeared that for about two hours after Captain Matthews had taken charge, as a volunteer, of Captain Dalyell's 80 men of the 42nd Native Infantry (on his being wounded, as before related), the enemy contented themselves with firing long shots occasionally from any point where their men could find shelter, from which no one suffered. Captain Matthews was watching the progress of Major Simmons's movements, as he issued from the pass, and was withdrawing his parties who had crowned the heights, when several men came running towards his post, calling out that the Affghans were carrying off the Company's gun-bullocks. Finding it was not far from his post. Captain Matthews instantly headed a party of thirty men, and, giving orders to the *subadar* to hold the hill, and having sent off a report to Major Simmons, pushed on at the double in the direction pointed out by the people. He proceeded about a quarter of a mile along the road, when the people shewed a pathway on the right, saying it was by that the Affghans had driven some of the cattle.

Entering the pathway with the few who had been able to follow, Captain Matthews came on four of the enemy, driving four of the bullocks: the men fled. Still pushing on, although only a *havildar* and two *sepoys* had been able to keep up with him and two Europeans, about a quarter of a mile, over an undulating country, covered with stunted shrubs. Captain Matthews and his small party came to a long, narrow valley, where nine more bullocks and two camels were recovered, under a smart fire front parties hidden amongst the bushes and rocks on the hills. Captain Matthews was shot through the leg, the ball grazing the bone. Two of Christie's Horse had fortunately come up before he was wounded, and he was put upon one of the *sowars'* horses; the cattle were driven back, and as Captain Matthews's party emerged from the low hills on to the main road, the rearguard was near at hand, and Captain Matthews was placed in a *doolie*. From this point, the country being more open. Major Simmons suffered no material interruption.

About two miles from Soorkab, the road is again commanded by hills on the left, and the enemy had assembled on one of them, keeping up an incessant fire. Major Simmons found it necessary to drive them off, previous to the passing of the artillery. The face of the hill towards the road was almost perpendicular; two companies of Her Majesty's 41st were, therefore, sent to turn their flank, whilst Lieutenant Brett's guns opened on them with shrapnel. The enemy were driven from their post, but it cost us a loss of one killed and two wounded.

The Light Company of the 42nd was posted early by General Nott on some hills to the right commanding the road on that side, and not very distant from our picquet on the hills above camp. There was no fighting beyond the hill last mentioned, but it was dusk when Major Simmons and his rearguard reached camp.

In Major Simmons's report of this day, he only mentioned the two guns of Captain Anderson's horse artillery, under the personal command of that officer, as left by me to keep the pass. The major afterwards wrote a letter to me on the subject of this oversight, in which he said he considered the keeping of the heights by the 43rd Native Infantry as having been the means of saving a great portion of the baggage, *godown*, &c., as well as many lives, and that, had I not made these arrangements, it is impossible to say what would have been the extent of our loss.

During this march, I wrote (being forced to do so) twice to General Nott; first, to report that I had found all his artillery at the mouth of the pass without a single file of infantry, and the heights unoccupied; secondly, to report that I had made arrangements for the safety of everything in his rear, but had only about 200 men to escort his whole artillery. The last note, I have reason to believe, gave the general great dissatisfaction. I think I may assert that I reached the pass only just in time to save the gates, the *godown*, and the baggage,—perhaps, the force from a reverse.

No division-order was issued on this occasion, nor was any notice whatever taken of the affair.

The force reached Gundamuck on the 20th October, and encamped at Jellalabad on the 25th. On the 27th General Pollock's force took their departure from that place, after destroying the fortifications, leaving General Nott's division still at Jellalabad, from which it commenced its march on the 29th to the Kyber Pass.

General Nott's force arrived at Lundee Khana on the 3rd November, having marched thither from Dukkah without a shot. From Lundee Khana, however, to Jumrood, it was one continued series of skirmishes.

The field-force orders of the 3rd directed the two infantry brigades to move together; but the 1st (or Brigadier Wymer's) brigade leaving early in the morning of the 4th, I was ordered to remain behind with my brigade (the 2nd), and bring up the artillery and the sandal-wood gates. This second arrangement did not appear in Orders, though it threw a very responsible duty upon the 2nd brigade, more particularly considering that the advance, or Brigadier Wymer's brigade, and all but two guns, reached the encamping-ground at Allee Musjid before I had got clear of the head of the Lundee Khana Pass; and when I did reach the top of the pass, I found myself deserted, and had, therefore, to make arrangements single-handed for the safety of my brigade, the baggage, the gates, and the *godown*, scattered over an extent of from seven to ten miles, and would have had to make my way with this responsible charge, without a gun, but that two of Captain Blood's battery were arrested by the enemy. Not only was I encumbered with the sandal-wood gates, but embarrassed by the rush of every description of baggage, the *godown*, camp-followers, &c., all in a state of the greatest alarm, and pushing forward with reckless disregard of orders.

On the morning of the 4th, the "general" beat at 5 a.m., and the "assembly" at 6 a.m. The force moved off in the following order:— The eight light companies of the eight infantry regiments, under Captain White, Her Majesty's 40th regiment; the cavalry, under Captain Delamain, 3rd Bombay Light Cavalry; the general and his staff; their baggage; the 1st (Wymer's) brigade of infantry; the Bombay troop of horse artillery, Captain Leslie; Captain Anderson's 2nd troop of horse artillery. Lieutenant Turner; the 9-pounder battery, Captain Blood; the sandal-wood gates of the Temple of Somnath; the 2nd (Stacy's) brigade of infantry; baggage and *godown*; the rearguard, under Major Browne, consisting of two horse-artillery guns, 250 cavalry, Her Majesty's 41st regiment, Major Simmons, and all the picquets and quarter and rear guards of regiments.

The advance, the general and his staff, their baggage, and the first brigade of infantry, moved off punctually at the moment. It was advisable to give them ample time and space, as Captain Leslie's troop of Bombay horse artillery had to follow, and any check to their progress, in a narrow and steep road, with a precipice on the right, might have been attended by disastrous consequences. The road from the base to the summit of the Lundee Khana Pass is cut out of the side of the mountain, conforming to all its tortuosities, with the exception of one or two places, where the action of the water, or the melting of the snows, had laid bare the rock, and where it had been found necessary to build up a causeway. The road is not of one uniform breadth, but on an average may be computed to be from twelve to fourteen feet wide.

I received a pencil note from the assistant adjutant-general, Captain Polwhele, intimating that General Nott wished me to take charge of the guns, *godown*, and Somnath Grates over the pass, and immediately moved to the mouth of the only road leading to the summit, and in person superintended the arrangements, which consequently delayed the second brigade. Sufficient space having been gained by Brigadier Wymer's brigade, Captain Leslie's troop of horse artillery started, always allowing some distance between every gun and waggon, in case of a standstill. This troop gained the top of the hill without assistance. Next followed Anderson's 2nd troop of irregular horse artillery (formerly in the service of Shah Shooja), commanded by Lieutenant Turner, which, owing to the inferiority of the cattle, could not run up of themselves.

Working parties from Her Majesty's 41st Foot and the 42nd Native Infantry were accordingly stationed at such points as were particularly steep or abrupt; they also acted as safe-guards, half of the men taking charge of the arms on any projecting ridge of rock, whilst the other half were on the drag-ropes. This troop soon passed the difficulties below, and a company of Her Majesty's 41st regiment, which had been sent with Captain Leslie's troop to the top of the pass, saw them safe to the summit. The 9-pounder horse battery (Bombay), commanded by Captain Blood, followed, and in consequence of the greater weight of metal, and the lightness of the cattle, much delay occurred in getting the gun over the lower part of the ascent, where the road was narrow and very steep, and the turns sharp and sudden. Working parties were stationed at short intervals, to relieve each other. This battery had been sent with the detachment of troops from General Nott's force, from Cabool into Kohistan, under my command, and consequently had not had, like the others, the advantage of a rest.

To take up the sandal-wood gates was a trying operation, and consumed still more time. However, by dint of bard labour, supported by good humour, this mass of wood was dragged to the top of the pass.

Nearly at the top, but in a ravine, on our right, lay the famous Jellalabad gun, the "*Cazee*," considered to be second only to the "*Zubber Jung*" of Ghuznee. It was off its carriage, and there being no available means of bringing it on, I resolved to burst it where it lay. I sent on the gates with the party of artillerymen belonging to the 18-pounders which had been destroyed, and on the carriage of which the Somnath Gates were piled, and halted at the head of the column, to arrange for the destruction of the Jellalabad gun. Whilst Major Simmons and Brigade-Major Dixon were in conversation with me on the subject. Major Sotheby, commanding the artillery with General Nott's force, happened to come up, and I pointed out to him the necessity of destroying the gun, and my determination to do so, and requested the services of an officer of artillery to superintend the duty.

Major Sotheby said the *Cazee* would be destroyed; but I was not satisfied. He then detailed the arrangements which had been made for the destruction of this gun, and, finding powder had been left for the purpose, and that the duty of bursting the *Cazee* had been entrusted to an artillery officer (Lieutenant F. Turner, horse artillery), I was satisfied, simply observing that I held Major Sotheby answerable that the gun should be destroyed.

It has been mentioned that Captain Leslie's troop of horse artillery effected the ascent without assistance, and that some delay occurred in getting Captain Anderson's 2nd troop of horse artillery to the top of the pass; more delay with the 9-pounder battery, and more still with the sandal-wood gates of Somnath. The advance, the general and his staff, and the general's and general staff baggage, the 1st brigade of infantry, Captain Leslie's troop of horse artillery, Lieutenant Turner's *ditto*, and four guns of Captain Blood's 9-pounder battery, had each pushed on, without any consideration for those in the rear, to Allee Musjid, as they reached the top of the pass, and arrived at Allee Musjid successively between half-past 11 a.m. and 2 p.m., 4th November.

It was about half-past 1 or 2 p.m. when my brigade, with the gates, after most severe labour, reached the summit of the Lundee Khana Pass, which opens on the plain between that and the mouth of the long defile ending at Allee Musjid. Not a gun or regiment was to be seen; even the two last guns of Captain Blood's battery, which had delayed the detachment considerably, had taken advantage of the level ground, and pushed on, and it was subsequently found that they were in a hollow, about a mile and a half in advance, held in check by the enemy.

The great fatigue the men of the 2nd brigade had undergone called for a halt, which was accordingly made, as soon as the brigade was sufficiently in advance to allow the baggage to pass on to the plain without interruption; the arms were then piled, and the men allowed refreshment.

The summit of a hill on the left was covered with armed men, but whether friends or foes, could not be known, as all dressed much alike, and no one had been sent with me to inform me on such matters. A strong party of Captain Thomas's *jezailchees* held the head of the pass. Interpreter and quarter-master Lieutenant Elliot, 43rd Native Infantry, officiating as commissary-general, in charge of the whole of the commissariat of the Bengal presidency, who had volunteered his services, and had attended me the whole of the morning, was accordingly sent back by me to bring one or two of Ferris's men to give some information on this point.

The whole brigade were seated on the ground; the baggage had just gained the head of the column, when a sergeant of the 9-pounder battery rode up at the gallop, inquiring for the brigadier. He reported that the last two guns and their waggons, with Captain Blood, were about a mile or two ahead, with only the Light Company of the 2nd Native Infantry, fairly held in cheek by the enemy, who shewed in force on all sides and had complete possession of the road. Her Majesty's 41st, under Major Simmons, was immediately despatched to their assistance, with orders not to proceed further on until I should join them. The baggage, which had been collected, was immediately ordered to the right flank.

Lieutenant Elliot quickly returned with two smart men of Thomas's *jezailchees*, who, being questioned as to the people on the hills to the left, instantly replied, "They are Affreedees, your bitter enemies; the men who attacked your last brigade." Captain Thomas's men at the head of the pass were too near at hand to allow of the enemy coming down on the plains at the spot near which the second brigade had been halted. The baggage having been shifted to the right, I moved on with the gates and my brigade for about half or three quarters of a mile, when, on a commanding ground, and quite near enough to keep up the communication with Captain Thomas's party, holding the head of the pass, and pretty well advanced on the plain, I stationed the 42nd Native Infantry, under Major Clarkson, facing the hill above mentioned, with orders to keep a sharp lookout after the baggage, right and left, as well as to the Affreedees in front.

About a mile from this post, my detachment came on the two guns of Captain Blood's 9-pounder battery and the light company of the 2nd Native Infantry. The enemy were retiring, after examining the country. The force moved on to a rising ground on the line of march, commanding a view of the country on three sides. Here I left the right wing of the 2nd Native Infantry, under Major Farrington, with similar orders to those given to the 42nd Native Infantry at the last post. Still moving on the road, an opening in the hills, both right and left, demanded attention.

Some baggage had already been carried off, and several bodies, shamefully mangled, marked the deadly hatred of this tribe to us and our followers. Selecting a suitable position, the other wing of the 2nd native infantry was posted on a commanding situation, about a mile or a mile and a half from the last post, with orders to keep up a communication with it. Still moving on, the remnant of the 2nd brigade came upon the Light Company of the 16th Native Infantry on an eminence, about half a mile from the entrance of the defile. Here also was a collection of irregular horse, baggage, camp-followers, amateurs, &c., vociferous about the immense numbers of the enemy who had met and driven them out of the pass. It was found necessary to strengthen this post, being the fourth on the plains. It consisted of but a single company; and the Light Company of the 2nd Native Infantry, which I had brought on, was accordingly added to the Light Company of the 16th Native Infantry.

It was impossible to deduct further from the brigade, with such a stake as that of the gates and guns in hand. The Light Company of the 2nd Native Infantry had been brought on to camp, as it had been skirmishing over the hills to the right all the morning, had driven the enemy back, and had only returned to the spot where I found them about half an hour before my arrival there. Some order being established, I moved into the defile with a company of Her Majesty's 41st, the sandal-wood gates, and the 43rd Native Infantry baggage. A party of 160 irregular cavalry were found here, who asserted that they had been driven back by ten times their numbers, posted on the hills, and consequently beyond their reach.

Small guards of infantry had been allowed to accompany the line of baggage at from twenty to thirty paces from the first. The horses of the 9-pounder battery, and the bullocks dragging the gates, were very tired, and the men had been on and off at the drag-ropes all day. Still there was never a moment's hesitation, when the guns, waggons, or gates required the assistance of the men; all was good humour and devotion to the service.

On entering the defile, there remained Her Majesty's 41st, less 100 rank and file picquet; the light company, completed to 80 rank and file; several small guards for baggage; in hospital about 70; quarter-master and rearguard, 40 each; so that less than 300 bayonets remained. The 2nd Native Infantry formed the second and third of the line of posts; the 42nd, the first of the line of posts. The 43rd Native Infantry were on duty over the gates, by field-force orders, which directed that a regiment should always form their escort. The enemy shewed pretty strong as the detachment wound down into the defile, but they were broken into parties of from twenty up to sixty, and many stragglers, making the hills alive.

Very soon after passing the beautiful *tope* on the left of the entrance of the defile, a company of the 43rd Native Infantry was left on a conical hill, commanding a view of the road on both sides, but out of reach of shot from the hills above. About a mile beyond this, at a turn in the road, another hill, possessing equal advantages, enabled me to leave a second company. Both these companies were withdrawn from the 43rd Native Infantry, on duty over the gates, the Light Company of which regiment was, it may be remembered, on the advance, and its picquet, and quartermaster and rearguard on duty with the rearguard of the force. Attempts to send an express had twice failed. From three to four miles of most difficult country remained to be passed through, and a third attempt was made by Lieutenant Elliot, who had volunteered, with some horsemen, and it proved successful.

I simply reported that, on arriving on the plain above Lundee Khana, I found myself deserted, and the enemy in such considerable force near the, head of the pass as to induce me to leave the 42nd Native Infantry in its vicinity; that with the 2nd Native Infantry, and with the two flank companies of the 2nd and 16th Native Infantry, which I found on the plain, I had completed a line of four posts to the entrance of the defile, each capable of holding their post against the enemy; that I had already taken two companies from the 43rd Native Infantry on duty over the gates, and since I entered the defile, I expected every moment to be forced to leave a third, to keep open the communication; that I understood three miles of the same country remained to traverse, and presumed to suggest the necessity of that distance being held by troops from the 1st brigade, at Allee Musjid camp, as I was reduced to the lowest possible numbers consistent with safety.

Shortly after the despatch of the third note by Lieutenant Elliot, some of the enemy had the madness to fire several shots into the column and among the baggage, from a gorge, which evidently was bounded by the hills, and from which there could be no escape but from the sides, being two spurs at right angles connecting it with the main ridge, which was almost perpendicular. The flankers had returned the fire, but, seeing the advantage I possessed, I determined to make an example of the assailants, and sounded the "cease-firing."

Three parties from Her Majesty's 41st were soon told off; two crowned the hills, right and left, whilst the third quietly entered the gorge; seven of the enemy were shot, and only one escaped, without any loss on our side. This success, however trifling, had an evidently good effect; for, afterwards, the enemy were observed creeping up the hills as fast as possible, nor was there a single shot fired into the column between the spot marked by this occurrence and Allee Musjid, a distance of about three miles.

In rather less than a mile from the spot from which I had despatched Lieutenant Elliot to Allee Musjid, the detachment came on the Light Company of the 42nd Native Infantry, and near at hand, but on the opposite side, found the Light Company of the 38th Native Infantry. The officers of both parties requested assistance. They were told the situation of the detachment, and that succour had been requested from the camp at Allee Musjid. My detachment met a squadron of the 3rd Bombay Cavalry, about a mile beyond those light companies, sent out by General Nott. The officer brought a note from the assistant adjutant-general, Captain Polwhele, saying the 16th Native Infantry would follow immediately. Cavalry were perfectly useless; they were therefore desired to fall into the rear of the column, and to return with the 2nd brigade to camp.

Lieutenant-Colonel MacLaren, with the 16th Native Infantry, soon met the detachment, and gave the first tidings of the sad loss suffered by one of General McCaskill's brigades, the night before.[5] Lieutenant-Colonel MacLaren, having received every information as to the location of the line of posts, lost no time in pushing forward to complete them, and to make such further arrangements as he might judge proper. I moved forward with my detachment, reaching Allee Musjid a little after sunset, after as hard a day's work as men could well sustain.

I reported the arrival in camp of the gates and the remaining two guns of Blood's 9-pounder horsed battery. The appearance of the detachment afforded an evident relief to many an anxious heart, for the disasters of the last evening had caused the most dismal forebodings as to the fate of the second brigade and the gates, whilst the jaded state

5. This affair is reported in the letters of Major-General McCaskill and Brigadier Wild, Nos. 541 and 542, Affghanistan Papers, p. 427.

of the cattle with Captain Blood's two 9-pounder guns justified an apprehension that they might have experienced a similar calamity. The line of posts in the defile already stationed there was strengthened, and Lieutenant-Colonel MacLaren placed others wherever the necessity of so doing was apparent. These arrangements enabled the baggage to continue moving along the road the whole of the night: the last camels, with the rearguard, did not reach Allee Musjid till past 7 a.m. on the morning of the 5th November.

To complete the details of this march, it is necessary to give an account of the proceedings of the rearguard from the time it marched from Lundee Khana until its arrival in camp at Allee Musjid the next morning, between 7 and 8 a.m. on the 5th November.

It was the good fortune of the advance of Major-General Nott and his staff, of Major Nott's baggage and the general staff baggage, the 1st (or Brigadier Wymer's) brigade, and the horse artillery of both Presidencies, and four of Blood's 9-pounder battery, to reach Allee Musjid between 11 a.m. and 2 p.m. on the 4th November. When they had attained in safety, and without molestation, the end of their journey at Allee Musjid, I had only got, with my crippled resources, my very responsible charge to the head of the Lundee Khana Pass, where I found myself deserted by everyone who could crawl in advance (save the two guns of the 9-pounder battery, held in check by the Affreedees), embarrassed with the cumbrous sandal-wood gates of the Temple of Somnath, and charged with the care of all the baggage, public and private; of the *godown* or provisions; and of what was of far greater consideration, the honour of the British arms, with not a fourth of the force to do the duty of the whole.

When my gallant brigade arrived, after sunset, at Allee Musjid, Major Browne, Her Majesty's 41st Foot, commanding the rearguard, was calling in the picquets and several guards of the Lundee Khana camps placed on duty at 10 a. m. on the preceding day, previous to following the last of the *godown* and baggage up the hill. It was 9 o'clock a. m. of the 4th November before the last men of the 2nd brigade entered on the narrow ascent which leads to the top of the Lundee Khana Pass; the cattle, baggage, and *godown* followed, and continued passing on till evening.

It was 6 p.m. before Major Browne, commanding the rearguard, commenced calling in the picquets. As it would be long before the last camels could reach the top of the pass, considering that the nature of the road rendered it necessary to travel at the slowest rate, and as it was nearly dark, some of the picquets were withdrawn by the pathway leading along the stream, and up the hills to the right, joining the made road at the highest point, and where it turns abruptly to the left. By this pathway many camels, *yaboos*, mules, bullocks, &c., had been crawling up the whole day.

The strong picquet on the higher hill on the left was reinforced, as the rearguard moved, by the two picquets below it, namely, by that on the lower hill, and by another which had been posted in the neck of a gorge in rear of the 43rd Native Infantry camp. On the sound of the bugle, the three moved off parallel to each other, the main column up the made road; the picquets right and left. By these precautions, the rearguard moved off unmolested; but the darkness of night and the irregularity of the ground enabled the enemy to creep on unperceived.

The party on the highest hill on the left, having a very circuitous route to make before reaching the road at the head of the pass, had been ordered to march so soon after the smaller picquets, joining a column abreast of them. This picquet had not moved off more than a quarter of an hour, when long shots from that direction passed over the column; the fire was returned whenever the glow of a match shewed above. At one time, during the ascent, several matches shewed together, and on one spot two companies of Her Majesty's 40th poured in a volley, which had the effect of silencing the enemy.

When the last section of the rearguard reached the head of the pass. Major Browne took all but those whose assistance was immediately required in the destruction of the Jellalabad gun, round the abrupt turn to the left, and there halted until the final arrangements for the destruction of the *Cazee* were completed. All being ready, this fatigue party rejoined the column. Everything had been ably managed, and after a few minutes of suspense the famous Jellalabad gun, the *Cazee*, was blown into as many fragments as his "uncle" (such was their reputed relationship), Zubber Jung of Ghuznee. The explosion was tremendous; but the sheltered position of our men shielded them from harm.

Before Major Browne made his last arrangements for the destruction of the *Cazee*, he sent on Captain Malet, of the 3rd Bombay Light Cavalry, with his detachment, to ascertain the state of matters ahead.

The column had been but a short time in motion, after the explosion of the *Cazee*, when a trooper returned from Captain Malet, with a note, saying that, notwithstanding the precautionary measures adopted by me in the morning, the baggage was attacked on the left, near the second post on the plain. Parties from Her Majesty's 40th Foot and the 16th Native Infantry were immediately pushed forward, with orders to pass on until they should arrive at the point of attack.

Major Browne, continuing to pass on, reached the plain separating the head of the Lundee Khana Pass from the entrance into the defile leading to Allee Musjid: desultory firing, sometimes heavier, sometimes lighter, was heard a short distance in advance. Soon after reaching the plain. Major Browne came on the 42nd Native Infantry, posted there by me in the early afternoon; he desired Major Clarkson to call in his men, and join the column. Proceeding on. Major Browne came on the second and third posts, each composed of a wing of the 2nd Bengal Native Infantry. It was as the rearguard neared the third post that the firing became more animated.

Between the third and fourth posts, the country opened considerably. The road from the head of the Lundee Khana Pass to the entrance of the defile leading to Allee Musjid was crossed by a valley at nearly right angles. It was at this point that several camels and their loads (chiefly belonging to Her Majesty's 40th Foot and the 38th Native Infantry) were carried off; three *sepoys* and several followers were killed, and two Europeans and eight *sepoys* wounded. At this point, also, baggage had been carried off in the early forenoon, before I checked the marauders by the line of posts which I left in passing along: the baggage belonged to officers and men of all regiments. Captains Webster, 43rd Native Infantry, and Christie, of the irregular cavalry, being the heaviest sufferers, having lost everything they possessed.

It was by the pathway to the right that these people, in full reliance on proper arrangements for their safety, pushed on and got between the advance and my charge. Many lost their lives; few reached camp in safety, but those who took refuge at the post where General Nott had placed Captain Gairdner, with the Light Company of the 16th Native Infantry, and which post I reinforced with the Light Company 2nd Native Infantry, under Captain Maclean.

The fourth of the line of posts was reached, and the rearguard entered the defile, with the main column in the rear of all, whilst small parties were interspersed, to check petty marauding, and give safety and spirit to the whole.

From the interval between the third and fourth posts, the firing almost ceased; long shots, at intervals, were fired into the column and baggage, but not a man was wounded from the time of entering the defile up to the arrival of the rearguard at Allee Musjid, between 7 and 8 a.m. on the morning of the 5th November.

No division order was issued on this occasion; no thanks were offered; no notice was taken of these different affairs, and of the successful accomplishment of a most difficult operation, beyond the following brief and cursory report of Major-General Nott to Captain Ponsonby, which appears in the papers laid before Parliament.[6]

> Camp, near Feshawur, November 8, 1842.
>
> Sir,—I have to acquaint you, for the information of Major-General Pollock, C.B., that the rearguard of my force, under the command of Major Browne, of Her Majesty's 41st regiment, was attacked by the enemy on marching to and from Ali Musjid. The arrangements made by Major Browne, assisted by Major Simmons, of Her Majesty's 41st regiment, appear to have been admirable, and the enemy were speedily defeated-
>
> I enclose a return of the killed and wounded. I directed the fort of Ali Musjid to be destroyed. The engineer's report is herewith transmitted.
>
> W. Nott.

As I reached the encampment, I ordered the corps to proceed to their respective lines, going to the left myself to report to General Nott. Several officers were standing opposite to the general's tent,-the Rev. J. N. Allen was one of them,[7]—and all congratulated me on my success. The general came out shortly after I dismounted; and said, "Well, Stacy, where are the gates?"

I replied, "I have sent them to their lines."

"And Blood's guns?"

"I sent them to their lines also." I reported my arrangements for the safety of the baggage, at which the general expressed his satisfaction, and shortly after, as it was growing dark, I took leave.

On the 6th November, the troops marched from Allee Musjid to Jumrood in the following order:—the eight light companies of the infantry regiments, Captain White; the cavalry. Captain Delamain; the

---

6. Papers relating to Military Operations in Afghanistan, No. 544, p. 428.

7. Mr. Allen has published a *Diary* of this march, and his work is as inaccurate in this portion as in many others. As Mr. Allen was fully aware of the anxiety felt in camp, and by no one more than General Nott, for the fate of the rear force, the gates, baggage, &c., and of the extraordinary difficulties which this part of the retiring army was left to grapple with singly, it might have been expected that his work would have done something towards supplying the deficiency of the public documents.

general and his staff; the general and staff baggage; the artillery, Major Sotheby; the 1st brigade of infantry; the 2nd brigade of infantry; the Gates of Somnath, escorted by the 38th Native Infantry, baggage and *godown*; rearguard, commanded by Major Browne, Her Majesty's 41st; three guns of 9-pounder battery. Lieutenant Terry; 250 cavalry, Captain Christie; Her Majesty's 41st Foot, Brevet-Major Cochran; also all picquets, rear and quarter-guards of the day before.

The rearguard was subsequently strengthened this day by two regiments of the 2nd brigade, furnished by me, namely, the 2nd and 43rd native infantry. The former regiment, under Lieutenant-Colonel Lane, was sent to occupy the heights on the right, which were only separated from those held by the Sikh troops by an opening, and which led round to a road, or water-course, running parallel to the made road. Lieutenant-Colonel Lane was directed to keep these heights until Major Browne, in withdrawing the picquets, should be able to relieve him. The other regiment (the 43rd) was added to the rearguard on an application from Major Browne to me for assistance before the brigade left the ground.

The encamping-ground at Allee Musjid was very confined, and surrounded on all sides by low hills, forming a concentric circle within a range of much higher ones. The lower range was occupied by our picquets, which were considerably increased. this day, as three sides of the higher hills were covered with the enemy, who had annoyed us a little during the night, and shots had been exchanged at intervals from 3 a. m. until the troops moved.

The "general" beat at 6 a.m. and the "assembly" at 6. About half an hour after the force had begun to move, the enemy commenced a series of attacks upon our picquets. The column was winding up the hill, when the firing on both sides became animated. One picquet was particularly hard pressed, and most of those on the right were partially engaged. Observing that the strength of the rearguard was inadequate, or unequal to the duties expected from it, I sent a proposal to Brigadier Wymer (General Nott having passed on, and the road being occupied by the horse artillery), that each should leave a regiment from our respective brigades, to reinforce Major Browne (who, in virtue of his seniority, assumed the command of the rearguard), the better to enable him to withdraw the picquets, after the gates, *godown*, and baggage should have left the basin, and reached the top of the first ascent. Brigadier Wymer declined this proposal.

About this time, it was supposed by those moving up the first ascent, that the rearguard of the 43rd, forming one of the line of posts on the right, had been driven in. Some of the men had gone to pick up some dry sticks to make a fire. It was only daylight, and they were a considerable distance from their guard, when a small party of Affghans, who had been concealed behind pieces of rock at the bottom of the hill, shewed themselves, and instantly fired on our men. The *sepoys*, of course; retreated on their post. The *jemadar*, commanding the guard, not content with simply firing on the enemy, advanced to meet their comrades, checked the Affghans, and returned to his post. Major Browne, thinking the great numbers of these Affghans might induce them to attack this picquet, strengthened this guard immediately.

On the foot of the first ascent. Brigadier Wymer met me. I urged him to leave a regiment, on the plea that the rearguard was much too weak to complete its duties without very severe loss, if they could do so at all, against the many heavy assemblages of Kyberries on the hills, the lowest calculation of their numbers being 3,000 men, but it was generally considered they had 5,000 collected here. Brigadier Wymer, however, refused, alleging that he had no authority to do so (neither had I), and he passed on, without stopping a moment. Left to my own resources, without hesitation, I took all the responsibility on myself, and sent Lieutenant-Colonel Lane, with the 2nd Native Infantry, to take possession of the heights on the right, and to hold them, till Major Browne, when withdrawing the rear picquets, should relieve him..

The firing had increased, and several of the picquets had been tried by the enemy. Major Browne sent to me (I was still on the ground), asking for assistance, and begged to retain the services of the 43rd Native Infantry, which he had halted, until the brigade orders should be received. I saw the necessity, or at least the wisdom, of the measure, and sent my brigade-major with orders to Major Nash, commanding the 43rd Native Infantry, to place himself under Major Browne's orders. Major Browne was now able to strengthen the line of picquets; these arrangements instilled a perfect confidence in our party; the enemy made several rushes on these posts, and in each attack was beaten back with very considerable loss.

In the meantime, the Gates of Somnath, the *godown*, and baggage were passing up by the made road, and Lieutenant-Colonel Lane, having possession of the heights on the right, *yaboos*, bullocks, and asses were enabled to ascend by the zigzag paths on the right and in front of the hill occupied by the Sikh headquarters.

The encamping-ground at Allee Musjid is very irregular, with a fine stream of water running through it. The basin is nearly divided into two, at the upper or northern end, by the proximity of the lower range of rocks, which approach to within about twenty yards of each other.

As soon as the fort of Allee Musjid was blown up, which was about noon, and as Major Browne was calling in some of the advanced pic-quets, Lieutenant Terry, Bombay artillery, went with a party to look out for a spot on which to place a gun, to keep in check a body of Kyberries, who appeared determined to cut in between the inner and outer part of the encamping-ground. In the performance of this duty, Lieutenant Terry was severely wounded, and ultimately died of his wound. He was a young man of great promise, respected and beloved by everyone in camp. Before the picquets were withdrawn, two guns were sent up and placed in position on the top of the first ascent facing the basin, and ready to play on the enemy should they follow, either by the basin or by the height on the right occupied by the 2nd Native Infantry.

As our picquets were withdrawn, the Kyberries appeared to gain courage, following in great force and occupying the posts as we quit-ted them. They assembled on the hills to the right in greater numbers than on any other spot. The Sikh army had several detachments skir-mishing with the Kyberries, who the whole day evidently meditated gaining possession of the road by the water-course to the right. They were allowed to remain unmolested until everything was ready with the rearguard to move on; the guns then opened on them with good effect, and before they could get out of range or under cover, they received three or four rounds. Most of the Kyberries were not visible to us after this; but the Sikhs had some sharp skirmishing to prevent their getting on our flank by the road along the water-course.

The Sikhs were opposed with great spirit by the Kyberries at this point; they had no assistance from Major-General Nott's force, and consequently suffered considerably. The left of the Sikh army rested on this water-course; if the Kyberries could have turned their flank, our rear would have been in jeopardy. The Sikhs behaved very well throughout the day; it was owing to their ignorance of tactics that they suffered so heavily; they lost thirty-six killed and had many wounded, one of .their chiefs, a very brave fellow, being hit very hard.

Major Browne, commanding the rearguard, assisted by Major Sim-mons and Brevet-Major Cochran, Her Majesty's 41st Foot, withdrew from the encamping-ground, suffering only a loss of one officer and seven men wounded, and a total loss throughout the day of one killed and fourteen wounded. The experience gained by the march between Lundee Khana and Allee Musjid was not altogether thrown away.

On this day, posts were left, and of sufficient strength, at different points of the road, to secure the force from loss. Major-General Nott left the light company of the Kelat-e-Ghilzie regiment on the crest of the first ascent, on the right of the Sikhs, and at the bridge over the ravine. Colonel MacLaren, commanding the 16th Native Infantry, was left with six companies to check the enemy in case they should attempt to cut in on the baggage at this point. Some of the *jezailchees* and some Sikh troops were also stationed here. Not a load was carried off this day.

Notwithstanding these precautionary measures, the Kyberries managed to get beyond the right of the Sikhs, and, pushing on, took possession of a hill much on this side the brigade, and which commanded the line of march. At first, no notice of this was taken, as only two or three men shewed on the heights; they were, it appears, waiting to be joined by others, for, on a sudden, the hill was covered and a sharp fire opened on the rearguard and baggage. Major Browne halted; the artillery officer got the guns in position, and two parties were quickly told off to crown the heights, one from Her Majesty's 41st and one from the 43rd Light Infantry.

As soon as these parties drew on them the fire of the Kyberries, Blood's 9-pounders opened, and soon forced the enemy to drop down the other side of the hill near the summit. They made one effort to drive back our parties, but in vain; the heights were disputed but a few minutes, when the enemy fled, and such of our men as could reach the crest of the hill fired into them until they were beyond reach. At this spot Lieutenant Chamberlain was very severely wounded. In storming the heights, only five men were wounded, two of them slightly.

Beyond this, the Kyberries did not shew, and Major Browne, with the rearguard, reached the camp at Jumrood about 4 p.m.

The amount of killed and wounded this day was only two officers and thirteen privates. No division order was issued on this occasion. General Nott's report is contained in the general despatch, (shown earlier in this section).

The troops marched from Jumrood on the 6th, and next day reached Koulsir, where they halted until the 12th, when they moved to Peshawur, and encamped there by divisions,—the first consisting of sappers and miners, Anderson's troop of horse artillery, park and foot artillery, 3rd Bombay Cavalry, Haldane's Horse, Her Majesty's 40th regiment, the 2nd and 10th Native Grenadiers, the 38th Light Infantry, and the Kelat-e-Ghilzie regiment; the second composed of Leslie's troop of horse artillery, Blood's battery, Christie's Horse, Her Majesty's 41st regiment, the 42nd and 43rd Light Infantry. By field-force orders of the 13th November, I was ordered "to furnish such guards as may be necessary for the duties of the second division."

The force marched from Peshawur on the 15th, crossed the Indus on the 18th, the Jelum on the 3rd December, the Chenab on the 8th, the Ravee on the 15th, and the Sutlej on the 22nd; and reached Ferozepore on the 23rd December, 1842.

On the 2nd of January, 1843, Major-General Nott having left Ferozepore to fill his appointment, at Lucknow, of Resident at the court of the King of Oude, the command of the Candahar force devolved upon Brigadier Wymer, and upon his quitting camp, to precede his regiment (the 38th), for Kurnaul, I succeeded to the command.

Section 7

Summary and Conclusion

A concise summary of the transactions recorded in the preceding sections will place those transactions, and my services in relation to them, clearly and distinctly before the reader.

The *khanat* of Kelat, having been taken by our forces under Major-General Willshire, towards the close of 1839, was made over to Meer Shah Newaz, the nominee of Shah Shooja-ool-Moolk; and Shah Newaz entered into a close alliance with the British Government. His rule, however, was distasteful to the chiefs and people, who, in the succeeding year, expelled him from Kelat, of which place possession was taken by Meer Mahomed Nasseer Khan, the only legitimate son of the late Mehrab Khan, and the British Government was set at defiance by them.

The retention of the country below the Bolan Pass in our interests and under our control was, at this juncture, of such importance to the security of our forces in Affghanistan and to the policy adopted by the British Government towards the countries bordering upon the Indus, that our envoy and minister at Cabool, the late Sir William Macnaghten, deputed Major-General Nott to retake the fortress of Kelat, which he accordingly occupied (finding it deserted) in 1840, and, leaving a garrison there, he returned with his army to Candahar.

The country of Kelat was at this time pervaded by an almost universal spirit of bitter hostility to the British, emanating from a deep-rooted distrust of our faith, or rather a conviction of our perfidy, owing chiefly to certain occurrences, detailed in the *Narrative*, which placed the British character in an equivocal light. The young *khan*, Meer Mahomed Nasseer, after abandoning Kelat, was still encamped, with a small force of Brahooes and Belooches, a short distance from the capital; the *sirdars*, to a man, peremptorily refused to submit to our supremacy, and the fierce, semi-barbarous tribes, who inhabited the country between our encampments to the north of the Bolan Pass and the Indus, maintained a harassing, desultory warfare, which threatened our communications, and confined our occupation of the country to those spots upon which our camps were actually pitched.

All the efforts of the British political agent in this quarter (the late Mr. Ross Bell) to establish a good understanding with the *khan*, to conciliate the chiefs and tribes, and to tranquillize the country, through which all the supplies from the Indus must be drawn, were completely baffled by this general repugnance, founded not merely upon an apprehension of our power and a suspicion of our motives, but upon a firm belief in our treachery; a sentiment which would have alienated civilized nations, and which makes ignorant and war-like people the deadliest and most dangerous of foes.

In this state of things, I spontaneously tendered my services, offering to go in the midst of these turbulent, irritated, and suspicious tribes, and endeavour to extinguish their hostility and mistrust, and teach them juster notions of our character. I was accordingly commissioned to negotiate with the *khan* and chiefs of Kelat, the objects in view being to induce them to submit to the supremacy of the British Government; to bring the country into a state of tranquillity, and to prevail upon the young *khan* to disband his army (thereby placing himself entirely at our mercy), and to wait upon the British political agent, in order to make arrangements with him for the future administration of the *khanat*. For the accomplishment of these important objects, I was provided with neither a military force to coerce the people, nor money to bribe the chiefs; I went unattended by a guard, or even a single *sepoy*; I trusted to no other protection than honesty of purpose, and employed no other force or influence than reason and persuasion.

The manner in which this very difficult and somewhat perilous office was successfully executed, is minutely detailed in the Narrative (which will not be without interest to the students of human character), as well as the unexpected embarrassments thrown in my way, whereby the difficulties and perils of the negotiation were greatly aggravated; and, perhaps, few diplomatic agents were subjected to severer trials of temper and discretion. Disregarding all personal sufferings and sacrifices, by a steady perseverance in the course of action which I deliberately adopted, I had the satisfaction of succeeding in all my objects. The predatory and desultory warfare was suspended (not a hostile shot having been fired in the country since I entered upon my mission); the *khan* was placed upon the throne of his ancestors; the Brahooe and Belooche tribes were taught to rely implicitly upon the honour, and integrity of a government which they had previously distrusted, and were converted from bitter enemies into confiding friends.

The sincerity of the *khan* and his chiefs, and the success of my negotiations, were severely tested by the calamitous events at Cabool, in 1842; but so firmly had I established throughout the country a trust in the British name and power, that these disasters, which cast a temporary cloud upon the lustre of our arms and tempted some of our allies to desert us, had no effect upon the *khan* and chiefs of Kelat, who even repelled the solicitations of the Shahzadeh Sufter Jung and the *sirdars* of Candahar to join them in a religious confederacy against us. In the hour of our supposed adversity (to use the words of Lord Ellenborough, the Governor-General of India), "the Court and chiefs of Kelat remained firm in their allegiance;" and although Beloochistan had, for eighteen months before, inspired the Indian Government with anxiety, if not with alarm; at a time when the whole of Affghanistan was in arms against us, animated by a contagious spirit of enthusiasm, to which a British army appeared to have fallen a sacrifice, the country beyond the Bolan Pass, inhabited by restless and barbarous tribes, had been soothed into unwonted tranquillity. It was, I believe, generally admitted that, if I had not succeeded in bringing in the Khan of Kelat, and conciliated the Brahooe and Belooche *sirdars*, not a man of our army above the passes would have returned to India.

Meanwhile, the success which had attended my negotiations with the *khan* and chiefs of Kelat, attended, or rather facilitated, my exertions in the Bolan Pass, the free passage of which became, in the unfavourable position of our affairs, a matter of vast importance, since this formidable defile was the route by which alone reinforcements and supplies could be sent to the beleaguered garrison at Candahar. For upwards of four months, I was engaged in the arduous task of completing arrangements with the tribes between the foot of the pass and the Indus, who had a multitude of real or colourable grievances to allege against the British authorities, and which had inflamed their animosity to the highest pitch.

After much difficult negotiation, the Bolan Pass was opened; our convoys were permitted to traverse it without molestation; the Doda Murrees, the most powerful of the tribes, and whose hostility was the most inveterate, were brought to accept our terms; treaties were concluded with them, with the Boogtees, the Doomkees, and other principal and minor tribes, the result of which was, their complete subjection to the authority of the *khan*, our ally, and the entire cessation of hostility and extinction of enmity on their part towards us; so that the country, singularly fitted by its physical features and the habits of its population to be the nest of political disorder, and which in 1840 was a scene of tumult and bloodshed, presented in 1841 the aspect of a settled and peaceful province.

The beneficial effects of this state of things, the fruit of my labours in Beloochistan,—brought about at a pecuniary cost utterly insignificant in amount,—were not restricted to the mere pacification of this particular country, and the transmutation of a vindictive people, mistrustful of our faith, into steady adherents to our interests; they exerted a material moral influence upon the operations of Major-General Nott at Candahar, whose bold and magnanimous movement from that city upon Ghuznee and Cabool would have been scarcely practicable but for the opening of the communication between Candahar and the Indus, and the tranquillization of a country which, in its former state, would have rendered the safety of all our troops above the Bolan Pass problematical. It will be seen from the *Narrative*, (section 3), that General Nott, a man not prone to exaggerate difficulties, told the Government that the check experienced by Major-General England at Hjkulzje (and which, I repeat, in my opinion, would not have happened if my suggestion had been acceded to) had produced a great moral effect throughout the country, and "had added considerably to the difficulties of his position."

The influence which my success, and I may justly add the means whereby it was attained, gave me amongst the chiefs and tribes of Beloochistan, operated (if I may so speak) as a species of talisman, in the march of Major-General England from Quetta to Candahar, the communication between which city and the posts to the south was completely closed, owing to the enemy's having taken possession of Killa Abdoolla. It was of essential importance that this communication should be reopened, and my acquaintance with the local chiefs, and especially with Meer Saloo Khan, who held paramount authority in the country, enabled me to bring them over to the British cause, and they were conducted by me, in the train of Major-General England's force, to Candahar.

The arrangements I had made with these chiefs were sanctioned and ratified by General Nott, and, to repeat the acknowledgment of

Major Rawlinson, the able political agent at Candahar, they "provided for the reopening of our *dâk* communication with India, and maintained that communication regularly and uninterruptedly during the remainder of our stay at Candahar."

The reopening of this communication is an incident in the history of this critical campaign which attracted the keen and experienced observation of the Duke of Wellington, who, in the House of Lords, passed a high eulogium upon the measure, the importance of which could not escape his discernment, although his Grace was not, of course, aware of even the name of the individual who had rendered this service.

In the triumphant march of Major-General Nott from Candahar to Ghuznee and Cabool, I had an active share in all the actions with the enemy, and after the arrival of that force at Cabool, I was selected to command the detachment furnished from General Nott's army for the expedition into the Kohistan of Cabool. In the attack on Istaliff, which has been described as one of the most brilliant and decisive actions of that campaign, I commanded the left column of attack, which, it will be seen from the *Narrative*, did eminent service both at the fortified village of Emillah and at the fortress of Istaliff, the strongest place in Affghanistan. If the army of Ameenoolla Khan had not been so effectually disposed of at this place (the killed alone of the enemy amounted probably to 1,000), they would have followed and harassed us as we retired, and occasioned our encumbered army much trouble, and perhaps considerable losses.

As it was, on the march of the British forces from Cabool to Peshawur, various attempts were made by the mountain tribes to impede their progress through the tremendous defiles. During this most painful and difficult march, my brigade was every day in the rear (the most arduous position, as even non-military men must know, in a retiring army), and in the Jugdulluk Pass, which has acquired a fatal celebrity, the second brigade, which I commanded, is entitled to almost the entire honour of having saved, by my arrangements, many lives, besides a large portion of the baggage and commissariat supplies, together with the Somnath Gates, a very precious, but a most cumbersome and embarrassing charge, and which nearly fell into the hands of the enemy.

In the march from Lundee Khana to Allee Musjid, the most dangerous and critical of all, owing to the desperate determination of the enemy, who saw their expected prey escaping them, and were elated by their success the evening before over a portion of Major-General

McCaskill's force, I was specially ordered by General Nott to take charge of the baggage, guns, gates, &c. My dispositions kept the enemy in check, and brought the long and heterogeneous train of baggage, supplies, artillery, and gates, together with the troops I had in charge, unharmed into Allee Musjid; and in the onward march from thence to Jumrood, the *Narrative* will shew that my resources were again most severely taxed to provide against the assaults of the Kyberries.

On one occasion, (section 6), I was obliged to act, though junior brigadier, upon my own responsibility. It is always difficult, and sometimes presumptuous, to predict what would have happened if certain measures had not been taken; but I am justified in affirming that, if I had not, upon that occasion, strengthened the picquets and rearguard with two regiments of my own brigade, the enemy *might* have cut in upon the gates, baggage, and *godown*, and inflicted upon us a severe loss of reputation as well as of property. I assert this with the more confidence, because it was generally acknowledged in the force that, but for the second brigade, the Somnath Gates and the greater part of the baggage would have been lost (besides the disgrace of a reverse) in the Jugdulluk Pass, in that of Lundee Khana, and near Allee Musjid. At Jugdulluk we had no orders, yet that affair has never been mentioned in any public despatch.

None of these transactions, indeed, have found any but a very penurious record in the official reports of General Nott. It is mortifying to the officers employed in Sir William Nott's army to observe the extraordinary contrast between his official reports and those of Sir George Pollock; the latter, full, complete, excluding no action or name from notice that had the smallest pretension to such a distinction; the former, brief, meagre, defective, and parsimonious. This contrast is not, however, a source of mortification merely, but of injury, inasmuch as it necessarily led to an incorrect estimate of the relative merits and services of the two divisions of the force, and by an inevitable consequence to an unequal distribution of those honours and distinctions which are the legitimate and much-coveted reward of military services. The disproportion of the distinctions conferred upon the officers of the two armies is enormous, being, perhaps, ten to one in favour of Sir George Pollock's.

When the distribution of honours to the Candahar force was promulgated, conceiving myself (as well as other officers of the second brigade, who had been entirely overlooked) to be unfairly treated,— having had the hardest work; having been taken several times out of my roster of duty, marching my brigade every day in the rear from Cabool to Jumrood,—I first addressed myself to Sir William Nott, calling upon him to see me righted. In his answer, he congratulated me upon my having received the Companionship of the Bath (for which I am most grateful), and declared that he made his reports of actions and officers according to the best of his judgment, and could not interfere with the arrangements of Government in the distribution of honours. It seems difficult to understand how, if Sir William did not interfere,—that is, did not recommend and point out the respective claims of his officers,—he discharged his debt of justice towards those who had so heartily co-operated with him and assisted him to win the high distinctions he received.

Disappointed in this application, I made an appeal to the Governor-General (Lord Ellenborough), and, failing there, I drew up, in July, 1844, a Memorial to the Honourable Court of Directors of the East-India Company, which I transmitted through the proper channels, setting forth the nature of my services, and soliciting that, through the Honourable Court, a representation of those services might be made to Her Most Gracious Majesty, whereby I might obtain such a mark of the royal approbation as my zeal and success might appear to deserve. In my letter to the Governor-General in Council, which accompanied this Memorial, I ventured respectfully to urge that, of the many difficult, yet successful, duties performed by me, both in the political and military departments, no adequate notice had been taken either by the Honourable Court or Her Majesty's Government; and added as follows:—

I am a cadet of February, 1804; have often been a volunteer, when active service was to be performed,[1] from the taking of the Cape in 1805-6. I was more recently a volunteer in the Army of the Indus, and served through the whole of the Trans-Indus campaign, from 1838 to 1842. During this period, it is my pride to say, that, as my opportunities of military service were frequent and of moment, so have they ever been successful, though frequently unacknowledged. And here I would beg most respectfully to remark that the different mode of proceeding observed by the two generals (General Pollock and General

---

1. I may mention that, in October, 1840, when Major-General Nott was preparing to move against Kelat, I volunteered to lead all storming parties; and again, in 1842, when the general resolved to move from Candahar upon Ghuznee and Cabool: in both instances, General Nott, who was much pleased, accepted my offer.

Nott) towards the officers under their respective commands, as regards the notice taken of their individual merits in their reports, must not only have left many officers of General Sir William Nott's force reason to complain of neglect as regards distinction, but must also have led to an erroneous estimation of the comparative services of the officers of the two armies by his Excellency the Commander-in-Chief, the Governor-General, the Honourable the Court of Directors, and the Home Government.

This Memorial has hitherto been ineffectual.

Let it not be supposed or suspected that there is any desire on my part to detract in the slightest degree from the merits of the late Sir William Nott, or to carp at the honours and distinctions bestowed upon him. His conduct merits the highest praise; he was brave and intelligent, and deserved all the Government gave him, perhaps even more; for by his gallant and adventurous move upon Ghuznee and Cabool (and the resolution was exclusively his own) he retrieved his country's honour. He may, nevertheless, inadvertently, have neglected an essential duty of a commander, that of bringing fully to the notice of the ruling authorities and of the public the services of his subordinate officers, and thereby caused temporary injustice, which it is still in the power of the Government to repair.

The design of this *Narrative* does not require that it should be pursued further. I may, however, briefly add that I commanded a brigade at the Battle of Maharajpore, near Gwalior, on the 29th December, 1843; that at the great and decisive action with the Sikhs at Sobraon, on the 10th February, 1846, I had the command of the 3rd brigade, belonging to Major-General Dick's division, and was ordered by Lord Gough to lead the advance against the enemy's intrenchments, which were forced by my brigade; that on the fall of Major-General Dick, at the fourth gun, on the right of the entrance, the command of the division devolved upon me, and I continued to command it until the close of the battle, at the passage of the Sutlej, while in the enemy's country, and up to the termination of the campaign.

Appendix

No. 1.

Descent of the Khans of Kelat from Abdoolla. Khan, Son of the Great Mehrab Khan.

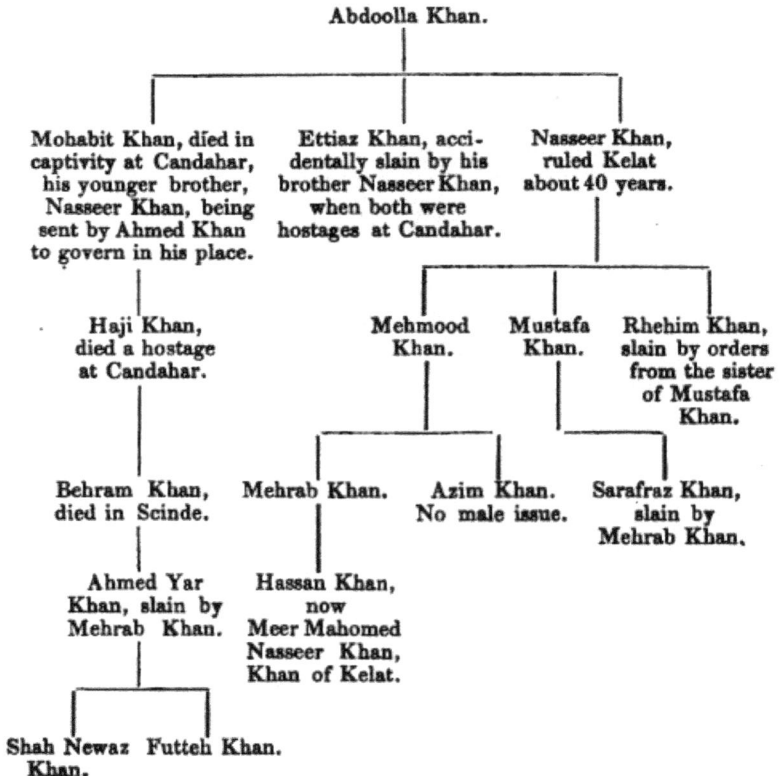

Abdoolla Khan.

Mohabit Khan, died in captivity at Candahar, his younger brother, Nasseer Khan, being sent by Ahmed Khan to govern in his place.

Ettiaz Khan, accidentally slain by his brother Nasseer Khan, when both were hostages at Candahar.

Nasseer Khan, ruled Kelat about 40 years.

Haji Khan, died a hostage at Candahar.

Mehmood Khan.

Mustafa Khan.

Rhehim Khan, slain by orders from the sister of Mustafa Khan.

Behram Khan, died in Scinde.

Mehrab Khan.

Azim Khan. No male issue.

Sarafraz Khan, slain by Mehrab Khan.

Ahmed Yar Khan, slain by Mehrab Khan.

Hassan Khan, now Meer Mahomed Nasseer Khan, Khan of Kelat.

Shah Newaz Khan.

Futteh Khan.

No. 2

Affair At Kotroo

The published account of this affair, in Field Army Orders, by Major-General Brooks, commanding the forces in Upper Scinde, dated "Camp, Sukkor, 6th December, 1840," is to this effect:—

> The major-general, having received authentic intelligence that Nasseer Khan, with the garrison of Kelat, about 4,000 men, had encamped in a strong position on the hills within eight miles of Kotroo, and that reinforcements to the extent of many thousands were on the road from Thull to join them, directed Lieutenant Smith, his *aide-de-camp*, to proceed express to Lieutenant-Colonel Marshall with orders to attack the *khan* in his position. The lieutenant reached Lieutenant-Colonel Marshall's camp on the 30th November, 1840, and the attack was made the following morning at daylight by the lieutenant-colonel at the head of 900 native infantry, 60 irregular horse, and two guns.

> The enemy were completely surprised; Nasseer Khan, with two followers, escaped on foot at the first alarm, but his chiefs and followers made a long and desperate defence, and it was not until four of the principal chiefs and upwards of 500 men lay dead on the field, and nearly the whole of the force had been put to flight, that the enemy's chief commander, Meer Boheer, with his son, six other chiefs, and 132 of their bravest followers, surrendered prisoners. The whole of the enemy's baggage and a large quantity of arms fell into the hands of the British in this "brilliant achievement."

The following is an account of the Kotroo affair, as detailed by the *khan's sirdars*, and which was confirmed by Darogah Gool Mahomed, Meer Boheer, Mahomed Husseen, Jan Mahomed, Dewan Ramoo, and Jysoo Moonshee, and I have reason to think it is substantially correct:—

> After we marched from Dadur, we came to Sooree Coombee. The Brahooes committed excesses on the Cutchee people, and the *khan*, finding they could not be restrained, considered it prudent to retire towards the hills; whereupon the *zemindars, bunneahs*, and *ryots* of Gujun, Gundava, Futtehpoor, Nowshara, &c., went in a body to Colonel Marshall, saying that, in consequence of the English being in their country, their lands and

property were plundered, and their people maltreated and killed. The colonel replied that it was not his affair; that the *khan's* country would be given to him again, and recommended them to go to the *khan*, make known their grievances to him, and ask him to send horsemen to protect them.

They accordingly carried their complaints to the *khan*, who was pleased at what they told him from Colonel Marshall, and he sent twenty *sowars* to prevent plunder in the villages, and despatched a Hindoo (Dewan Ramoo) to Kotroo, with compliments to Colonel Marshall, who received Dewan Ramoo kindly, and at his suggestion, the *sowcars* (bankers) of Shikarpore sent supplies of money and grain to the young *khan*, who was thereby induced to regard the English as his friends. A day or two afterwards, Mahomed Husseen and Jan Mahomed (a servant of the Khyrpore Nawab, Rustum Khan) came to the *khan's* camp with a letter from Mr. Ross Bell to the *khan*, full of friendship, and informed him that they were desired by Mr. Bell to give kind assurances on his part.

These messengers were treated with the greatest respect and kindness by the *khan*, and they remained in the camp, conversing with the chiefs, until half the night had passed, when they went to the quarters assigned them. At daybreak, a *sowar* came galloping from the English camp, calling out loudly that the English army was coming. Reshed Khan's and Meer Boheer's camp lay between the English and the young *khan's*. At this time, the *khan* and Darogah Gool Mahomed were in conversation. Upon hearing the intelligence brought by the *sowar*, everyone got ready, and all eyes were turned to Mahomed Husseen and Jan Mahomed, who were asked to explain how it was that they came with a friendly letter and message from Mr. Ross Bell, and that yet the English were coming to attack them.

They both pleaded ignorance; whereupon Gool Mahomed desired Jan Mahomed to gallop towards the English army and stop them, adding, 'It is not the custom to send proposals of peace and friendship in the evening, and next morning make an attack.'

Jan Mahomed accordingly galloped off and reached the English army when it was little more than a musket-shot from Meer Boheer's camp, and on his remonstrance it was halted. He then returned towards the *khan's* camp. In the meantime the English had advanced a little further and then halted again. When they were in motion, some three or four matchlock-shots were fired, but the *khan*, the moment he heard the first report, gave orders to cease firing. Mahomed Husseen and Jan Mahomed were then sent by the young *khan* to Colonel Marshall, to remonstrate.

The colonel, after a conversation, ordered Jan Mahomed to write to the *khan*, desiring him to come to Mr. Ross Bell, to make his *salaam*. There was nothing in the note about terms; nor was it signed or sealed; but it was brought by Jan Mahomed to the *khan*, who affixed his seal to it, telling Jan Mahomed that he agreed to whatever Rustum Khan and Mahomed Husseen arranged, and returned it by Jan Mahomed to Colonel Marshall. Upon the colonel's receiving back his note with the young *khan's* seal affixed to it, he went back with the troops. Another detachment was advancing by another route, and when Colonel Marshall received back the note, he mounted his *moonshee* on one of his own horses, and sent him to order their return.

Shortly after, Mahomed Husseen returned to the *khan's* camp, and finding that the *khan*, who had retired to a hill, still remained there, he sent a message to him, telling him to return to his tent, as the English army had withdrawn. He came accordingly, and that night, Mahomed Husseen and Jan Mahomed remained in the *khan's* camp, and as soon as order was restored, they met Gool Mahomed, to discuss the occurrence. The latter was very angry, and required the two *vakeels* to explain it. They both strenuously denied any prior knowledge of the movements of the English troops.

After a time it was settled that they should both go to Colonel Marshall, and arrange terms, telling him also that the *khan's* cattle were worn out and that he was in want of money, and that it was hoped that, as an act of friendship, he would fall back upon Baugh, and allow the *khan* and his troops to occupy Kotroo and Gundava, when he would make his arrangements and subsequently go to Mr. Ross Bell; or, if this was objected to, that he would send supplies of provisions and money. The two *vakeels* accordingly proceeded to Colonel Marshall, who replied that he must send the propositions to Mr. Ross Bell, and wait his answer.

In reply to Mahomed Husseen's application for money, the

colonel said he would send 2,000 *rupees* to the *khan* if he had a receipt, and Mahomed Husseen sent to the *darogah*, requesting that Dewan Ramoo might come to receive the money, which he did, and Maliomed Husseen gave a receipt for it. Dewan Ramoo laid out part of the money in the purchase of grain, which he brought, with the balance, to the *khan's* camp, and informed Darogah Gool Mahomed, that Mahomed Husseen requested he would come to Kotroo the next morning to consult about terms.

The *darogah* was unable to go in the morning, and about eight in the afternoon, a man came to the *khan's* camp and stated that preparations were making by the English to come against them the ensuing day. No one believed him, as Mahomed Husseen and Jan Mahomed were in the English camp, arranging terms of peace, and the people went to rest. Others, however, arrived with similar intelligence, and it was resolved that a couple of horsemen should be sent to Kotroo to ascertain its truth. At break of day, the *sowars* returned with the news that the English army was advancing. The young *khan* was sent to a hill close by, and the women and children were ordered to move in the same direction.

Darogah Gool Mahomed ascended the hill, where he observed troops advancing from Kotroo, who directed their attack upon Meer Boheer's camp. Who shall say how many men were killed, wounded, and taken; how much property was seized, or what was the extent of our misfortunes?

No. 3

Seizure of Beejar Khan

The statement made to me by Beejar Khan, Doomkee, of the circumstances of his seizure, is as follows:—

Syud Ameer Shah brought me a *purwanah* to the effect that I was to go to Mr. Ross Bell without any fear, and make my *salaam*; and he told me that he had been desired by Mr. Postans to reassure me, and to send me to Mr. Ross Bell, and that whatever offences I had committed were forgiven, and that I should obtain back my country. Under this guarantee, I went to Captain Amiel, and he seized me and made me prisoner.

The statement which Syud Ameer Shah made to me is to this effect:—

I was living at Lheree, when Mr. Postans sent for me. I went to him. He desired me to bring in Beejar Khan for a visit. I answered that Beejar Khan was in a state of great alarm, and that perhaps he would not come, but if he (Mr. Postans) would write a letter to reassure him, I would take it. He did so, and told me to take it, and not to be alarmed. I went to him, and reassured him, and persuaded him to come in. He came to Captain Amiel to make a *salaam*. Mr. Amiel did not say anything for four or five days, and Beejar Khan, taking courage from his reception, sent away most of his followers; but in four more days he was seized by Captain Amiel's servants.

No person who knew the parties could suspect the late Captain Postans of deliberate treachery, in sending a *syud* to bring in Beejar Khan, or that Mr. Ross Bell was aware he was committing a breach of faith in the orders he issued. But the question is, what construction the natives were entitled to put upon the act, according to their own principles and habits. Every one acquainted with Mahomedan notions must be sensible that the sending a *syud* was equivalent, in their opinion, to a guarantee of safety, and that the detention of the chief after such a virtual guarantee would be construed a breach of faith.

No. 4

Translation.

This is a treaty concluded on oath. At the present time, we, Islam Khan and Ahmed Khan, have come, on the part of our father, Beelbaruk, Boogtee, and Meer Husseni and the Muzzarees and Notanees, and have made our *salaam* to the *khan* and Colonel Stacy, and have become obedient and subservient. We will in future refrain from robbing and doing injury to the country of the *khan* or in that of the British. This practice we have relinquished, and should any of our tribes, Boogtees or Notanees, do injury or wrong in the country of the *khan* or the British, on the Bolan route or in other places, then are we responsible, and they shall suffer punishment, and we will cause them to repent of and refrain from such evil practice; so that again they shall not harbour any idea of doing injury in the country of the *khan* or the British.

The enemies and bad wishers of the *khan* we shall esteem enemies to ourselves, and evil-doers and robbers of any tribe, Belooche or Brahooe, shall and no refuge near us; we will drive

173

them out from among us. Should any tribes, Belooche or Brahooe, cause injury or evil in the *khan's* country, then will we
collect and repel them. Should they, however, be stronger than
us, then shall we look for assistance from the *khan's* troops, that
the enemy may be destroyed. While we live, we will not quit
the circle of our obedience and submission to the *khan*. On
these accounts, this treaty has been concluded on oath, on the
part of our father and tribe, on the 16th day of *Zul-Kadur*, A.H.
1257 (corresponding with 1st January, 1842).

No. 5

Extract of a letter from Lieutenant-Colonel Stacy to General England, dated "Quetta, 23rd March, 1842."

It will be necessary to take guides from this, as we must expect
to find every village on the line of march deserted. Which route
do you propose to march by? I fear you will find the water at
Hykulzye cut off. Hykulzye is supplied from the hills east of
Niah Bazaar, and the head of the water is about eight miles
from Hykulzye. There are spots where it may be had by digging
from two to three feet; this, I fear, would not answer, when you
have so many horses and camels, and consequently we might
have to march a second stage after our action with the enemy,
which we must expect at Hykulzye.

This extract will shew that I knew perfectly well how to take the
general to a place with plenty of water.

No. 6

The Affair at Htkulztb.[1]

The official despatch of Major-General England relating to this
affair is as follows:—

Major-General England to Mr. Maddock.

Camp, near Quetta, April 2, 1842.

Sir,—I have the honour to acquaint you, for the information
of the Right Honourable the Governor-General in Council,
that having advanced from hence on the 26th *ultimo*, with the
troops mentioned in the margin.[2] I arrived at the entrance of a
defile which leads to the village of Hykulzye early on the 28th,

---

1. Papers relating to Military Operations in Affghanistan, pp. 187, 820—223.
2. Four guns, horse brigade; 1 troop 3rd Light Cavalry; 5 companies Her Majesty's
41st regiment; 6 companies Bombay native infantry; 50 Poona horse.

at which place I had intended to await the remainder of the brigade now in progress to this place through the Bolan Pass.

2. From the total impossibility which now evidently prevails in obtaining any sort of information of the numbers and position of the enemy, and from the stern silence observed on such subjects by even those whose interest seems to depend on our success, I had no reason whatever to suppose that the people visible on these hills near Hykulzye were more than an assemblage of the scouts and marauders which are thus placed on all parts of this country wherever our troops traverse it; and the principal men of the village of Hyderzie, which is but six miles from the defile in question, and who received us on the preceding day with the greatest apparent cordiality, carefully kept from our knowledge, though much questioned on the subject, that Mahomed Sadig, the insurgent chief south of Candahar, was strongly posted in the pass above mentioned and contiguous heights, for the express purpose of opposing our progress.

3. It became evident, as we approached, that there was some preparation made for resistance by the insurgents on the commanding ground which flanked our line of march at this point; and, after a rapid reconnoissance, I proceeded to attack the principal hill by four light companies, including that of Her Majesty's 41st regiment, supporting the attack by the remainder of the wing of that corps, under cover of the four guns of Captain Leslie's horse artillery; the remainder of the troops being duly distributed for the protection of the baggage.

4. The enemy kept his strength concealed behind a succession of breastworks improved by a ditch and abattis, until our advance reached the crest of his exterior defence, when a crowded body suddenly sprung up, and made the contest so unequal, that it was immediately evident it could not be advantageously maintained.

5. The light companies fell back, therefore, on the small supporting column of Her Majesty's 41st regiment, which, on the appearance of the enemy's cavalry, which now rushed out from behind the hills, formed square, and gallantly resisted the efforts which were made to penetrate and break it; the matchlockmen of the enemy still keeping up a sharp and destructive fire from the heights.

6. To persevere in a second attack on the now developed strength of the enemy, with the small numbers I had disposable for such an operation, I deemed to be unwarrantable; and I therefore determined to move by my right to the ruined village of Bazar, three miles to north-north-east, in which direction the baggage was first ordered to proceed, and the troops followed across the plain in *échellon* of squares, the artillery protecting by alternate guns, and the whole covered by as good a display of cavalry as we had at command.

7. The steady manner in which this movement was made prevented any close molestation from the enemy; neither did they make any attack on us during the night.

8. I here discovered that 400 men, principally cavalry, had joined the insurgents' forces, from Candahar, the day before my arrival, and that, with a view to resist us, Mahomed Sadig had collected also at this point, from Shoranent and Shawl, 500 men, and that Mirza, a Kakur chief, with 100 of that tribe, also formed part of his force; the rest of the enemy's strength was made up by the Atchukzye horse, formerly in our service, by armed villagers of the neighbourhood, making an estimated total of at least 1,500 or 2,000 men. Many officers, however, consider it to have been much greater.

9. I moreover discovered that the defences within which the enemy fought, had been works of two months' preparation, and I have seldom seen better cavalry than those, which, for the first time, displayed themselves, when the light companies fell back on Her Majesty's 41st, at which moment several of the enemy were bayoneted in their attack on the square of that half-battalion.

10. On the morning of the 29th, it was perceptible that the insurgents had been collecting further reinforcements of armed villagers during the night, and that arrangements were making by them on an increased scale to resist any renewed assault on our part; and it being evident that the object of my remaining in the Pisheen Valley was negatived, whilst its resources and communications were thus in the hands of an enemy much stronger than myself, and that the latter could not be dislodged from the important heights he occupied without incurring severe additional losses, I felt I should best serve the views and interests of Government by falling back to my position at this place until reinforced; and I am happy to say that this difficult operation has been accomplished, although encumbered with a train of 1,500 baggage animals and camels, and four and a half *lacs* of treasure, and many wounded men, notwithstanding the constant presence of the enemy, without hurry, and without incurring the loss of any baggage or article of public property beyond such as might reasonably happen in any ordinary march in India.

11. In passing near some strong ground yesterday near Koochlach, a company of Her Majesty's 41st regiment ascended a steep hill on our left, and killed sixteen of a party of the enemy, from whom our column was receiving some annoyance in its progress, many others being wounded.

12. Having now detailed the circumstances belonging to the military events in this vicinity for the last few days, I solicit the favour of bringing to the notice of the Right Honourable the Governor-General in Council, the good conduct of the troops generally, and the gallantry of Her Majesty's 41st in particular, under Major Browne. I had every reason to be also satisfied with the good practice of Captain Leslie's efficient battery; and Major Apthorp, of the 20th Bombay Native Infantry (severely wounded, and since dead), led the light companies to the attack in the best possible style.

13. I have received from Major Wyllie, assistant adjutant-general; Captain Boyd, assistant quarter-master-general; Captain Davidson, deputy commissary-general; and the rest of the officers of the staff, very valuable and zealous assistance.

14. I beg to enclose a return of killed and wounded, as well as a copy of a letter which has this day been addressed to me by Lieutenant-Colonel Stacy, of the 43rd Bengal Native Infantry, who has been a volunteer with this force during its recent operations, and I quite concur in the sentiments expressed in the 6th paragraph of the lieutenant-colonel's communication.

15. I further beg leave to submit, for the information of the Right Honourable the Governor-General in Council, a copy of a letter which I have this day addressed to General Nott.

I have, &c.

R. England.

Extract of a Letter from Lieutenant-Colonel Stacy to Major-General England.

Quetta, March 31, 1842.

I have said the affair of the 28th, however distressing, has not been unproductive of good; it has shewn us, besides other facts, that our intelligence is next to nothing, our information so imperfect, that the existence of the intrenched position, which it appears the enemy had been engaged on the last two months, was utterly unknown to us; nor should we, I believe, have learnt that similar works have been prepared in the Kojuck, but for an advance on Hykulzye. Let it be observed, that our ignorance of the existence of this intrenchment, and the time necessarily taken to prepare it, prove, no less, our want of common information beyond our picquets, than the astonishing unanimity which is leagued against us.

Major-General England to Major-General Nott.

Camp, near Quetta, April 1, 1842.

Sir,—I wish to acquaint you that the insurgents are so strongly posted and stockaded in a defile which leads from the village of Hykulzye to the plains in this direction, that I am of opinion that it is not to be forced by less than a strong brigade; and such brigade should be equipped with mortars. I had no information whatever of this defensive arrangement on the part of the insurgents until I was stopped by it, with some loss of men, in my way to the village of Hykulzye, at which place I had intended to wait for my reinforcements, now in progress through the Bolan; and then to proceed to Killa Abdoolla with some treasure, &c., for the use of the force under your command.

I shall again attempt this operation with a brigade lightly equipped, and without knapsacks, as soon as I hear from you that you are prepared to meet it on the northern side of the Kojuck, and that this aid of treasure is absolutely necessary to you; but it would in my opinion be most prejudicial to the safety of Quetta, if I remained longer from it than merely to perform this service. I beg to advise that the force you send to meet me at Killa Abdoolla should be strong with mortars, if you can spare them, as I have none, for I am credibly informed that the Kojuck is stockaded.

It is, however, possible I believe to turn it. I have had no intelligence from Candahar since the 19th.—I have, &c.

R. England.

The letter of the Governor-General of India to the Secret Committee, dated "Benares, April 21st, 1842," contains the following paragraphs:—

In consequence of the scarcity of funds in the treasure-chest at Candahar, and the difficulty thence arising of negotiating bills on Shikarpore and other places, but at heavy loss, and in consequence also of a deficiency in some essential articles of medicine for the use of the hospitals, much anxiety had been expressed by the authorities at Candahar for the early transmission of an escort from Upper Sinde through Quetta in charge of supplies of cash and medicines. Major-General England, commanding in Upper Sinde, had been preparing to advance with a complete brigade to Shawl, in support of Major-General Nott, whether with a view to cover his retreat, if he decided on retrograding, or to keep up the communication with him if he resolved to maintain himself at Candahar.

The major-general did not expect to be able to commence his march from the valley of the Indus before the latter end of March, and he was averse to move his troops forward in detachments, but intended to carry up through the Bolan Pass a complete brigade, and to convoy to Candahar, or to the Kojuck Pass, about twenty *lacs* of treasure, besides various supplies of medicines and stores. At the pressing instance of the political agent. Major Outram, backed by the requisition of Major-General Nott, Major-General England at length consented to commence his advance with the troops detailed in the margin,[3] leaving the remainder of the troops to follow when their commissariat and other arrangements should be completed.

He accordingly commenced his march on the 7th *ultimo*, and arrived at Quetta without difficulty on the 16th *ultimo*.

The state of affairs at Candahar, as then known at Quetta, was not such as to have made an immediate effort to push on a portion of the treasure and supplies indispensably necessary; and Major-General Nott had declared his intention not to detach a party from his force to meet and relieve the escort on the road

---

3. Four guns horse artillery; wing of Her Majesty's 41st Foot; troop of 3rd Light Cavalry; wing of 6th Native Infantry; a detachment of 100 Poona horse.

between Quetta and Candahar, and there was accordingly no obvious object of importance to induce Major-General England to advance beyond Quetta, before he was strengthened by the arrival of his reinforcements from Sinde.

He, however, moved out from Quetta on the 26th *ultimo*, and met with slight opposition till his approach to Hykulzye, where he found Mahomed Sadik's force strongly posted in a position difficult of approach, on the defences of which much previous labour has been spent. The general's despatch of the 1st instant from Quetta will give your Honourable Committee all the details of the failure of his attempt to force the enemy's position; the subsequent abandonment of the effort, and his retreat, without further loss or serious molestation from the enemy, to the post of Quetta.

Some excitement is said to have prevailed among the tribes about the Bolan Pass, and the feeling in parts of Cutchee and Sinde appears to be hostile; but no actual disturbances of any serious nature have taken place, and the Brahooes and all under the influence of the Khan of Kelat maintain an attitude of friendship and confident reliance on the British power.

No. 7.

Subjoined are extracts from testimonies furnished to me by Major Boyd and Major Wyllie, relative to this affair.

From Major Boyd to Lieutenant-Colonel Stacy,

17th May, 1843.

I understood from you that you were authorized to act in a political capacity on your arrival in the Valley of Pesheen, and that you were most anxious for the attendance of Rheimdad with the force proceeding with Major-General England into the valley; but that your application for his services had not been complied with, and I recollect you imputed the failure at Hykulzye, or rather the collision with the enemy, to his not being with us.

I cannot positively assert that I was present when you volunteered to lead up the hill after our repulse; but I remember during the time we were in front of the enemy your telling me you had, as second senior officer, thrice offered to lead up a body of men, and take the enemy's position, which offer the general refused. I am not aware who procured the information regarding the village of Bazaar, to which we retired, and possessed all the advantages you describe.

I can state that, when Major-General England determined upon retiring to Quetta, and wished to march at midnight, you strenuously opposed his doing so, as it would materially injure the British cause, and give the enemy confidence, and that, if the general would agree to advance, you would take the troops by the road which you shewed me, and which would turn the enemy's position. The reason for not moving at midnight was the impossibility of conveying the commissariat stores, after the heavy rain of the preceding evening.

I believe it was you who shewed us the cross-road from Bazaar to Hyderzye, which took us out of reach of the enemy's fire.

On the morning on which we marched into Quetta from Koochlaq, the major-general told me to lead the column, and should the Moorza Pass be occupied by the enemy, I was to lead round by the hills, and follow a guide who was brought by Moorj Mull, the commissariat contractor.

I can with perfect confidence state that your influence with the Belooche tribes was the cause of the road being again opened for the transmission of the *dâks*, and that you met the brother of Saloo Khan, Moolla Attah Oolla, at Killa Abdoolla, and brought him on to Candahar. Had it not been for your influence and character with the tribes, I do not think arrangements for opening the road could have been accomplished. With reference to the state of the Bolan Pass during the autumn of 1841, I can safely say it was impossible to go through it without a strong guard, as it was in October I was employed in surveying the road leading into the Bolan from Kelat, and it was during this time that the Kaukers were so troublesome, and committing murders in the pass.

From Major Wyllie to Lieutenant-Colonel Stacy,

31st May 1843.

I was informed at Quetta that the services of Rheimdad, the Naib of Shawl, had been refused you by the assistant political agent; but I had no knowledge then of your instructions relative to that district. Rheimdad did not accompany Major-General England's force to Hykulzye when the major-general met with a check at that place, in March, 1842.

If I remember rightly, the detachment under the major-general was taken to the deserted village of Bazaar by Moorj Mull, the commissariat camel contractor, and the road pointed out by his men, and the information relative to the cross-road to Hyderzye from Bazaar, alluded to in the 8th para. of your letter, was also furnished by the same individual. Captain Davidson, deputy commissary-general, having on this occasion proceeded at the head of the column.

I heard you volunteered to the major-general to lead a party against the enemy's position at Hykulzye, after the light companies had retired.

You were averse to the major-general moving from Bazaar at midnight, and stated it accordingly.

I am not aware who shewed the road from Koochlaq to Quetta to the right of the Moorza Pass.

On the advance of Major-General England's force to Candahar the second time, I am well aware that you opened a communication at Killa Abdoolla with one of Saloo Khan's relatives, who accompanied you to Candahar, and before which period the *dâk cassids* could not travel between that place and Quetta; but on the arrangement alluded to being made, the communication was opened, and to the best of my recollection remained uninterrupted.

No. 8

Major-General England to the Assistant Adjutant-General, Candahar.

Camp at Lora River, April 29, 1842.

Sir,—I have the honour to acquaint you, for the information of the major-general commanding the troops in Lower Affghanisan and Sinde, that I yesterday attacked the enemy's strong position in front of the Hykulzye, with the troops mentioned in the margin,[4] and dispersed them in all directions.

2. The three columns of attack were led by Major Simmons, Her Majesty's 41st regiment; Captain Woodburn, 25th Bombay Native Infantry: and Major Cochran, Her Majesty's 41st; the latter being accompanied by a wing of the 25th Bombay Native Infantry, under Captain Teasdale, commanding that corps.

---

4. One troop Bengal horse artillery; 3rd Light Cavalry; Poona horse; Her Majesty's 41st regiment Light Battalion; 25th regiment Native Infantry.

3. The reserve was in the hands of Major Browne, commanding Her Majesty's 41st regiment.

4. Nothing could be more successful than the combinations; and the insurgents, after a short resistance, fled into the rugged mountains in their rear, leaving their standards, and being closely and gallantly pursued by the 3rd Light Cavalry, under Captain Delamain.

5. The practice of Captain Leslie's horse-artillery battery was, as usual, most effective; and the conduct of the troops excellent.

6. I beg to annex a list of the casualties which have occurred in this affair.—I have, &c.

R. England.

<h2>No. 9.</h2>

Major-General Nott to Mr. Maddock.

Camp, Goaine, 38 miles S.W. of Ghuznee,
August 31, 1842.

Sir,—I have the honour to acquaint you, for the information of the Right Honourable the Governor-General of India, that Shumsoodeen, the Affghan governor of the fortress of Ghuznee, brought nearly the whole of his army, about 12,000 men, into the vicinity of my camp yesterday, at 3 o'clock p.m.

I moved out with one-half of my force; the enemy advanced in the most bold and gallant manner, each division cheering as they came into position, their left being upon a hill of some elevation, their centre and right along a low ridge until their flank rested on a fort filled with men: they opened a fire of small arms, supported by two six-pounder horse-artillery guns, which were admirably served: our columns advanced upon the different points with great regularity and steadiness, and, after a short and spirited contest, completely defeated the enemy, capturing their guns, tents, ammunition, &c., and dispersing them in every direction. One hour's more daylight would have enabled me to destroy the whole of their infantry.

Shumsoodeen fled in the direction of Ghuznee, accompanied by about thirty horsemen.

I enclose a list of killed and wounded on the 28th and 30th instant; also a return of ordnance, ammunition, &c. &c. taken from the enemy.

The behaviour of the troops, both European and native, was such as I anticipated, and afforded me complete satisfaction.

I beg leave to bring to the favourable notice of the Right Honourable the Governor-General of India, the under-mentioned officers : many of them have served under my command for the last three years, and have been conspicuous for their zeal and gallantry in the various affairs which have occurred with the enemy during that period, and especially in the action of the 12th of January last, and have invariably upheld the reputation of our arms, and the honour of our country.

Brigadier Wymer, commanding the 1st Infantry Brigade; Lieutenant-Colonel McLaren, commanding 16th regiment Native Infantry; Major Hibbert, commanding Her Majesty's 40th regiment; Captain Burney, commanding 38th regiment Native Infantry; Captains Christie and Haldane, commanding corps of Bengal Irregular Cavalry; Major Sotheby, commanding the artillery; Captain Blood, commanding Bombay Foot Artillery; Major Sanders, Bengal Engineers; Lieutenants North and Studdert, Bombay Engineers. Majors Leech and Rawlinson, of the political department, attended me in the field, and rendered me great assistance in conveying my orders.

My best thanks are due to my staff. Captain Polwhele, deputy assistant-adjutant-general; Captain Waterfield, *aide-de-camp*; Lieutenant Tytler, deputy assistant quarter-master-general.

Annexed is a letter from Brigadier Wymer, speaking in the highest terms of his brigade-major. Captain T. H. Scott, of the 38th regiment Native Infantry. I fully appreciate this excellent officer's merits; he has been with me in four actions. I trust I shall not be thought presumptuous in expressing a hope that he will receive some mark of the favour of Government, by brevet or otherwise.

I cannot close this despatch without expressing my admiration of the dashing and gallant conduct, rapid movement, and correct practice of Captain Anderson's troop of Bengal horse artillery,—nothing could exceed it; and I beg leave to bring this officer, and Lieutenant Turner, attached to the same troop, to the particular notice of his Lordship, as officers who have on many occasions rendered me most essential service.

I have, &c.

W. Nott.

Brigadier Wymer to Major-General Nott.

Camp, Chuppakhana, September 1, 1842.

Sir,—Adverting to division orders of yesterday, expressive of your praise and thanks to the troops employed under your command in action with the enemy on the afternoon of the 30th instant, I hope you will not consider it ill-judged on my part, bringing to your favourable notice the valuable assistance I derived from the active services of Captain Scott, major of brigade to the 1st Infantry brigade under my command, whose exertions during the fight on that day demand and merit my best praise and acknowledgments. This being the second time of the display of Captain Scott's abilities when in action with the enemy, as my personal staff, will, I hope, plead my apology for recommending him to your notice, and the favourable consideration of Government, in any way you may have it in your power to mention him as a meritorious and deserving officer.

I have, &c.

G. P. Wymer.

No. 10

Major-General Nott to Mr. Maddock.

Camp, Ghuznee, September 8, 1842.

Sir,—My despatch of the 31st *ultimo* will have informed you of my having defeated the Affghan army commanded by Shumsoodeen.

On the morning of the 5th instant, I moved on Ghuznee. I found the city full of men, and a range of mountains running north-east of the fortress covered by heavy bodies of cavalry and infantry: the gardens and ravines near the town were also occupied. The enemy had received a considerable reinforcement from Cabool, under Sultan Jan.

I directed Major Sanders, of the Bengal Engineers, to reconnoitre the works, under escort of the 16th regiment Native Infantry, and a party of irregular cavalry. This brought on some smart skirmishing, in which our *sepoys* behaved to admiration. Captain White, of Her Majesty's 40th regiment, commanding the light companies of the army, was pushed forward, accompanied by Anderson's troop of horse artillery, to support the reconnoitring party, and I at once determined on carrying the enemy's mountain positions before encamping my force. The troops ascended the heights in gallant style, driving the enemy before them until every point was gained.

The village of Bullal is situated about 600 yards from the walls of Ghuznee, upon the spur of the mountain to the north-east, and observing it to be a desirable spot for preparing a heavy battery to be placed 300 paces in advance, I ordered it to be occupied by two regiments of infantry and some light guns, and retired the columns into camp.

The engineer officers, sappers and miners, and infantry working parties were employed under the directions of Major Sanders, during the night of the 5th, in erecting a battery for four 18-pounders: these guns were moved from camp before daylight on the morning of the 6th; but, before they had reached the position assigned them, it was ascertained that the enemy had evacuated the fortress.

I directed the city of Ghuznee, with its citadel, and the whole of its works, to be destroyed. I forward the engineer's report.

In these operations our loss has been much less than might have been expected from the numbers and positions of the enemy, and the fact of the troops having been necessitated to move under the range of the guns of the fortress.

I enclose a list of the killed and wounded.

The exertions of Major Sanders, of the engineers, were, as usual, most zealous, and my thanks are due to him and the department under his charge.

I beg to notice the following officers: Brigadier Wymer; Major Hibbert, commanding Her Majesty's 40th regiment; Captain Evans, in temporary charge of the 16th regiment Native Infantry; Captain White, Her Majesty's 40th regiment, commanding the light companies of the force; Major Sotheby, and officers of the artillery.

I have every reason to be satisfied with my staff. Captain Polwhele, deputy assistant adjutant-general; Captain Waterfield, *aide-de-camp*; Captain Ripley; and Lieutenant Kay, deputy judge-advocate-general.

I continue to receive the greatest assistance from Major Leech.—I have, &c.   W. Nott.

P.S.—I have recovered about 327 of the *sepoys* of the 27th regiment Bengal Native Infantry, who had been sold into slavery, and dispersed in villages forty miles round Ghuznee.

No. 11

Major-General Nott to Major-General Pollock.

Camp, Urghundee, Sept 16, 1842.

Sir,—I have the honour to acquaint you that, Shumsoodeen. Sultan Jan, and other Affghan chiefs, having assembled about 12,000 men, occupied a succession of strong mountains intercepting my march upon Beenee Badam and Mydan, on the 14th and 15th instant. Our troops dislodged them in gallant style, and their conduct afforded me the greatest satisfaction.

The artillery distinguished themselves; and I beg to mention the names of Captain Leslie, Bombay horse artillery; Captains Blood, Bombay foot artillery, and Anderson and Turner, of the Bengal horse artillery, and the 38th and[5] 43rd Bengal Native Infantry.

I beg to bring under the favourable notice of Government Captain White, of Her Majesty's 40th regiment, in command of the light companies of Her Majesty's 40th and 41st regiments, and of the 2nd, 16th, 38th, 42nd, and 43rd Bengal native regiments, for the able manner in which he carried my orders into effect, and for the gallantry displayed by him and the companies under his command, in ascending the mountains and driving the enemy from their positions. I had every reason to be pleased with the conduct of all troops, European and native. I forward a list of killed and wounded.

I have, &c.

W. Nott.

No. 12

Major-General McCaskill to Captain Ponsonby.

Camp, Istalif, September 30, 1842.

Sir,—I have the satisfaction to acquaint you, for the information of Major-General Pollock, C.B., that the troops under my command yesterday made themselves masters of the strong and populous town of Istalif, totally defeating the numerous levies collected for its defence, under the infamous Ameer Oollah Khan Loghuree, Kaojie Ameer Kotwal, Hazin Khan (an assassin of Sir Alexander Burnes), Hazir Alee Khan, Khuleefa Ibrahim, and many other chiefs of Cabool and Kohistan.

The major-general is aware that the force detailed in the mar-

---

5. So in the original; but a name seems to be omitted.

gin[6] was placed at my disposal for operations in these valleys, on the 25th. The two brigades formed a junction near Khwaja Rawash on the 26th; moved to an encampment near Zimuree on the 27th, and pitched their tents within four miles of this place on the 28th.

The same evening I reconnoitred the enemy's position. It is impossible to conceive ground naturally stronger. The town of Istalif, consisting of masses of houses and forts, is built on the slope of a mountain, in the rear of which are yet loftier eminences, shutting in a defile which leads to Toorkistan, and in no way can this place of abode of 15,000 people be approached but by surmounting ranges of hills separated by deep ravines, or traversing, by narrow roads, its gardens, vineyards, and orchards, fenced in with strong enclosure-walls; the whole of them, with the mountain-side and tops of the houses, were occupied by *jezailchees*; and the strongest proof is afforded that the enemy, after this disposition, considered the place as unassailable, by their having retained within the town the wives and children not only of the inhabitants, but of thousands of refugees from Cabool.

The observations which I was enabled to make under a sharp *jezail* fire, and the report of Major Pottinger, induced me to determine to assault, the next morning, the right of the enemy's extensive position, as it was there that I could hope to bring the artillery most effectively into battery. Arrangements were made with this view. The troops were formed into two columns of attack and reserve; Brigadier Tulloch's brigade and the mountain-train composed the right; Brigadier Stacy's and Captain Blood's battery, and the 18-pounders, the left; these were sup. ported by the third column, under Major Simmons, Her Majesty's 41st, consisting of a wing of his regiment and the cavalry under Major Lockwood: Captain Christie's corps protected the baggage. The troops moved soon after daylight, and traversing the plain in perfect order, passed nearly from the left to the right of the

---

6. Artillery.—Captain Backhouse's mountain-train; Captain Blood's battery of 9-pounders (Bombay), two 18-pounders. Cavalry.—Headquarters and two squadrons of Her Majesty's 3rd Light Dragoons; 1st squadron 1st Light Cavalry; Captain Christie's (late S. S. 2nd regiment) corps of cavalry. Infantry.—Brigadier Tulloch's brigade (with the addition of Captain Broadfoot's sappers and miners, and the exception of the 60th Native Infantry); Brigadier Stacy's brigade.

enemy's position. Our light troops and guns repressed the occasional attacks of their *jezailchees* from the gardens, who were numerous and most audacious; but when the column arrived in front of the village Ismillah, I resolved to make a combined attack on this point; Brigadier Tulloch's brigade assailed its left, and Brigadier Stacy, making a long detour, attacked the right

I cannot express in adequate terms my admiration of the style in which the former column, covered by skirmishers, rushed upon the gardens, filled with bold and skilful marksmen.

Her Majesty's 9th Foot, the 26th Native Infantry, and Captain Broadfoot's sappers, vied with each other in steady courage; and their rapid unhesitating advance soon left the enemy no resource but flight.

Very shortly after this assault, the three light companies of Her Majesty's 41st, the 42nd and 43rd Native Infantry, covering their own column, got into action, and, on their side, stormed the village and vineyards with distinguished gallantry. The combination was steadily persevered in, and though I had few opportunities of using the artillery with effect, I had soon the gratification of seeing the enclosures, forts, heights, suburbs, and town successively won by the two columns.

The enemy were driven from them, and pursued with a rapidity which left no time to rally, and a singular spectacle was then presented in the escape up the mountain-side of the women and children, from the place, to which no interruption was offered; but, as detached parties of the beaten Affghans still occupied some very lofty heights, the mountain-train ascended them by a dizzy pathway, and dispersed the fugitives by its effective fire.

Our reserve was now established on the lower heights, and the whole of the place; filled with property of every description, much of it plundered from our army in 1841, was in the hands of our force; two guns (brass field-pieces) were also taken, and one of them was seized with such promptitude, that its captor. Lieutenant Elmhirst, Her Majesty's 9th Foot, turned its fire upon the fugitives with some effect. I directed the town to be set on fire in several places, after taking out various supplies which might be useful to our troops, and the work of demolition is still proceeding under the direction of Major Sanders, of the engineers.

Our loss has been trifling, for the advance of our officers and men was too rapid and decisive to allow of the sharp fire of the enemy telling much upon them; and, deceived by the direction of the reconnoissance of the 28th, the Affghans had expected the attack on their left, and posted their guns and the *élite* of their force in that quarter.

I have now the pleasing task of expressing the amount of my obligation for their exertions in the field, to Brigadiers Tulloch and Stacy, commanding brigades and columns; to Lieutenant-Colonel Taylor, K.H., Her Majesty's 9th Foot; Major Huish, of the 26th Native Infantry; and Captain Broadfoot, of the sappers, commanding corps on the right, which bore the brunt of the action; to Major Simmons, Her Majesty's 41st Foot, commanding the reserve; to Captain Backhouse, commanding the Mountain-Train, and Captain Blood, commanding the battery of 9-pounders; this last was ably aided by Lieutenant Terry.

I have received valuable assistance throughout our operations from Major Pottinger, C.B., and Major Sanders, engineers; and yesterday from Captain Mackenzie and Lieutenant Airey, Her Majesty's 3rd Buffs, and Lieutenant Webb, 30th regiment Madras Native Infantry, temporarily attached to me; and, since we marched from Cabool, as on former occasions, from my own staff, departmental and personal, *viz..* Captain Havelock, deputy assistant adjutant-general; Lieutenant Mayne, deputy assistant quartermaster-general; Lieutenant Pollock, artillery, *aide-de-camp* to the major-general, who volunteered his services with me; and Lieutenant Bethune, Her Majesty's 9th Foot, my own *aide-de-camp.*

Regarding the last-mentioned officer, I take the opportunity of rectifying an oversight on my part. I ought specially to have reported to Major-General Pollock, Lieutenant Bethune's valuable services in the recent affair at the Huft Kotul, in which I was entrusted with the command of the main column. Brigadier Tulloch reports, in very strong terms, the good conduct on the present occasion of Captain Smith, Her Majesty's 9th Foot, his brigade-major. I enclose a return of the killed and wounded, and of the two guns captured.—I have, &c.

John McCaskill.

No. 13

Major-General McCaskill to Captain Ponsonby,

Camp, Khwaja Rawash, October 6, 1842.

Sir,—The troops entrusted to my charge for a special service in the Kohistan having pitched their tents at this place, previously to returning to their respective encampments, I take this opportunity of requesting you to solicit the attention of Major-General Pollock, C.B. to some points, which, in the hurry of our active operations, I had neglected to dwell upon. I have already intimated, that Brigadier Stacy's report of the part borne by his brigade in the capture of Istaliff, on the 29th *ultimo*, did not reach me till the 2nd instant.

It will ever be matter of regret to me, if this accidental delay should prevent the merits of some of the officers and troops under me being prominently brought to the notice of the Right Honourable the Governor-General, and his Excellency the Commander-in-Chief. The brunt of the action certainly fell on the infantry corps, and sappers, of Brigadier Tulloch's brigade; but the credit of turning the enemy's extreme right,—of allowing him no respite or breathing-time on that line;—of aiding in completing the capture of the town, when its possession was hotly disputed from behind walls and from the tops of houses, from courtyards and in winding streets, built on steep declivities, is due to the regiments under Brigadier Stacy.

My commendations have been especially earned by Major G. Browne and Her Majesty's 41st regiment, for the share they took in these gallant efforts, and for the exemplary humanity displayed by the men towards the unfortunate families of the vanquished. That corps was zealously emulated and supported by the 42nd Native Infantry under Major Clarkson, and the 43rd under Major Nash.

In addition to the services of Major Sanders, as field engineer, I ought to have remarked on the distinguished gallantry with which he accompanied the heads of columns in the advance of Brigadier Tulloch against the gardens and town. Neither must I leave without record the marked intrepidity of Lieutenant Mayne, deputy assistant quarter-master-general, in pointing out the path of the same column amidst the hottest of the fire, and in aiding in following up the victory. I have before mentioned, that the light companies of Her Majesty's 41st, and the 42nd and 43rd Native Infantry, covered the manoeuvres of their own brigade. This onset was led very bravely by Lieutenant Evans, who was afterwards killed in the town (and was succeeded in command by Lieutenant Madden), and by Lieutenant Woollen, 42nd Native Infantry, and Captain Macpherson, 43rd Native Infantry.—I have, &c.

John McCaskill.

No. 14.

Major-General Nott to Captain Ponsonby.

Camp, Giant's Tomb, October 15, 1842.
Sir,—I beg to report, for the information of Major-General Pollock, C.B., that the rearguard of the force under my command was yesterday attacked by large bodies of the enemy in the Huft Kotul Pass. I sent 200 *sepoys*, and a wing of Her Majesty's 40th regiment, and two companies of Her Majesty's 41st, under command of Major Hibbert, to the assistance of Captain Leeson, of the 42nd regiment Native Infantry, who had charge of the rear. Our *sepoys* defeated and dispersed the enemy. Captain Leeson speaks in high terms of the gallantry of the officers and *sepoys* under his command.

Major Hibbert, and the wing of Her Majesty's 40th regiment, and the two companies of Her Majesty's 41st, under Captain Blackburne, behaved with their accustomed gallantry: my thanks are due to all the troops engaged. I enclose a list of killed and wounded.—I have, &c.

W. Nott.